BATTLEGROUND
SUSSEX

To Lynne

*   *   *

Battleground Sussex tells the story of one county from
the earliest days of recorded history through to the
dark days of the Second World War.

This book traces the various conflicts and military influences
that have helped shape Sussex and its people. It brings to life
conquerors, warriors and statesmen, alongside the struggles and
sacrifices of the ordinary folk who have populated and defended
the region throughout the ages. From the days of Celts, Romans
and Saxons, to the Battle of Hastings; from the dawn of
democracy to the English Civil War; from Napoleon to Hitler,
Battleground Sussex explains how the county of Sussex has so
often been on the nation's front line.

Richly illustrated throughout, this action-packed book will
appeal not only to those interested in the history of this county,
but also to enthusiasts of British military history as a whole.
Much of what happened in Sussex ultimately shaped the future
of the whole country – events that can all be found in fascinating
detail within these pages.

BATTLEGROUND
SUSSEX

*A Military History of Sussex
from the Iron Age to the
Present Day*

JOHN GREHAN
& MARTIN MACE

With a Foreword by
Dame Vera Lynn OBE, DBE

Pen & Sword
MILITARY

First published in Great Britain in 2012
By Pen and Sword Military
an imprint of
Pen and Sword Books Ltd
47 Church Street
Barnsley
South Yorkshire S70 2AS

ISBN 978 1 84884 661 6

A CIP record for this book is available from the British Library

Printed and bound in England
by MPG Books Group in the UK

Typeset in Ehrhardt by
Chic Media Ltd

Pen & Sword Books Ltd incorporates the imprints of
Pen & Sword Aviation, Pen & Sword Family History, Pen & Sword Maritime,
Pen & Sword Military, Pen & Sword Discovery, Wharncliffe Local History,
Wharncliffe True Crime, Wharncliffe Transport, Pen & Sword Select,
Pen & Sword Military Classics, Leo Cooper, Remember When,
The Praetorian Press, Seaforth Publishing and Frontline Publishing

For a complete list of Pen and Sword titles please contact
Pen and Sword Books Limited
47 Church Street, Barnsley, South Yorkshire, S70 2AS, England
E-mail: enquiries@pen-and-sword.co.uk
Website: www.pen-and-sword.co.uk

Contents

List of Images

LIST OF IMAGES

16. The barbican and gatehouse of Lewes Castle. The castle is on the north side of Lewes High Street (TQ414101).
17. The motte and remains of the keep of Lewes Castle.
18. The helm-shaped monument to the Battle of Lewes in the grounds of Lewes Priory.
19. Winchelsea's Pipewell Gate which is situated to the north-west of the town (TQ 905174).
20. The Strand Gate at the eastern corner of Winchelsea town, overlooking the River Brede.
21. Rye's Land Gate which is in the north-eastern corner of the old town at the junction of Landgate and Tower Street (TQ 922202).
22. The Ypres Tower at the south-eastern corner of Rye old town, adjacent to the church. In the foreground is a cannon in the Gun Garden (TQ 922202).
23. The front view of Bodiam Castle, showing the main gate and barbican. Bodium Castle is signposted from the B2244 to the north-east of Robertsbridge (TQ 785256).
24. The southern face of Bodiam Castle.
25. One of the two "demi-culverns" that were placed in a battery within the outer bailey of Pevensey Castle at the time of the Spanish Armada. The gun is on display inside the castle (TQ 664048).
26. A modern reproduction of a fire beacon. This example is at West Wittering Beach (SZ 768984).
27. A French cannon of a type used in the Battle of Beachy Head. It fired a 5–6 pound ball and was located on the upper decks of the ships. It is on display at the entrance to the Eastbourne Redoubt.
28. Amberley Castle's main gate. The castle is situated off the B2139 (TQ 031132).
29. The medieval gate-tower and moat of Michelham Priory. The Priory is situated to the east of Upper Dicker on the road towards Hailsham (TQ 558093).
30. Herstmonceux Castle. The castle is signposted from the A271 to the east of Herstmonceux village (TQ 646104).
31. Cowdray House. The ruins of this fortified manor house are only open to the public at specified times. They can be viewed from a public footpath that leads off the main A272 road (SU 892217).
32. The beautifully restored castle at Arundel. Note the large, round keep in the centre of the castle and the bailey on either side (TQ 017074).
33. The remains of the gatetower of Bramber Castle. The castle is located near the roundabout on the A283 at Bramber (TQ 184107).
34. An aerial view of Camber Castle, which clearly shows the Tudor rose

configuration. The castle can be reached by footpath from Rye Harbour Road (TQ 922185).

35. A view of the north-western front of Camber Castle. The Castle sits on the Winchelsea Beach Nature Reserve.

36. A gun emplacement and magazine of the 19th century Lower Battery at Newhaven, which is now adjacent to the West Beach car park (TQ 448001).

37. The remains of the fort at Littlehampton that can be seen today (TQ 027012). Just visible beneath the undergrowth is the loop-holed Carnot Wall and part of a caponier. Access is provided by the Rope Walk along the western bank of the River Arun.

38. Two gun pivots which once formed part of the defensive armament of the Langney Redoubt. These are standing at the end of the seafront promenade at Langney Point, Eastbourne (TQ 642011).

39. The scant remains of a gun emplacement from the Langney Redoubt, situated at the end of the promenade at Langney Point.

40. A section of the Royal Military Canal at Pett Level (TQ 894139).

41. An early painting of what appears to be Martello Tower No.28 at Rye Harbour. Though in poor condition, the tower can be seen adjacent to the car park at the end of Rye Harbour Road (TQ 942188).

42. Martello Tower No.74 on the seafront esplanade at Seaford (TQ 485985).

43. Martello Tower No.55, at Norman's Bay, which stands between the seafront properties that back onto the minor road from Pevensey Bay (TQ 684053).

44. Caponier and ditch at the Eastbourne Redoubt. The Redoubt is situated on the promenade to the east of Eastbourne town centre (TV 623997).

45. Shoreham Redoubt, showing the loop-holed Carnot wall and caponier. The redoubt is at the end of Fort Haven at the eastern extremity of Shoreham Beach (TQ 233045).

46. The gun emplacements for the Emergency Coastal Battery at Newhaven located on the cliff top to the west of Newhaven Fort (TQ 4477001).

47. A 6-inch gun in its emplacement on the ramparts of Newhaven Fort.

48. The battery observation tower for the Emergency Coastal Battery raised in 1940 at Pett Level. Access to the battery position is through the Pett Level Nature Reserve (TQ 891135).

49. A Type 24 infantry pillbox. The one shown here can be seen near Wadhurst, at the junction of Partridge Lane and the B2099 (TQ 606336).

50. A Second World War 25-pounder pillbox, located 400 yards north of Betley Bridge, near Henfield (TQ 197178).

51. A photograph of an Emergency Coastal Battery at Shoreham-by-Sea in 1940.

The battery was located next to the Shoreham Redoubt on Shoreham Beach (TQ 233045). The searchlight tower can still be seen.

52. The old plaque of Ford airfield when it was the Fleet Air Arm base of HMS *Peregrine*. The plaque was photographed in one of the accommodation blocks in what is now HMP Ford (SU 998027).

53. Situated two and a half miles east of Arundel in West Sussex, the Chain Home station at Poling was one of the first twenty planned before the Second World War. However, it had not been completed when war broke out. This view of three large transmitter towers at Poling was taken from the south side. Poling's receiver rowers, which numbered four in total, are just out of the picture to the right. The remains of the radar station are on private land adjacent to Poling Street (TQ 045052). Some of the defences built to defend the radar station can still be seen to the south of the site.

54. A painting of the control tower at Tangmere airfield. The tower can still be seen on private land to the north of the old runways at the end of a road which runs beside the present-day aviation museum (SU 913066).

55. A Matilda tank of 'B' Squadron, 44th Tank Battalion, in the village square at Findon on 31 December 1940 (IWM H7680)

56. A 12-pounder breech-loading gun in its emplacement on the cliff-top ramparts of Newhaven Fort (TQ 448004).

57. A hangar at the former Ford airfield, which was photographed in the grounds of HMP Ford.

58. Don't touch! Accompanied by three soldiers, a police officer inspects a 2-inch British mortar bomb that was found lying in the open on the South Downs near Pyecombe, north of Brighton.

59. The letter written by Mr Abel to the Chief Constable of Eastbourne's Police following the events of Wednesday, 2 October 1940.

60. The pall of dense black smoke that hung over Ford airfield after the attack on Sunday, 18 August 1940.

61. The memorial to those killed in the raid on Ford airfield on 18 August 1940, which was erected at Clymping Church in 1942 – note the camouflaged hangers in the background and the barbed wire perimeter fence. Arthur Cunningham's name is listed on the right-hand panel. The attack resulted in one of the most serious death-tolls from a *Luftwaffe* raid on a British airfield during the Second World War.

62. The site of Poling radar station was decommissioned in 1949 but did not officially close until July 1956. By the late 1960s very few of the original wartime buildings had survived. This receiver block is perhaps the most important

exception, though its blast walls have long since been removed and it has been put to use as a workshop and garage. This building, in effect the nerve centre of the site, housed two receivers along with a plotting table. Since this photograph was taken in the 1990s, this structure has been converted to private housing.

63. Despite the best efforts of anti-aircraft gunners, six Focke Wulf Fw 190s of 10/JG 2 attacked the gas holder, housing and hotels in Worthing on 9 March 1943. A number of properties were badly damaged and the Working Mens' Club received a direct hit and was flattened. This photograph was taken from the cockpit of one of the attacking aircraft – the photographer's own aircraft is machine-gunning the town's gasholder at extreme low-level before heading south back across Worthing. Note the flashes caused as his bullet or cannon fire hits the structure.

64. Drama off the South Coast, 21 March 1940. The Eastbourne lifeboat *Jane Holland* pictured alongside the *Barn Hill* as firemen on the tug *Foremost No.22* play their houses on the still-burning merchant ship. The duties of a lifeboat and its crew were difficult and perilous during peacetime, but the addition of a world at war, and the fact that that the enemy could be just twenty-two miles away, only served to make some situations that much worse. The extent of the damage to the steamer can clearly be seen in this picture.

65. In the hours after the bombing, the badly damaged *Barn Hill* gradually drifted north-east, finally running aground near Langney Point. On the Saturday following the attack, the ship finally broke her back, spilling out some of her precious cargo.

66. A tunic of a sergeant of the Royal Sussex Regiment from 1876. On the tunic is the Indian Mutiny campaign medal of 1857-8. The tunic is on display in the Redoubt Fortress and Military Museum, Eastbourne.

67. A photograph of the 1905 camp of the Sussex Yeomanry at Lewes.

68. A Sussex soldier: the monument to the 2nd Battalion Royal Sussex Regiment which can be seen near the pier, off Grand Parade, in Eastbourne. The statue dates from 1906 and commemorates soldiers from the 2nd Royal Sussex Regiment who lost their lives in military operations in Malta, Egypt and India between 1882 and 1902.

69. Bexhill Barracks. Above the door is the badge of the Royal Sussex Regiment. The barracks are on the A259 in the Old Town area of Bexhill (TQ 737080).

70. The Keep of the Roussillion Barracks on the A286 to the north of Chichester, (SU 895065).

71. A reproduction of the "bombard" found in the moat of Bodiam Castle. It is currently on display in one of the towers of the Castle.

72. One of a pair of cannon which originally stood at the entrance to a depot built

Maps

Foreword

Having spent a large part of my life in Sussex, and having experienced those uncertain days of the 1940s, I know only too well what the people of this county must have endured during Britain's finest hour. Yet the Second World War was not the only time that Sussex has been on the nation's front line. Being so close to mainland Europe has meant that every invader, potential or actual, has viewed the open, stony beaches of Sussex with a view to conquest. As a consequence almost every previous generation has had to face the grim realities of war.

There can be few counties in England where so much fighting has taken place, over so many centuries. The great battles of Hastings and Lewes changed the course of British political and social history. Throughout the Hundred Years War the coastal towns of Sussex were under regular attack and such places as Rye and Winchelsea were ransacked. When the King of Spain attempted to crush England with his Armada the fire beacons on the heights of Ditchling and Crowborough signalled the news to London whilst the militia men stood to arms along the coast.

Nor was Sussex spared the internal conflict of the Civil War with Royalist forces besieged at Chichester and Arundel succumbing to the overwhelming strength of the Parliamentarians. With the age of Napoleon Bonaparte, invasion threatened Sussex once again and forts and barracks sprouted in every major town and port.

But it was the two world wars of the twentieth century, and especially the second, which had the greatest impact upon the ordinary folk of Sussex. Almost everyone in the county was affected in one way or another – Eastbourne, for example, was one of the most frequently bombed coastal towns in Britain.

I well recall that summer and autumn of 1940 and the dashing exploits of the RAF that saved Sussex, and Britain, from yet another invasion. It is because of the courage and sacrifice of such men and women that the people of Sussex have lived in peace for almost seventy years and warfare has been consigned to history books such as this one, which I am pleased to endorse.

Dame Vera Lynn OBE, DBE

Introduction

The Military Geography of Sussex

From its south-eastern tip Sussex is little more than sixty miles from continental Europe and the county's coastline, some seventy-six miles long, occupies a large part of Britain's southern frontier. Before the days of Macadam and the Turnpike, water travel could prove more certain than land transportation and the seas that define the borders of our nation aided, rather than deterred, the invader. Though the last successful invasion of Britain took place almost 1,000 years ago, the gently shelving beaches of Sussex have tempted the prospective invader with the promise of both an easy disembarkation and a short and direct route to London.

The repeated threat of invasion from the Continent has shaped the very landscape of the county. The rounded tops of the Iron Age hill forts, the sheer walls of the medieval castles, the squat stumps of Martello towers, the moulded Vaubanesque contours of the Palmerstone redoubts and the crouched concrete blocks of the Second World War pillboxes constitute the visible evidence of Sussex's position on Britain's front line.

Over the centuries, the coastline has changed. Selsey was once an island – its Old English name was Seolesig, or Seal Island. Pevensey Castle, now around a mile from the coast, once stood on a small peninsula that projected into the sea. To the east of Pevensey, the town of Old Winchelsea was swept away by mighty storms and an entirely new town had to be built away from its once magnificent harbour, the Camber.

Storms, shingle and silt also blocked Hastings harbour and coastal erosion took away part of the cliff where its castle once towered above the sea. The estuaries of the rivers Arun and Adur have shifted a number of times, driven by westerly winds and strong currents. The mouth of the River Ouse was once at Seaford. It is now at Newhaven.

Inland from the coast lies Sussex's most prominent geographical feature. Running for seventy-two miles from its origins deep in the heart of Hampshire to its conclusion, at the cliffs of Beachy Head high above the Pevensey Levels, is the chalk mass of the South Downs. Eight hundred and eighty-eight feet tall at its highest point, and between five and seven miles wide, this natural defensive

INTRODUCTION

The South Downs – defensive barrier or Iron Age super-highway? This is a view from the Norman motte and bailey castle at Fulking looking towards the hill fort at Devil's Dyke.

barrier was, like the sea, as much an aid to communication as an obstacle.

To the north of the Downs is a narrow strip of greensand and then the Weald, once a vast, virtually impenetrable forest jungle which was almost devoid of lateral pathways. Only along the foot of the Downs, or across their lofty peaks high above the Wealden plain, could Neolithic and Iron Age man travel easily from east to west across Sussex and it was upon the broad peaks of these hills that the early inhabitants of this area built the first defensive fortifications. At Mount Caburn, The Trundle, Cissbury and half a dozen other sites the remains of the earthen ramparts and deep ditches of the hill forts can still be traced.

The Downs are dissected by three large rivers – the Arun, Adur and Ouse. These waterways were all navigable for a considerable distance inland from the sea and to guard the passage of these important commercial and strategic avenues great castles were constructed on dominating heights at the points where the rivers cut through the Downs. At a later date, when the paths of these rivers had settled, their estuaries were also guarded by solid Victorian forts.

Some of these defensive works have been all but destroyed yet at Arundel,

Shoreham, Lewes and Newhaven the walls of once-mighty fortifications still stand proudly in their historic settings. A fourth river – the Cuckmere – also passes through the Downs but the river is not navigable and is so close to the eastern limit of the Downs that it possesses little strategic value and no fortifications protect its upper reaches. However, the wide, flat estuary of the Cuckmere, known as Cuckmere Haven, was considered to be a likely disembarkation point, and pillboxes and machine-gun posts dating from the Second World War now blend into the nearby cliffs.

Further to the east, close to the Sussex border with Kent, is the River Rother. As with all of Sussex's major rivers it flows from north to south, exiting into the sea. At its estuary Winchelsea developed into one of the county's most important ports until the storms and the drift of shingle diverted the mouth of the Rother eastwards to where the town of Rye now stands. Throughout the Middle Ages and until the sixteenth century, Rye was considered to be one of the bulwarks of the nation. The prevailing winds in the Channel are from the west and the silt and shingle closed in upon Rye harbour, narrowing its passage and reducing its scour until the port was left far from the sea.

The Rother, with its tributaries the Brede and the Tillingham, marks not only the eastern extremity of the county, but also the limit of the most extensive region of flat land along the south-east coast – the Romney Marsh. The Rother, as the only defensible feature in the area, was of considerable military significance and its course was commanded by the most sublime of Sussex's fortified buildings, Bodiam Castle. The line of the Rother was also incorporated into the most ambitious military structure of the nineteenth century, the Royal Military Canal. The Canal, really a massive wet ditch and rampart, effectively isolated Romney Marsh and removed it from the military equation.

Confusingly, there is another River Rother in Sussex. This second Rother is in West Sussex. It is a tributary of the River Arun, which it joins near Pulborough. A station was built by the Romans at the junction of these rivers on Stane Street, the great road from Chichester to London. A Norman motte and bailey castle was also built near here.

Another river, the Lavant, has its origins in the western Downs, running southwards to meet the sea at Chichester. In early times the Lavant estuary, sheltered by Selsey to the east and Thorney Island to the west, was the most important waterway along the Sussex coast. It was here that the Romans built their regional capital, the fortified stronghold of Chichester.

At the eastern end of the Downs the hills fall away to the flat, low terrain around Pevensey and Eastbourne which travels on beyond the borders of Sussex and across the Romney Marsh. This is an area that is difficult to defend and every

INTRODUCTION

actual or potential invader from William of Normandy to Adolf of Germany has regarded the beaches of East Sussex and Kent as the best available landing ground. Here can be seen the powerful Roman fort at Pevensey which was one of the Saxon Shore forts built to deter the barbarian raiders. The castles of Hastings, Camber and Rye, and the seemingly endless chain of Martello towers, still look out from this shoreline.

Paradoxically, the low-lying nature of the ground in this area lent itself to defence. The drainage ditches here are sealed by sluice gates and if invasion threatened the area could be flooded by opening the gates. Though this was official policy in the eighteenth century and early nineteenth century, it was never put into practice.

Northwards beyond the beaches and the Downs is the clay soil of the Low Weald which, in wet weather, turns into a heavy, glutinous mud. A travelling barrister in 1690 described Sussex as "a sink" which receives all the water from two long ranges of hills on both sides of it – i.e. the North and South Downs.

A hundred years later, in 1751, a Dr John Burton, in an account of his journey through Sussex, asked: "Why is it that the oxen, the swine, the women and all other animals are so long-legged in Sussex? May it be from the difficulty of pulling the feet out of so much mud by the strength of the ankle, that the muscles get stretched as it were and the bones lengthened?"

The extreme north and north-eastern side of the county, bordering Kent and part of Surrey, is occupied by the High Weald. This is a broad belt of sweeping sandstone hills and narrow valleys of clay or shale. Campaigning across such terrain would have been extremely difficult especially as the Weald was also partly covered in a dense forest (the word Weald means wood) which in Saxon times was recorded as being 112 miles from east to west and thirty miles across. The mud and the trees alone were a sufficient deterrent to any invaders from the north and few fortifications are found in the north of the county.

Despite its former inaccessibility this area has contributed significantly to the military history of Sussex. It was upon the Wealden hills to the north of Hastings that Harold and William fought for the crown of England, and the flat lands of the Low Weald played a part in the greatest conflict of all – the Second World War. At Hammerwood near East Grinstead and on the flat fields of Chailey, small, temporary airfields were formed and used from 1943 until after D-Day.

Like the Sussex coast, the Sussex Weald has changed considerably. Most of the great forest has gone, devoured by the iron workers and shipbuilders of previous centuries and the property developers of more recent times. The great medieval hunting grounds of the Ashdown Forest have been preserved, however, and these rolling heathlands have been a training ground for the British Army since the First World War.

The other low-lying region in Sussex is the strip of land between the Downs and the sea. This coastal plain widens from the east until it reaches its broadest point at Chichester where it stretches for ten miles towards Selsey across what is known as the Manhood Peninsula. Here, during the First World War, were seaplane and airship bases to protect allied shipping crossing the Channel, and a generation later this coastline, so close to Nazi-occupied Europe, was the home of six airfields including Tangmere – the second most important fighter base in the south during the desperate months of the Battle of Britain.

At the western end of the Sussex coastline the featureless and almost rectangular-shaped projection of Thorney Island also proved to be an ideal base for the RAF. The airfield was used by Coastal Command and then Fighter Command from 1938 until 1976 and Thorney Island is still occupied by the Army. Ford airfield was formerly the Fleet Air Arm's HMS *Peregrine*, and Shoreham airport was once the home of Hurricanes and Blenheims.

CHAPTER 1

Celts and Centurions:
The First Invasions of Sussex

There are few records to tell us of the conflicts that may have occurred in the Sussex area before the Battle of Hastings in 1066. The large number of fortifications that were built on the Downs, the High Weald and along the coast, however, clearly indicates that the threat to the local population of armed assault was indeed a real one.

The first defensive works that can be found in this area date back as far as the New Stone Age. These are the "causewayed" enclosures of Neolithic man. There are at least four such New Stone Age camps in Sussex, at The Trundle (north of Chichester), Barkdale (above Bignor), Whitehawk (Brighton racecourse) and Coombe Hill. They were sited on the Downland summits and they were formed with earthen ramparts above one or more ditches. The entrances were approached along causeways which bridged the ditches and cut through the ramparts to reach the interior.

These camps were also used as corrals for rounding up cattle. Populations were small in Neolithic times and it is likely that conflicts between tribes were not common. It is therefore possible that ranching was the main reason for the existence of the enclosures, as with the Bronze Age camps such as Ranscombe near Lewes, defence being of only secondary importance.[1]

There can be no doubt, however, about the primary purpose of the Celtic forts of the Iron Age. The remains that we see today at places such as Hollingbury, Wolstonbury and Highdown were made by the Celts who arrived in the Sussex area around 550 BC towards the close of the Bronze Age in Britain. These forts were of a similar construction to the causewayed enclosures, with deep ditches hewn out of the chalk and high ramparts made from the excavated earth, topped with wooden palisades.

The earthen walls were revetted with timber and in at least one fort – that at Hollingbury – the revetments were reinforced with flint walls. Other Iron Age forts have also been identified in the Weald – notably the promontory forts at High Rocks and Iping and the hill fort at Garden Hill in Ashdown Forest – which does indicate that this area was not the uninhabited wilderness that it was once believed to be.[2]

To defend such a fort, the defenders would hurl stones, and possibly javelins, from the ramparts. Pits filled with suitably-sized stones, the equivalent of magazines in fortresses of more recent times, have been found at excavated sites.[3] The weakest points in the defences of a hill fort were the entrances and it was against these that attackers concentrated their efforts. As Julius Caesar in the first century BC has explained, the attackers would attempt to drive the defenders away from the entrance with a hail of stones. Then, under the cover of their shields, they would try to set fire to the gate. Gateways, therefore, became increasingly sophisticated.

Often the actual gate was set well back from the edge of the ditch with the walls flanking the entrance and gateway. It is even possible that elaborate gate-towers were built above the entrance to enable the defenders to throw stones onto the heads of the approaching enemy. At The Trundle, for instance, excavations have revealed that the gates had inverted entrance passages and that, when the last improvements were made to the fort around 200 BC, the gates were made even stronger and the passages longer.

Though some hill forts were permanently occupied fortified villages, most were likely to have been administrative or trading centres during times of peace. There is no evidence to suggest that they were the strongholds of local chieftains but more probably places of refuge for the community if threatened by an aggressor. Gradually, the smaller hill forts fell into disuse with the larger ones becoming tribal headquarters.

Around 250 BC a second group of Celtic warriors crossed the Channel. They came from the Marne area of France and were armed with a new and formidable weapon – the horse-drawn chariot.[4] In the face of this invasion the local Celts built more hill forts and strengthened the existing ones but the Marnians could not be deterred. The invaders successfully occupied the western and central Downlands establishing their capital at Cissbury (near Worthing) where they built the second–largest Iron Age fort in Britain.

The walls of this impressive structure are a mile in circumference and encompass an area of seventy-eight acres. The surrounding ditch was originally eleven feet deep with ramparts thirty feet wide, towering twenty to thirty feet above the ditch. It took approximately 60,000 tons of earth and stone, reinforced by between 8,000 to 12,000 timbers, to form the walls.[5] It would have taken a huge number of warriors to man these defences adequately.

Cissbury was also England's second most productive flint-mining site. Flint was Neolithic Man's axe-head, arrow-head, spear tip and dagger. Cissbury was a great regional arsenal where weapons were made and stored and the site must have been as important in the Stone Age as it was in the Iron Age.

The Celts were the dominant nation of the pre-Roman era throughout Europe.

CELTS AND CENTURIONS

The ramparts and ditch that are typical of a Downland hillfort. This photograph is of Mount Caburn which can be reached by foot from Glynde (TQ 445089).

They were a mixture of racial types linked by a common language and their settlements extended from Asia Minor to the Atlantic. Celtic society was not as uncivilized or barbaric as the Romans, who supplanted them, have led us to believe. In general the Celtic leaders were elected to office and it was their duty to administer to the community.

When a tribal group occupied a territory the land it held belonged to the tribe as a community and the ground was shared out by the drawing of lots. Their religion was Druidism which was one of the first religions to preach the doctrine of the immortality of the soul. Many Romans considered that it was this belief in immortality that led to the Celts reckless bravery in battle. Indeed, the Druids would accompany them into battle.

The Celts were excellent iron-workers, able to produce weapons that were lighter, stronger and sharper than the bronze weapons of the people in the regions they overran. Their leaders fought on horseback armed with throwing spears (or javelins) and long iron swords. They were considered to be the finest light cavalry in Europe using their javelins in hit-and-run raids against enemy infantry formations. The lower orders operated on foot. They used both thrusting spears, which could be up to seven feet in length with an iron head and wooden stave, and shorter throwing spears. The latter was the principal ballistic weapon of the period as the longbow was regarded as a hunting implement.

Round, or sometimes rectangular, wooden shields with protruding domed or conical iron bosses were carried by warriors of all ranks. Body armour was limited to linked iron rings threaded onto cloth or, later, loose chain mail – though some warriors fought naked. According to Julius Caesar the British Celts covered themselves in blue woad to give them a more frightening appearance in battle.[6] Tall helmets were worn, at least by the nobility, some being embellished with ridges, studs and horns.

The Celts' most feared weapon was the war-chariot. Julius Caesar has left us an excellent description of these terrifying military vehicles in action. "The chariots of the Britons," wrote Caesar, "begin the fighting by charging over the battlefield. From them they hurl javelins; although the noise of the wheels and chariot teams are enough to throw any enemy into panic. The charioteers are very skilled. They can drive their teams down very steep slopes without losing control. Some warriors can run along the chariot pole, stand on the yoke and then dart back into the chariot."[7] After this impressive display the chariot teams would dismount and engage the enemy on foot. The chariots were then kept in readiness for a rapid retreat if the battle went against them.

By the start of the last century BC, Britain had become divided into a number of large tribal groupings and armed conflict was more likely to have occurred between these groups than their component parts. Yet the greatest threat to the Celts came not from their own internecine struggles but from the mightiest military force of the ancient world – the Roman Empire.

Celtic warfare was seen as an opportunity to display individual bravery and it was not unusual for battles to be decided by single combat between the champions of opposing tribes. With such a philosophy, subtle tactics and complex manoeuvres were both despised and pointless. When they faced the disciplined Roman legions they opposed them with nothing but their courage and their strength.

Julius Caesar's two early campaigns against Britain were little more than extended raids designed to intimidate the tribes who were giving support to the Celtic Gauls in their war against Rome. But his military victories enabled him to impose restrictions upon the Celtic leaders which guaranteed a degree of stability in Britain. The principal British chieftain at this time was Cunobelin, the ruler of the Catuvellauni tribe that occupied the Thames Basin.

Cunobelin appears to have generally complied with Caesar's impositions but upon his death his sons, Togodmunus and Caratacus, in violation of Caesar's treaties, moved against the Celts of the Sussex region, a Belgic tribe known as the Atrebates. The Atrebates had invaded Sussex four years after Julius Caesar's second British campaign. They were led at the time of their occupation of Sussex by Commius who was strongly pro-Roman.

The Catuvellauni drove the Atrebates southwards until they were left clinging to the Sussex coast and the new Atrebatic leader, Verica, sought refuge in Gaul – appealing to Rome for assistance. It is possible that during this time, when the Atrebates were being hard-pressed by the Catuvellauni, that a series of defensive dykes were created to the north of Chichester.

Now known as the Chichester Dykes (or the Devil's Ditches) these once-considerable earthworks form a discontinuous line over ten kilometres long. The Lavant estuary was an important inlet in early times and these dykes could well have formed the defences of the main harbour of Verica's kingdom located somewhere in the Chichester-Selsey region. It has also been suggested that the dykes were built when the Atrebates first occupied the Selsey peninsula in 50 BC and that they were a form of beach-head to protect their landing base.[8]

The unrest in Britain prompted the Romans to mount a full-scale invasion of the island under the pretext of supporting their ally Verica. This time, though, the Romans intended not merely to restore the previous order but to conquer.

In 43 AD the Emperor Claudius sent four legions across the Channel under the command of Anlus Plautius. The Britons, led by Caratacus, were decisively beaten in a battle near the River Medway and the Romans quickly subdued south-eastern Britain. Plautius then sent the Second Legion (*Legio II Augusta*), commanded by the future emperor Flavius Vespasian, southwards to form a base in preparation for the conquest of the Isle of Wight and the West Country.

The most obvious place for such an encampment was at the principal Atrebatic port at the mouth of the Lavant. This site was close to the Isle of Wight, could be easily supplied by sea and was located in friendly Atrebatic territory. It is even possible that as soon as the Catuvellauni had been defeated and the Roman presence in Britain was firmly established, supplies were being shipped to the Lavant estuary in anticipation of Vespasian's arrival.

A Roman legion numbered around 5,300 men to which were added native auxiliaries – in this case quite probably revengeful, or booty-seeking, Atrebatic Celts. The legion was divided into cohorts. The No.1 cohort was a crack fighting unit of 800 men, the other cohorts numbering only 480. Each cohort was split into centuries of originally 100 men, but by this date nearer eighty, under the command of a centurion. Centuries were composed of ten sub-units called conturbernia of eight to ten legionaries each.

Legionaries were armed with two 7-feet-long javelins (or pila) which had an effective throwing range of thirty yards. They were made with a thin iron shaft which bent on impact with a solid object. If the pila struck the shield of an enemy the weapon would bury itself into the shield and then buckle. The bent pila could not be removed easily from the shield which now had a seven-feet-long iron pole hanging from it. Inevitably, in the heat of battle, the shield would be quickly discarded. The legionaries would then move in upon the shield-less enemy and finish them off with their swords.

Legionaries were heavily armoured with metal plates on the chest, back and across the shoulders, all three plates being held together with leather straps. Below this was a skirt of leather and metal throngs and, above, a bronze or iron helmet. His defensive armour was completed by a large, convex, rectangular shield.

The legion was an infantry formation. Its cavalry arm was formed from the native auxiliaries. These were armed with both spears and swords. Flat, oval or hexagonal shields were also carried. The auxiliaries also provided small cohorts of light infantry, a contingent of archers and even some troops armed with slings.

Roman field artillery consisted of *catapultae* and *cheiroballistae*. The former were huge bows which were tensioned by handspikes and could propel a javelin 1,000 yards. The ballista was a spring-loaded gun that fired foot-long metal bolts. It has been stated that the Second Legion may have had as many as sixty ballistae and used them to great effect against the Britons.

It has been estimated that Vespasian commanded 8–10,000 men. His camp on the Lavant estuary was therefore of a considerable size with a well-palisaded earthen perimeter and wooden barracks. The legion moved off from the camp to seize the Isle of Wight around 44-5 AD. The Second Legion is known to have fought a number of battles and to have taken twenty British strongholds.

Though most of these engagements were against the Belgae and Durotriges of Hampshire and Dorset, it is possible that Flavious' march through Catuvellaunian-held territory in Sussex was not without incident. It is certainly possible that they met some opposition at Mount Caburn where Roman scabbards have been found next to the charred remains of the fort's wooden gateway.

The camp on the Lavant estuary continued as an important Roman base and the harbour, with its associated buildings, began to take on a more permanent appearance. But it was not until the second century that the town of Noviomagus Regentium was properly fortified. Running for one and a half miles, the original walls were made of earth faced with flint and mortar. In the third century these were replaced with massive stone walls, the foundations of which still encompass the centre of what we now call Chichester.

The Roman policy of allowing local chieftains to remain in power in their own provinces was extended to Britain. Though they adopted Latin names, wore Roman

Chichester's "Palace" bastion in the south-west quadrant of the city. The bastion can be seen from the "Walls Walk" which is accessible from numerous points around the city (SU 858045).

robes and lived in luxurious villas, these leaders were still Celts. After the occupation of the south-east the Celt Cogidubnus was installed as the client king of the area previously ruled by Verica. His capital was Noviomagus Regentium.

Noviomagus means "newmarket" and the place became an important commercial centre. From its once-mighty walls the famous Stane Street began its long journey to London, cutting through the dense forests of the Weald. At some time in the fourth century, probably after AD 367 when Barbarian raids against the English coast increased, bastions were added to the city walls. The bastions were built to house ballistae. Around the entire defensive perimeter a deep and wide ditch was also dug. To serve the ballistae Chichester must have maintained a permanent garrison.

Barbaric simplicity gave way to Romanesque sophistication and for almost four hundred years peace reigned throughout most of present-day England. Yet the grandeur that was Rome proved too tempting a prize to both barbarian and citizen. *Pax Romana* could not be sustained. Internal divisions and external assault led to the Roman legions being withdrawn from Britannica. Attacks from the Germanic nations of northern Europe led to the development of defensive works along the coast of southern Britain.

A series of forts, each protecting a good harbour, was built from Norfolk to the Isle of Wight. Under the command of a Count of the Saxon Shore, the walled city of Chichester and the great fort at Pevensey (Anderida) formed part of a defensive network designed to repel the barbarian hordes.[9]

Chichester was merely a fortified city but Pevensey was a purpose-built military fortification. Encompassing some nine acres of land, the fort's irregular oval trace followed the line of what was once a promontory that reached out into the sea. It had walls thirty feet high linked to ten bastions. Each, no doubt, mounted a great *catapultae* or ballistae.

With the withdrawal of the last Roman legions in 410 the Emperor Honorius wrote to the British towns and told them that they would now be responsible for their own defence. In 367 the country had suffered from attacks by the Picts, Scots, Francs and Saxons acting in concert in what has become known as "the great barbarian conspiracy".[10] To help combat the barbarian hordes the Britons introduced mercenaries from the Continent to defend the Saxon Shore. Pevensey Fort, for example, was garrisoned by warriors of unknown origin called the Abulci.[11] The defences of the Saxon Shore proved inadequate, however, and the Germanic invasions of Britain began.

An aerial view of the Roman fort of Anderida, with the medieval castle of Pevensey occupying its south-eastern corner. (By kind permission of English Heritage and Skyscan Photography.)

CHAPTER 2

South Saxons:
A County Created

To counter the barbarian incursions of the fifth century it is believed that Ambrosius Aurelianus, High King of the Britons, erected what has been called the Ambrosian barrier around the south-eastern coastline. This possibly took no more than the form of concentrations of troops to defend a particular area. It has been proposed that these points can be identified by the prefix Amb. Thus at Amberley, Ambersham and possibly Amberstone (near Pevensey Castle) were established the most southerly garrisons of the Ambrosian barrier.[1]

Despite these precautions the Saxons crossed the Channel in three ships landing at a place called Cymensora in the year 477. They were led by Aelle and his three sons, Cymen, Wlencing and Cyssa (or Cissa). It would seem that the landing was opposed by the Britons – to the Saxons they were simply Welsh, or foreigners – many of whom were killed and the rest driven into the Weald (the Andresweald). Cymensora is believed to have been near Selsey but the reference in the Anglo-Saxon Chronicles to the Britons retreating into the Weald would indicate that Aelle's landing was further to the east and it is certainly possible that Aelle landed somewhere between the Arun and the Cuckmere rivers.[2]

The Saxons' first objective would have been Noviomagus. By this time the city was slipping into ruin, though it was still the most important urban centre in the region. Cissa later rebuilt the city which became Cissa-ceaster and eventually Chichester. It is possible that the old British hill forts, particularly Cissbury Ring (Cissbury means "Cissa's fort") and Mount Caburn, were reoccupied at this time by the Britons.

Over the course of the next thirteen years the Saxons consolidated their position and extended their territory eastwards, though it would seem that the Ambrosian barrier restricted the invaders to the coastal plain. It is known that they fought at least one battle by the unidentified "Mearcredes" stream. Rivers have always been of considerable tactical importance and a fight at a river crossing was typical of the warfare of the period. This battle was fought, almost certainly, on the banks of either the Arun, the Adur or the Ouse.

Whilst at least one authority states that this encounter took place at Seaford near

9

The east gateway of the Roman Saxon shore fort of Anderida at Pevensey.

the Ouse, local tradition tells us that the Britons clashed, unsuccessfully, at Slonk Hill to the north-east of Shoreham. The origin of the word "slonk" is found in the Saxon word for slaughter. Thus Slonk Hill is slaughter hill. Yet Slonk Hill is not defensible and if the Britons did attempt to stem the Saxon advance the more likely battlefield would be the adjoining Mill Hill which overlooks the River Adur, possibly the Mearcredesburna of Anglo-Saxon tradition. Certainly the large number of Saxon burial sites between Shoreham and Pevensey may indicate that the invaders encountered stiff resistance from the Britons throughout this area.[3]

At Slonk Hill the invaders were successful and they continued eastwards until they reached the Roman fort at Pevensey (the fort of Anderida). Here Aelle and Cyssa stormed the defences and, according to *The Anglo-Saxon Chronicle*, "killed all who were inside, so there was not one Briton left". This was no easy victory for the Saxons. According to a twelfth-century writer, Henry of Huntigdon, the fort was besieged for many days with the Saxons finding themselves under attack by the natives using the Andresweald as cover from which they mounted hit-and-run raids. The invaders were only able to take the fort when they divided their forces in two – one to keep the British guerrillas at bay, the other to assault the walls.

The capture of Pevensey is recorded in the year 491 AD though dates in the early pages of the *The Anglo-Saxon Chronicle* are unreliable.[4]

SOUTH SAXONS

The territory conquered by Aelle and his sons became known as Suthseaxe which means the South Saxons. In time Suthseaxe became Sussex. Aelle himself became the leader of all the Germanic tribes south of the Humber and the first man to carry the title of Bretwaldas (Broad-Wielder), or High King of the English.

The Germanic invasion, which had swept across eastern and southern Britain, encountered a determined resistance in the west in the form of the legendary British warrior, Arthur. Though evidence of Arthur's existence is scanty, what is quite certain is that the Saxon advance was met with great force. It was against this force that Aelle led a confederation of Anglo-Saxons from Sussex and Kent.

The opposing armies clashed at Mount Baden (Mons Badonicus) which is possibly somewhere to the north of Bath. For three days battle raged with Arthur and his Britons achieving a momentous victory. Aelle's defeat was so complete that the Saxon conquest of Britain was halted and for the next seventy years the invaders were left in occupation of only East Anglia, Kent and a narrow strip along the Sussex and Hampshire coasts.

Gradually, however, the whole of the Sussex area came under Saxon control. This was probably through a process of confrontation rather than integration as there are few place names in Sussex that are of Celtic origin. Strung out in their small communities along the Downs and the edges of the Weald, the Britons would stand little chance against the organised Saxon forces.

It would seem that the marshland to the west of Pevensey marked the limit of the South Saxons' domain. Beyond this area, in and around present-day Hastings, a separate Germanic group, the Haestingas, maintained an independent existence until they were conquered by Offa of Mercia in 771.

From the archaeological and pictorial evidence available it has been concluded that the weapons, and therefore the tactics, employed by the Britons and the Saxons were largely the same. The relative scarcity of swords and hand-axes amongst the British and the Anglo-Saxons may indicate that these weapons were the preserve of the nobility, and the word Saxon was probably derived from the Seax, a single-edged, long dagger (about eighteen inches) carried by the Saxons. Saxon body armour was usually no more than a thick leather jerkin and helmets do not seem to have been worn.

Warfare at this time was conducted at close quarters. The Saxons fought almost exclusively on foot with their shields forming a protective wall. The British still fought both on foot and on horseback. The objective of each side was to break through their enemy's shield wall without compromising the integrity of their own defensive formation. The numbers of men engaged in the battles with the Saxons were not great.

Aelle and his sons disembarked at Cymensora from just three ships with probably

11

no more than fifty men in each vessel. There had been a movement away from the Roman towns back to the countryside where communities were comparatively small and isolated. Thus it was possible for a band of just 150 warriors to establish a beach-head from which the whole of Sussex was eventually conquered.

After subjugating or driving out the Britons, the Saxons began fighting each other. At one time the territory under the control of the South Saxons included the Isle of Wight. This was lost to Wessex in 685 when the West Saxon leader Caedwalla invaded Sussex and killed the king of the South Saxons, Aethelwalh. From this time onwards Sussex appears to have been closely associated with Wessex, eventually becoming an integral and important part of that powerful kingdom – though at one time Sussex came under the authority of the midlands kingdom of Mercia. Certainly Sussex, confined by the sea to the south, the marshes to the east and the Wealden forest to the north, was too small to maintain its independence. In 823 Sussex was fully incorporated into Wessex and little is known of its subsequent Saxon history.[5]

Initially the Saxons, unlike the Celts, did not feel the need to build any fortifications of their own. They had conquered by offensive action and, confident of their military prowess, they had little interest in defensive structures. The Saxon shield wall was considered to be defence enough for these fearsome warriors. The Saxons, however, were followed by another warlike nation from northern Europe – the Danes.

As raiders the Saxons could concentrate their strength upon a single point and overwhelm the inhabitants. But when the Saxons had themselves become settlers they were as vulnerable to the Danish incursions as the Britons had been to the Saxon attacks. The long series of wars against the Norsemen, therefore, resulted in the erection of a number of defensive "burgs" situated at points of strategic importance.

Almost certainly erected during the later years of the reign of Alfred the Great (871-99), the burgs were rebuilt on old Roman sites or were entirely new structures. They were designed to hold provisions and provide shelter for the local population. A permanent garrison or, burghware (the men who keep the burgs) was formed to defend them, assisted by the local population. Once built, the residents and the people of the surrounding area were required to keep the walls of the burg in good condition. Each man was assigned a particular section of the wall (roughly four feet) to maintain and, if necessary, to defend.

An early tenth century document, the Burghal Hidage[6] lists five burgs in Sussex at Burpham, Chichester, Lewes, Hastings and "Heorepeburan" which is probably Pevensey. Many of these forts were no more than natural or man-made mounds, on top of which were wooden stockades. More than thirty burgs were established and it was said that no one lived further than twenty miles from the protection of a burg.[7]

Sussex appears to have suffered less from the depredations of the Norsemen than many other areas of England. It is known that the Vikings attacked Chichester in 894. The brief reference to this raid in the *Anglo-Saxon Chronicle* states that "the town-dwellers put them to flight, killed many hundreds of them, and seized some of their ships".[8]

Another battle is alleged to have taken place at Kingley Vale to the north of Chichester and the great Yew forest of the Vale was planted in commemoration of the Saxon victory.[9]

In 896 two ships, which had formed part of a raiding party that was returning to the Continent from attacks against Devon and the Isle of Wight, ran aground in Sussex. The Danes were captured and taken to Winchester where Alfred ordered them to be hanged. In 998 the Danes occupied the Isle of Wight and from there they raided Hampshire and Sussex to obtain food. Eleven years later "the force", as the Scandinavians are called in the *Anglo-Saxon Chronicles*, "ravaged and burned as was their custom", in Sussex, Hampshire and Berkshire.[10]

The Viking attacks compelled the various Saxon groups to fight together and eventually to combine under a single leader. The effect was the forging of the English nation.

The unification of the Anglo-Saxon tribes can be traced back to 867–8 when the Mercians of the midlands and the West Saxons of Wessex under Ethelred joined forces to hold off a large Viking attack from Northumbria. This combined force was strong enough to hold back the Danes.

Three years later Ethelred died and Alfred became king of Wessex, the most highly developed part of the country still in Saxon hands. The Vikings attacked Wessex repeatedly but were fought to a standstill. For fourteen years from 880 onwards, Wessex enjoyed a sustained period of peace that it had earned on the battlefield. Alfred's authority extended throughout Somerset, Wiltshire, Hampshire, Sussex and most of the southern and eastern half of the country not occupied by the Danes. Sussex, held continuously throughout the Danish wars by the Saxons, guarded Alfred's southern flank and it was at Westdean, three miles from Alfriston (Alfred's tun), that Alfred is supposed to have established one of his courts.[11]

It was during these years of peace that Alfred organised a regularised military system throughout his kingdom. This was based on resurrecting the Saxon fyrd which was an established, part-time army. Every man that held land was obliged to undertake military service in the fyrd. In theory, only warriors who had actively fought to defend their country or fought on behalf of the king had the right to hold land and dispose of it as they pleased upon their death i.e. hereditary rights. Any persons who refused to fight forfeited these rights.

It would seem that this was a personal service that had to be performed. Unlike other obligations such as burghbote (the maintenance of the burgs) or brycegeweore (the upkeep of bridges) which a wealthy thegn could have performed for him by one of his men, the landholder himself had to undertake the military service (fyrdfaereld) in the field alongside his king.

There was a second group of free men and cottars who held land from their overlord, be it a thegn, or an ecclesiastical body or person (such as a bishop), who were also obliged to perform military service. The thegn or lord was responsible for ensuring that the persons under his authority attended the fyrd. As all land ultimately belonged to the king, desertion or failure to comply with military service by individuals of this group resulted in the person's land being confiscated and returned to the king.

The number of men that an overlord had to supply to the fyrd depended on the amount of land the lord held. If the Berkshire Doomsday record is typical, the requirement was one man per five "hides" of land. These men were paid for their service from funds raised by their fellow landholders. Their length of service was two months a year. If more than one person had a share in the five hides then the person that represented them on fyrd service was assisted by the others with regards to weapons, provisions and pay. Each fyrd was centred round a burg.[12]

By this time the seax had become a secondary weapon, spears being the principle armament of the low-born Saxons. Swords remained the preserve of the wealthy. They were expensive items and were handed down through the generations. Some were given names (for example Excaliber!) and were elaborately inlaid and overlaid in silver and gold.

In 893 the Danes returned to the offensive. Again Alfred – justifiably called "the Great" – fought the invaders to a standstill, both on land and at sea. At the age of just 50, Alfred died. His long series of battles had saved England from being overrun but the struggle for control of the country continued for another 100 years with the last Viking raid against the Sussex coast being delivered against Hastings in 1011.[13]

Sussex had been in the forefront of the fight against the Danes with the Sussex thegn, Wulfnoth Cild, being appointed by King Ethelred the Unread to lead a large contingent of Sussex ships against the Danish leader, Cnut. According to the *Anglo-Saxon Chronicle*, Wulfnoth was "betrayed" and driven into exile.

Wulfnoth, however, took with him many of his ships and the king sent his navy to oppose the rebel thegn. Ethelred's ships were hit by a severe storm which forced them aground, enabling Wulfnoth to destroy the stranded vessels. Though it would seem that with this victory Wulfnoth won his way back into royal favour, the loss of ships was disastrous for England, allowing the Danes to raid the length of the south coast.

Finally, in 1017, the last of the great Wessex kings of the Saxons, Edmund Ironside, died. With his demise all resistance to the Danes ended, and the Danish leader, Cnut, was acknowledged King of England.

For over twenty years the Danes ruled England until the sudden death of Cnut's son Harthacnut left the throne vacant. A protracted, though bloodless, power struggle resulted in the restoration of Alfred's royal line in the form of Edward the Confessor. Edward's accession brought together all the feuding elements as his father (Ethelred the Unread) was English and his mother, Emma of Normandy, had also married Cnut the Dane.[14]

Edward had lived in his mother's country for most of his life and he continued to maintain his connections with the Normans. Though nominally part of France, Normandy was, in fact, an independent Nordic country, its territory having been won from the French in the late ninth century.

A few years after his assumption of the throne it is thought that Edward invited his friend William, Duke of Normandy, to England. It may have been during this visit that Edward promised William that he would succeed him as King of England. William, as Edward's cousin once-removed, through his great-aunt Queen Emma, was the closest adult male relative to The Confessor and, arguably, the rightful heir to the English throne.

At this time another famous figure first makes his appearance upon history's stage. Harold Godwin (or Godwinson), Earl of Wessex, was Edward's most powerful subject and the country's leading military commander having beaten the Welsh and extended Edward's rule into south Wales. From comparatively obscure origins Harold's father (who was probably of English descent, possibly the son of Wulfnoth Cild) married into a branch of the Danish royal family and in time became one of Cnut's most trusted subordinates.

When Edward became king, Godwin, as Earl of Wessex, established himself as the unrivalled power behind the throne. His relationship with Edward was a stormy one which reached a head in 1048 when Godwin openly defied the King.

One of Edward's Norman friends, Eustace of Boulogne, was returning to France from a visit to Edward's court when he entered Dover and demanded accommodation for himself and his entourage. One of the townsfolk refused to admit an armed foreigner into his house and a fight broke out. Others became involved and at the end of the dispute nineteen Normans and twenty English lay dead.

Eustace demanded retribution and, as Dover fell within Godwin's domains, Edward ordered Godwin to punish the townspeople. Godwin, quite understandably, refused and the enraged Edward banished Godwin from his kingdom.

Godwin was now seen as the champion of the English and when a year later he returned to England and sailed along the shores of his old earldom he gathered considerable support at Pevensey, Hastings and along the Kent coast. The strength of Godwin's force compelled Edward to reconsider his support for the Normans and all Godwin's previous rights, lands and privileges were restored.

Shortly after his showdown with Edward, Godwin died and his eldest son Harold took not only his father's title of Earl of Wessex but also his position as Edward's chief advisor. As the years passed Edward's participation in government decreased and the affairs of state were administered almost entirely by Harold who was given more titles and greater authority. At one time the Godwin family held four of the five largest earldoms in England but two of Harold's brothers disgraced themselves – Tostig because of his harsh rule and Swegen for seducing the abbess of Leominster – and they were driven into exile. This could not have happened without Harold's authorisation and it turned Tostig into a bitter enemy.

In 1064 Harold set off by ship from Bosham harbour near Chichester. His destination and his reasons for travelling have never been satisfactorily established but strong winds blew his ship along the French coast to Ponthieu where Harold and his retinue were captured and imprisoned.

Duke William managed to secure Harold's release from the Count of Ponthieu and made him welcome at his palace at Rouen. During his stay in Normandy Harold fought with the Norman army in an attack against Brittany and in return was knighted by William. It was later recorded in, the text accompanying the Bayeux Tapestry, that at this time, Harold took an oath upon some holy relics. This may therefore have implied, as William was subsequently to allege, that Harold would support the Duke's claim to the English throne in the increasingly likely event that Edward died without an heir. In response to this William confirmed Harold in his earldom and allowed him to return to England.

Whether or not Harold made such an oath, or whether it was made under duress, is not known, but as his liberty was entirely dependent upon William's goodwill, it was hardly likely that Harold could have refused such a request.

At the beginning of the fateful year of 1066 it was clear that Edward was dying. He had no obvious heir and the only legitimate contender was a distant relative (his nephew Edgar) who was still a child. So, on his deathbed, Edward gave his hand to Harold and, it was claimed, offered him the throne of England.

CHAPTER 3

Fight for the Throne:
The Battle of Hastings

On the night of 4 January 1066, Edward the Confessor died. The following morning he was buried at the new abbey of West Minster. Edward had personally planned and supervised the construction of the great building and he was the first man to be interned within its walls. That same afternoon Harold Godwinson was crowned King of England in the same building. Though his succession was endorsed by the Witan (a gathering of the leading noblemen and clergy) others were to dispute his claim and Harold must have known that he would have to fight to keep his crown.

Harold's claim to the throne, apart from Edward's deathbed endorsement, was based on the fact that his father had married the sister of Ulf who was Cnut's brother-in-law. Edward's Queen Emma was also Harold's sister. If these tenuous links with the Danish and English royal lines were justification for Harold's succession then Harold's younger brother Tostig, the recently disgraced and exiled Earl of Northumberland, also had a claim. So too did Ulf's son Svein, King of Denmark, as did Duke Willliam of Normandy whose mother Emma had married that great warrior Cnut and to whom Edward may have once promised the English throne.

The Norwegian king, Harald Hardrada, also cast his eyes across the North Sea. The Vikings had a long record of successful attacks upon England and many people of Norwegian descent had settled in the north-east of the country where he might attract some support.

Fortunately for Harold, Svein, who was Harold's cousin and friend, did not press his claim. But Tostig immediately began to canvas for support and William made preparations to invade England and claim what he genuinely seemed to believe was his rightful inheritance.

England had proven to be vulnerable to the Viking raids of previous generations and its reputation as a fighting nation cannot have been high. But it was no mere raid that William of Normandy proposed to his barons when they met the Duke in the castle of Lillabonne at the beginning of spring. He planned to attack and subjugate an entire country, a country far larger than his own. Such an operation would require a huge army and a massive fleet to transport it across the perilous waters of the Channel. William had neither and it was obvious that he would need assistance from outside Normandy.

If the Duke was to persuade enough men to join his adventure he would have to convince them that such an enterprise would succeed. Yet the scale of the operation and the obstacles that stood in William's way were unprecedented.

Not since Caesar, a thousand years earlier, had a general attempted to transport an entire army across the Channel. It would be almost another thousand years before such an enterprise would be repeated when the Allies invaded Normandy in 1944, and that was the single largest combined military, naval and air operation ever mounted.

Though William's barons had little choice but to offer their backing, without the approval of his overlord, the King of France, he could not leave his territory unprotected. So, following the meeting at Lillabonne, William rode to the great capitals of western and northern France to garner support for his expedition and assurances from his rivals that they would not attack Normandy in his absence. A deputation was also sent to Rome where the Pope was persuaded to condemn Harold for breaking his sacred oath and to sanction William's claim to the English throne. This was a critical decision as William could now seize the moral high ground. The Witan may have chosen Harold but William had been selected by a higher authority – by God.

Despite the obvious perils of the proposed invasion, with the offer of estates and titles to those men who would follow him, William soon found plenty of ambitious knights prepared to join his growing army, especially since he had received papal approval. From as far north as Flanders and as far south as Italy they flocked into Normandy to join William's great enterprise. Men he now had, but his greatest problem was transportation. No one had ever tried to ship a medieval army such a distance (from the harbour at Dives to the English coast is approximately ninety to ninety-five nautical miles) and it was clear that he would need to build hundreds of vessels, and that would take time.

Time, by contrast, was exactly what Harold did not need. As early as April, Tostig, possibly in collusion with William, had crossed the Channel with some sixty ships and had raided the coastal settlements of Sussex and Kent. Harold called out his forces but his brother then sailed up the east coast, no doubt hoping to draw Harold away from the south. The new king of England was not deceived. Tostig's force was small and could be left safely to the fyrd of Mercia and Northumbria.[1] The real danger had yet to materialise.

Harold was fully aware that William intended to invade as he had received a number of threatening letters from the angry Duke. The English king had assembled a large force of infantry and his entire fleet of around 400 ships at the Isle of Wight. All summer long he waited for the Normans to appear. The prevailing winds in the Channel throughout the summer months blow from the south-west and any invasion force from Normandy would be carried by these winds to the beaches of Sussex and Kent.

By placing his fleet at the Isle of Wight those same winds would sweep Harold down the coast and upon the rear of the invaders. Harold had called out the fyrd to defend their country and his force on the Isle of Wight amounted to around 10,000 men with other warriors watching the tides along the coast. Their obligatory military service was two months each year, and for more than eight weeks the men of the fyrd had waited with growing impatience for the threatened attack. At some point Harold would have to allow his troops to return home but soon it would be autumn and then winter when no invader would dare put to sea.

By early August William was ready. He had put together a huge fleet in the harbour at the mouth of the River Dives. It is impossible to know how many ships William may have had. Figures in early accounts range from 696 to 11,000 vessels and between 10,000 and 60,000 men. As William fought at Hastings with possibly around 8,000 men historians have estimated that the Franco-Norman fleet could have been no larger than that of the English and probably little more than 350 strong.

Their armies assembled, the two great men waited on their respective sides of the Channel for the wind that would carry them both to the shingle beaches of Sussex. The Norman ships, clearly defined in the Bayeux Tapestry, had long, shallow keels and single masts bearing a square sail. Such vessels would have limited ability to sail to windward and their shallow keels would have little effect in preventing leeway. William therefore had no choice but to wait for the wind to blow from the south or the south-west.

Meanwhile, Tostig, after suffering a heavy defeat in Lincolnshire, continued up the east coast to Scotland. Though Tostig probably appreciated that he would never be able to command enough support in England to seize power for himself, he seems to have persuaded the Scottish king, Malcolm, and then the Norwegian king, Hardrada, to join him in an attempt to invade northern England. It is possible that Tostig hoped to recover at least part of the Northumbrian earldom from which he had been banished. Malcolm, no doubt, saw an opportunity to annex territory around the English border and Hardrada must have wished to emulate the achievements of the great Viking warrior-kings of the past.

Back in Normandy, the great fleet at last set sail from Dives-sur-Mer on 12 September, but strong westerly winds blew the ships along the Norman coast. Some ships were lost and a number of men were drowned. The invasion fleet found shelter at St Valéry in the Somme estuary, more than 250 kilometres to the east of Dives.

William buried his dead (in secret, presumably so as not to dishearten the rest of the troops) and waited again for a favourable wind. But the wind blew from the north and running with that wind was a dreaded old enemy. Accompanied by Harold's embittered brother Tostig came the Vikings and the most fearsome warrior of his age, Harald Hardrada.

It was now the middle of September and with the onset of the northern gales Harold dismissed the fyrd. The invasion season was over for the year and the Anglo-Saxon warriors returned to their homes and their farms. Harold, who was a Sussex man, went to his family home at Bosham for a few days before riding with his household troops back to London, only to learn that the Norsemen had landed in Northumbria.

Harold collected as many of his men as he could muster and started for the north. The English army marched 190 miles from London to York in just four days. This was a considerable achievement but it must not be assumed, as many have, that the journey was made on foot. The Anglo-Saxons, from Alfred the Great to the Duke of Wellington, have excelled as infantry and Harold's army was no different. But the men that accompanied Harold were men of rank and paid retainers.

These were elite troops, not foot-sloggers. They would have ridden to York. The English despised the horse in war as it was too easy for cavalry to escape the terrifying slaughter of a medieval battlefield. The Anglo-Saxons stood and fought. The horse was seen as a means of transportation and it was on horseback that Harold travelled from London to York.

Harald and Tostig had landed at Riccall and advanced towards York, the great capital of the north. A combined force raised by the northern English earls marched from York to meet the invaders and the opposing armies clashed just outside York on 20 September at Gate Fulford, which is now a suburb of the city. Here the English were soundly beaten and the two earls, Edwin of Mercia and Morcar of Northumbria, made peace with Hardrada.

Meanwhile Harold Godwin had reached Tadcaster, less than ten miles from York, on 24 September. There he rested overnight and early the following morning he marched through York and fell upon the unsuspecting Vikings. At Stamford Bridge, ten miles beyond York, Saxons and Vikings stood toe to toe and swung their battle-axes and swords in mortal conflict. The invaders had been taken completely by surprise and many of the Norsemen had been caught without their shields and swords.

The invaders were pushed back to their longboats after suffering terrible losses. Tostig was killed and Hardrada was shot through the throat by an arrow. It is said that the Norsemen sailed to England in 300 ships yet they needed only twenty-five of those ships to take the survivors back to Norway.

Harold had earned a remarkable victory against an enemy force probably larger than the one that William had assembled in Normandy. It was not often that an English army defeated a Norwegian horde but the invaders were so decisively beaten that never again would the Vikings threaten the shores of England. If its memory had not been overshadowed by the events that followed, the Battle of Stamford Bridge would have been regarded as the greatest victory ever achieved by the English Saxons. So with unbridled confidence, though diminished numbers, the Anglo-Saxon army marched back to the south because the wind had changed in the Channel and William of Normandy had landed at Pevensey Bay!

Instead of entering London in triumph, Harold went to Waltham Abbey to contemplate and to consider his next move. We can only guess at his state of mind at this time. After his great victory against the Vikings did he consider himself invincible or, after two weeks of marching and fighting, was the news of the Franco-Norman invasion a crushing blow to Harold's belief in his right to the throne?

Harold knew that he would have to fight again but his men were exhausted. The most prudent policy open to Harold was for him to find a defensive position near to London and allow his troops a few more days to recuperate. William would have no choice but to march upon London where he would find the English army rested and ready for battle, supported by the population of the nation's capital.

Instead Harold committed a fatal blunder and decided to drive his warriors forward again. Without even waiting for the troops of the northern earls which were already marching southwards, Harold set off from London on 12 October. With just his paid retainers and men of the London fyrd – possibly as few as 5,000 men – Harold crossed the Thames and rode down to Rochester and through the Weald. The Sussex and Kent fryd were told to join Harold's force at a well-known point on the Wealden Hills where the districts of Baldslow, Ninfield and Hailesaltede met – the place of the Hoar (grey) Apple Tree on Caldbec Hill. To this place most, if not all, of the fighting men of Sussex must have made their way to do battle for their king.

William's fleet had sailed from the harbour of St Valéry-sur-Somme on 27 September, making landfall at around 09:00 hours the following morning at what is now called Norman's Bay. His force was composed of possibly 3,000 mounted knights, 1,000 archers and 4,000 foot soldiers.

William's great achievement, from a military standpoint, was in crossing the Channel with such a large body of cavalry. No medieval commander had dared attempt such an operation. But the mounted troops were the flower of the Norman army and William had to take them with him if he was to have any chance of success. In the end, it would be these men that would tip the scales of victory in favour of the invaders.

A Norman archer on the battlefield of Hastings at Battle.

Armed with lances and long, heavy swords or iron maces, the cavalry were protected from neck to knee in chain mail, their heads covered with iron helmets and nose-guards. Long, tapering shields were also carried. The comparatively recent introduction of the stirrup had increased the fighting effectiveness of the mounted soldier considerably. Not only did the stirrup give the rider a more secure seat and greater control of his mount, it also enabled him to get the full weight of his body behind his lance when charging an enemy and when striking at an opponent with a sword or mace.

With the aid of this simple invention the mounted knight would dominate European warfare for much of the Middle Ages. The Norman infantry, being of lower rank, were not so heavily armed and some may have carried just a single weapon, be it either sword or spear. Many of the archers wore neither protective mail nor helmets.

William must have expected his landing to be opposed by the English and his disembarkation was conducted in true military fashion, as Robert Wace explained just 100 years later: "The archers were the first to land, each with his bow bent and his quiver full of arrows slung at his side ... The knights landed next, all armed, with their hauberks on, their shields slung at their necks and their helmets laced."[2] Shortly after landing William, with an escort of just twenty-five men, including William fitzObern, one of his key military advisors, undertook a reconnaissance of the area.

The Normans immediately erected a wooden fort within the confines of Pevensey Castle. It has been suggested that the wood was brought from Normandy already pre-cut so that the walls could be assembled very quickly. His beach-head thus secured, William waited for the attack that he believed was imminent.

But Harold was still moving down to London from Yorkshire and it was at least two weeks after the Normans had landed that the English army assembled on the High Weald. Whilst they waited for Harold's force to appear, the invaders moved along the coast to Hastings, scavenging for food and ransacking many of the villages between Pevensey and Hastings on the way.

At Hastings William ordered another castle to be built, this time using conscripted local labour. William could not leave the coast to seek out Harold. He did not have any idea where the English might be and every step that he took further inland took him deeper into hostile territory. Also, and of over-riding importance, was the fact that he dare not leave his fleet unprotected for fear that it could be captured or destroyed.

Whilst they waited, the Normans plundered the region around Hastings. This may simply have been the troops foraging for supplies to keep the army and its horses fed. It has also been suggested that the Normans undertook such destruction in order to induce Harold to move against them immediately, for the longer that they remained in one place the more difficult it would become for them to find food in the area.

Sussex was part of Harold's hereditary earldom of Wessex and he could hardly remain inactive whilst his people and their homes were being destroyed. In fact the ravaging of the countryside was one of William's principle tactics and one that he had employed previously to great effect, particularly in 1063 when William had successfully attacked Maine.[3]

Such actions were commonplace in medieval Europe and it had led to the building of castles throughout the Continent. Before the advent of gunpowder and the introduction of heavy ordnance into siege warfare, the walls of stone castles were extremely difficult to breach. Faced with invasion, the defending forces could retire into the safety of their castles. The invaders would be free to harry the countryside but they would not be able to settle in the invaded land because the defending army would still be intact and able to counter-attack as, and when, the opportunity presented itself.

It was said by Oderic Vitalis[4] that the English were severely disadvantaged by the lack of stone-built fortifications. This view is supported by the fact that the Normans began building castles from the day that they landed.

The prospect of plunder would attract large numbers of men to join the army of a successful commander. Though some of William's supporters had been promised great estates, not all of his men could be given land. Many must have followed William just for the chance of unlicensed rape and pillage. Yet, if William of Malmesbury is to be believed,[5] Harold did not share out the spoils of war after the victory at Stamford Bridge and as a result few men, other than his household troops, followed him south to face the Normans.

This could possibly explain why Harold, king of a large and well-populated country, faced William with only a few thousand soldiers. It may well be that Harold had sealed his fate at Hastings with that decision at Stamford Bridge.

At last, on 13 October 1066, the English army could be seen gathering on Caldbec Hill, some eight miles to the north-west of Hastings. In a campaign of this nature, in relatively unknown territory, early warning of the approach of the enemy was crucial to the invaders and William's cavalry scouts were clearly pushed far and wide. The sudden and rapid approach of the English caused William to withdraw his foraging parties and advanced pickets and he concentrated his army in readiness for an immediate onslaught by Harold.

Throughout the night of the 13th, the Normans, fearing a surprise attack, stood to arms. At this time William also learnt that Harold had sent his fleet round the coast to cut off the Normans' retreat and prevent any reinforcements being sent from France.

An artist's impression of a wooden Norman tower, typical of those used in early motte and bailey castles. (By kind permission of the Director, Hastings Castle.)

Some historians have criticised Harold for concentrating his army too close to the Norman encampment. Yet his position was ideal for defence and was near enough to the Norman camp to force William to attack without delay. It is also possible that Harold had hoped to attack the Normans and catch them unprepared as he had caught the Vikings at Stamford Bridge. But William's cavalry pickets had spotted the English army approaching across the Weald. The similarities in Harold's march to Tadcaster and his march to Caldbec Hill could also support the view that Harold hoped to surprise William as he had Tostig and Hardrada.

BATTLEGROUND SUSSEX

The subject of the English deployment is one of considerable interest. At some point in time, possibly on the morning of the 14th, Harold moved southwards from Caldbec Hill down to Senlac Hill (also now known as Battle Hill). Why this movement occurred is not known. It may have been that Harold, having assembled his forces on Caldbec Hill, was continuing his advance upon Hastings and that the only reason why he stopped on the Senlac ridge was because he had seen the Normans marching to meet him. It has been stated that the vanguard of William's army spotted the English coming out of the woods on Caldbec Hill and emerging onto the Senlac ridge that crossed the Hastings road.

Such statements have led some to claim that Harold was taken by surprise and his men were still taking up their positions when the Normans began their attack. It is certainly difficult to understand why Harold moved from Caldbec Hill if he intended to fight a defensive battle. Caldbec Hill, at 300 feet above sea level, is higher than Senlac Hill and its sides are steeper.

Harold had already rejected the suggestions of his advisors to remain on the defensive at London and wait for William to attack him. Therefore it seems extraordinary that Harold would march so purposely – without waiting for the northern earls to join him – all the way from London just to take up a defensive position near Hastings.

It has been stated by some historians that Harold took up a defensive position on Caldbec Hill whilst he awaited the reinforcements which he knew would reach him in a day or two. Indeed, one chronicler claimed that by the 13th Harold still had only one-third of the total force that he expected would eventually join him.[6]

It is more likely that Harold planned to attack the Normans and take them by surprise – as he had the Vikings – but when he saw thousands of mounted knights approaching at the head of William's army he realised that he could not operate in open order against such a large body of cavalry. He took advantage of the terrain and assembled his force upon Senlac Hill. No other course of action fits the known facts.

There are no accurate records to tell us the size of the English army. Military experts have examined Harold's position and they have estimated that, standing shoulder to shoulder and eight men deep, no more than seven or eight thousand men could have formed a battle-line upon the Senlac Hill. In the *Chronicon ex Chronicis* of 1118, Florence of Worcester declared that many Englishmen left Harold's army before the battle because the hill was already too crowded. The English and Norman armies, therefore, were roughly the same size. It was in their composition and their tactics that the opposing forces differed.[7]

Harold's army was composed entirely of foot warriors. They carried battle-axes, swords and spears as their principle armament, with throwing axes, javelins and even stones tied to sticks as their missile weapons. There were few archers in Harold's army. It is usually stated that this was because the bow was used in England mainly for hunting and was not considered to be an instrument of war. This is not entirely true. That there were fewer English archers than Norman at the Battle of Hastings seems certain. The accounts written after the battle and the Bayeux Tapestry all agree on this point. The bow would indeed have been used for hunting but it was also considered to be a weapon of war. It was used by the English at Stamford Bridge (Hardrada, remember, had been killed by an arrow) and it was used at Hastings. But it was seen as a weapon of the lower classes and a large part of Harold's army was composed of men of rank so the bow was not their weapon of choice.

Equally, the archers that had fought so successfully at Stamford Bridge would not have been able to march from York with the mounted retainers. The forces moving down from the north to join Harold later may well have included large numbers of archers.

Though the bulk of the English army was made up of fyrdsmen the King also possessed a number of retainers that lived on the royal estates whose military duty included the provision of their own arms and horses. These were the famed housecarls.

As both Earl of Wessex and King of England, it is thought that Harold would have been able to support the cost of approximately 3,000 housecarls. Some of these would have fallen at Stamford Bridge and it has been calculated that no more than 2,000 could have been present on 13 October 1066. Harold's brothers, Gyrth and Leofwin, who held earldoms in East Anglia, Kent and Surrey, together may have been able to provide another 2,000 of their own housecarls.

This force of well-armed and well-paid professional soldiers formed the backbone of the army. Alongside these fearsome warriors stood the wealthy landowners, also well armed. The Bayeaux Tapestry shows some of the English wearing chain mail and helmets, and these would be the thegns and housecarls but others, the fyrdsmen, appear with no armour, possessing just shields for protection.

If the English were to fight a defensive battle then their tactics would be simple. From behind their shield wall the men, packed into one massed formation, would swing their mighty battle-axes and throw their javelins. If the men held their ground (and their nerve) the enemy would be unable to make much impression upon such a body in hand-to-hand combat alone.

Such tactics did not require a complex command structure. All each man had to do was stand and fight. It cannot be said that Harold directed his troops other than by personal example and they would not be capable of any manoeuvre other than a wild change. By contrast, William's army, with its large proportion of mounted

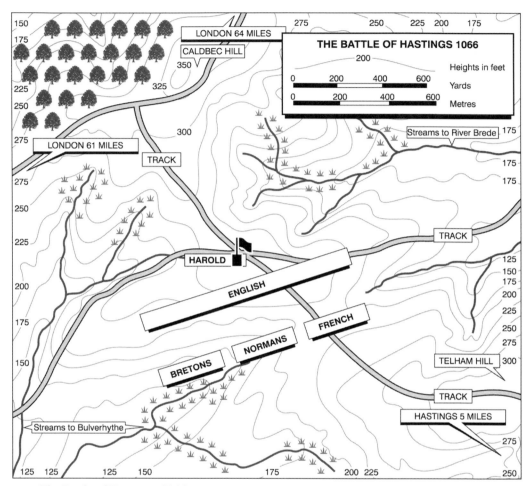

The Battle of Hastings, 1066.

troops, was an offensive force and needed careful handling. Its three arms, the bowmen, infantry and cavalry had to be organised, disciplined and controlled to be truly effective.

William, therefore, split his army into three divisions. The main division, led by William himself, was entirely Norman. Of the other divisions, one was a French and Flemish force (with a small Norman contingent) under Count Eustace of Boulogne, and the other was a mixed body of mercenaries from Brittany, Anjou and Maine.

This last division was commanded by a Breton called Alan Fergant. Each division was a well-balanced force of all three arms though the centre division, under William, was possibly twice the size of the other two.

There does not seem to have been the same formal and clearly defined military structure in Normandy as the semi-feudal system of Late Saxon England. It appears to have been an ad-hoc arrangement. Individuals were granted land, or inherited land, in return for which they supplied a fully armoured and mounted knight or knights depending on the terms of the arrangement between themselves and their overlords. The length of military service each year also seems to have been arbitrary. Forty days was regarded as the usual period of time but it is likely that the men served for as long as they were required or faced penalties as a consequence.[8]

Whatever the differences, the same basic principles applied in both armies. In return for land or money the recipients fought for their lord or sovereign when ordered to do so.

At dawn on Saturday 14 October, the leading units of the Franco-Norman army marched out of Hastings. William's army was soon strung out for many miles along the narrow track that led passed the Senlac Hill on its way to join the London Road. By the middle of the morning most of William's force had assembled at the foot of Harold's position.

Running for approximately 750 yards, with a width of some 150 yards, the Senlac ridge rises gently to some sixty feet above the foot of Telham Hill. The ground to the left of the ridge is steeper than the main ascent and to the right, where the slope is easier, was an area of marshy ground. Behind the ridge lay part of the dense Andresweald forest. William's options were therefore limited.

His main strike force was his mounted knights and they could not operate effectively on the difficult terrain that flanked Harold's position. The Duke had no choice but to mount a frontal assault.[9] It would be a brutal battle of attrition until the English line broke.

It was stated that a wall surrounded the English position and this is usually interpreted as being the shield wall, though one historian, E.A. Freeman[10], positively asserts that this was a palisade erected around the hill. For this assertion to be true the troops, who had marched all the previous day, would have had to spend the evening cutting trees. They would also have already planned a defensive battle.

Whilst neither of these actions are impossible what rules out such a supposition is that the English would already have had it in mind to fight their defensive battle on Senlac Hill, not on Caldbec Hill where they spent the night. For if they prepared their palisades for use on Caldbec Hill they would have had to pull them up to move forward to Senlac Hill the following morning. This simply does not make sense, nor is there any recorded evidence of it happening. The shield wall was the only wall that Harold's men stood behind.

A Norman knight waits at the foot of Senlac Hill. In the background are the remains of Battle Abbey where Harold's army stood. The battlefield of Hastings is part of the English Heritage property of Battle Abbey, Battle (TQ 448001).

As they came down the northern face of Telham Hill the Normans deployed into battle order to the left of the track, facing their enemy. William would not have been able to identify Harold in the midst of the English army but he could see the Dragon banner of Wessex and Harold's personal flag of The Fighting Man flying above the centre of the ridge. Defiantly, William set his standard directly opposite that of his enemy.[11]

The battle opened at around nine o'clock with a volley of arrows from the Norman archers. They used a short bow with an effective range of around a hundred yards. It was most probably from this distance that the first volley was fired. The housecarls, forming the front ranks of the English army, raised their shields in an interlocking barrier and few arrows found their mark. Volley followed volley but the shield wall remained unbroken. With few arrows being returned by the handful of English bowmen, the Normans soon began to run out of missiles. At around 10:30 hours William called off his archers and ordered the attack.

To the cries of "Dex Aide!" ("God help us!") the Normans marched up the gentle slope of Senlac Hill with the papal banner leading the way. "Out!", "Out!", "Out!", was the English war cry.

Ahead of the Normans rode a man known as Taillefer, or Cleaver of Iron, who had received permission from William to be the man to strike the first blow. Throwing his sword into the air and catching it again, he galloped into the English line. He may have struck the first blow for William, but it cost him his life. As the Normans approached the English line, the defenders "hurled their javelins and weapons of all sorts;" wrote Guy of Amiens, "they dealt savage blows with their axes and with stones hafted on handles".[12]

All three divisions of William's army attacked simultaneously and the clash of arms, the shouts of defiance and the screams of agony and terror, reverberated around that fatal hill. "With great vigour the [English] held those who dare attack them hand to hand and with their swords began to drive them back", wrote William of Poitiers, just seven years after the battle. "The Norman infantry turned in flight, terrified by this savage onslaught, and so did the knights from Brittany and the other auxiliaries on the left flank. Almost the whole line of the Duke fell back."[13]

As the Normans retreated, the Breton knights panicked and their horses bolted into the marshy ground to the west of the battlefield. Seeing the disorder amongst the Bretons, part of the fyrd broke formation and charged down the hill in pursuit of the fleeing Frenchmen.

Whether this move was a reckless act undertaken by ill-disciplined troops overwhelmed by the excitement of battle, or was an intentional counter-attack ordered by Harold, will never be known. But it would have been difficult for Harold to transmit orders along the packed ranks on the hill and any attempt to do so would have the potential to cause confusion. It is safe, therefore, to assume that Harold told his troops to stand their ground at all costs, and nothing more.

The English charge, reckless or not, nearly won the day. In the confusion William was thrown off his horse and the Normans, thinking that their leader was dead, continued to retreat. If Harold would have followed up the retreating invaders at this moment, the entire course of English history might have been changed. But the Anglo-Saxon King failed to take advantage of the confusion in the Norman ranks and William re-mounted his horse, threw back his nasal-guard to make his presence known, and then rallied his troops.

The Normans turned on their pursuers and encircled them. Unsupported and outnumbered, the valiant (or reckless) men of the fyrd were slaughtered. Harold had shown his weakness as a commander. William had shown his strengths as a man.

Both sides now re-grouped. Losses amongst the English front ranks were replaced from the rear and the Norman archers recovered all the arrows that they could find. With the shield wall still intact William decided to change tactics. Instead of a mixed infantry and cavalry attack, the second Norman assault would be made entirely on horseback.

The Duke led the mounted knights – the flower of his army – back up that blood-soaked hill. The opposing ranks hacked at each other with swords and axes in a heavy and prolonged period of action. Though Harold's two brothers, Gyrth and Leofwine, were both killed, the English line held firm. In the savage fighting William had the first of three horses killed under him.

According to William of Poitiers, and others, the Duke, seeing no prospect of breaking down the shield wall, faked a retreat in order to draw some of the defenders out of position. As the knights fell back down the hill, a thousand or more English warriors, despite witnessing the massacre of their comrades earlier, left the crest and chased after the Normans. At this point William ordered his knights to turn round. The English were surrounded and butchered.

A number of historians have argued that such a tactic as a feigned retreat would have been impossible for cavalry of the eleventh century to perform.[14] They believe that it would require not only a great degree of discipline but also a considerable amount of practice and even planning to accomplish such a manoeuvre in the confusion of a medieval battle. Yet this is exactly what had happened. At the battles of Arques in 1053 and Messina in 1060, Norman knights, including some of those who fought at Hastings, had indeed performed this exact tactic. It was not a new development in warfare and this manoeuvre had been known and practised in Europe by horsemen since Roman times.

Furthermore, it is probable that this manoeuvre would not have been undertaken by all the Norman knights at once but by subunits which, in their feigned retreats, would have enticed small numbers of English from their positions and then cut them down. Rather than one large-scale planned general action it would be a succession of localised clashes.

It is hard to believe that the English would repeat their earlier mistake and this scene is not depicted in the Bayeux tapestry. Yet no authority has refuted the story and it is hard to understand how Harold could have been beaten unless large numbers of his troops broke formation.

As William of Malmesbury quite correctly wrote: "The English ... formed an impenetrable body, which would have kept them safe that day, if the Normans had not tricked them into opening their ranks by a feigned flight."[15] The reason why the English were so easily duped was because the Anglo-Saxons were accustomed to fighting on foot and had not previously encountered a large and disciplined body of mounted knights such as they faced at Hastings.

The battle had decidedly turned in William's favour. With the destruction of the English right, the western end of the hill would no longer be held by the defenders. The shield wall would not have been extended to re-take this ground, quite the reverse was the case. As losses mounted, so the shield wall contracted to ensure its integrity. So now the smaller body of defenders would have been concentrated into a position holding the central and eastern parts of the hill. The open western end of the hill, which has the most gentle gradient, could be climbed easily by the Norman horses, and the knights would no longer be forced to fight uphill. At last on the same level as the English, the mounted Normans could now strike down upon the defenders from the height of their saddles.

Realising this, William staged a massive assault on the English line with his entire army. The archers were ordered to fire high into the air over the head of the front ranks to assail the lighter-armed troops behind the housecarls. The defenders would have responded to this by raising their shields above their heads. Though the shields would have protected the English, raising them above their heads meant exposing their bodies as well as making it more difficult for them to wield their weapons. At the same time, therefore, the Norman infantry and cavalry were to attack the front and both flanks of the English line.

The battle had now been raging for many hours, but still both sides fought with great energy. Most medieval battles lasted no more than an hour or two before one of the opposing forces broke off the engagement and retired to the safety of its own strongholds. But there was no avenue of escape for the Normans.

With their ships now surrounded by the English fleet, the invaders had to win or they would certainly die. The English dared not break formation to flee because the Norman cavalry could outpace them. They had seen the fearful consequences of such action when their comrades had chased after the Norman knights only to be slaughtered. The Normans had nowhere to run and the English could not run. So the battle continued throughout the afternoon but the English line was visibly shrinking with each attack and William's troops were able to assail every part of Harold's position with ease.

It must have been evident to every combatant that the English had lost too many men to hold their ground much longer. The defenders were under constant attack from all sides and it could only be a matter of time before the line was broken.

Harold could not win the battle and he should have ordered a withdrawal. There were woods to the rear of Senlac Hill which the Norman knights would have found difficult to penetrate. He still had thousands of men under his command and darkness was approaching. If he had retreated into the woods and escaped through the night back to London, he could have formed another army from the northern forces that were marching south. But Harold stood his ground and fought on until, sometime in the late afternoon and as the light was beginning to fade, he was struck in the eye by an arrow.

Harold, we are told,[16] pulled the arrow out of his eye but the incident was spotted by the Normans and William ordered his knights to finish off the wounded king. The Normans charged the centre of the English line. It was reported that at least half the knights that tried to fight their way through the housecarls surrounding Harold were killed in the attempt but, finally, four Normans reached the weakened English monarch: "With the point of his lance, the first pierced Harold's shield and then penetrated his chest, drenching the ground with his blood," wrote Guy of Amiens, "with his sword, the second cut off his head ... the third disembowelled him with his javelin. The fourth hacked his leg off at the thigh and hurled it far away."[17]

Harold's body was so badly mutilated that his lover, Edith Swan Neck, was the only one who was able to identify it after the battle.

The housecarls fought on until, at around 17:00 hours, the English tried to escape under the cover of darkness. From the account of William of Poitiers it seems that the army did not keep together in an ordered withdrawal but it was a case of every man for himself. The Duke, again showing sound leadership, did not allow the English to re-form and he sent his knights off in pursuit.

One party of knights that had ridden northwards through the woods saw a group of housecarls on a slight rise beyond Caldbec Hill. The knights charged after the housecarls but they plunged into a hidden ravine. Many horses and men were killed in the fall, others by the housecarls who pelted them from above.

The housecarls were only driven from their position by an organised attack from Eustace of Boulogne and William himself. Eustace was wounded in the encounter and carried from the field. This ravine was later termed the Malfosse (the evil ditch) though its exact location has not been satisfactorily established.

The English army melted away into the night and William returned to the battlefield where he spent the night amongst the dead and the dying. His banner now flew above Senlac Hill on the very spot where the Royal Standard of Wessex stood only hours before.

Losses on both sides had been horrifically high, and Hastings is regarded as having been one of the bloodiest battles of the age.[18] It has been estimated that William's casualties amounted to more than 30 per cent of his original force and the English losses higher still. William's army, though victorious, was therefore much reduced in numbers. He had to hope and pray (which no doubt he did) that the English would now accept his right to the throne. Another such battle would ruin him.

Fearing a renewal of hostilities, William withdrew from the battlefield to his camp at Hastings on 16 October. He was in a perilous position in a hostile country with supplies running low. But reinforcements were being shipped from France to Dover and after an anxious week of inactivity, William marched eastwards along the coast.

At Dover William learnt that the grandson of Edward Ironside, Edgar Aethling (Aethling meant a son of royal blood), had been proposed as Harold's successor and London was preparing to resist the invaders. Over the course of the next few days the expected reinforcements arrived at Dover and William waited no longer.

On 31 October he captured Canterbury, the ecclesiastical heart of the country, and sent a large detachment to cut off all the main routes into London. William marched with the rest of the army to Winchester, with his fleet tracking his movements along the coast to Chichester or Portsmouth, and occupied the old Wessex capital.

With London surrounded and the other two most important cities in the hands of the invaders, the leading English figures, including the Archbishop of Canterbury and Edgar Aethling, submitted to what they considered was the inevitable. They invited William to accept the throne. It was, as Wulfstan of Worcester remarked, "as though with Harold had fallen also the whole strength of the country".[19] William was crowned King of England on Christmas Day.

William had won his crown with the sword and with the sword he was compelled to defend it. Over the course of the next fifteen years he faced uprisings from the south-west to the north of England, including two attacks by Danish forces under Swein, their king. William met every revolt with force, burning villages and destroying crops and farm implements in reprisal. It has been suggested that as many as 300,000 English died or were killed during William's reign as a result of these tactics.

Few could argue that the Battle of Hastings was one of the defining moments in world history. It brought an introverted race that had been the subject of successive waves of invasion into the mainstream of Western Europe. For hundreds of years after Hastings the kings of England were the overlords of Normandy and much of France. The invaded became the invaders until their empire stretched around the globe.

On 14 October 1066 a new nation was born, one that eventually became the greatest power on earth.

CHAPTER 4

Conquerors and Castles: Medieval Sussex

With the Norman conquest of England a more structured form of feudalism overtook the system of rights and traditions of Anglo-Saxon days. All land was the property of the king who granted estates to his leading followers in return for their military service and these powerful barons maintained bodies of armed retainers to enforce their authority over the potentially rebellious English.

As the vital bridge between London and Normandy, as well as the ancestral home of Harold Godwinson, Sussex had to be secured against revolt and William divided the county into five (later six) districts or baronies, known as Rapes, each of which was held by a Norman knight on William's behalf. Each Rape was centred around a formidable castle. These castles formed a network of strongholds which, as well as deterring insurgency within the civil population and preventing invasion, were used as regional administrative centres. There were also a large number of lesser landholders who held their property from their Rapal lords. These minor landholders also built their own castles again in return for the provision of military service, or the furnishing of soldiers in times of conflict, the terms of which were generally dependent upon the size of the estates they held.

Castles were virtually unknown in England before the Conquest but in Europe they were of enormous importance in medieval warfare, as was reflected in William the Conqueror's erection of a small castle at Pevensey as soon as he landed and at Hastings which became his operational base.

At first the castles in Sussex were built of wood with the most important ones being replaced by huge stone structures. Many of the smaller castles were abandoned as estates became amalgamated or the need for defensible structures was no longer considered necessary. The result is that across Sussex there are some forty castles. Some of these are magnificent structures, the remains of which still dominate the skyline. Many others are lost almost beyond trace.

Generally these structures were composed of a mound or motte, usually man-made, upon which a wooden fort or "keep" was erected. This was where the great Lord would reside and was the last line of defence in a siege. Around the motte was

The motte and part of the east wall of Hastings Castle. The castle is on the cliffs above the town and can be reached by car via Castle Hill Road or on foot from the West Hill lift (TQ 822094). (By kind permission of the Director, Hastings Castle.)

an area of open ground which was the bailey. The bailey was enclosed by a tall wooden wall. Surrounding the bailey wall was often, though not always, a wet or dry ditch. A ditch was also sometimes dug around the base of the motte. The size and height of the mottes varied enormously, as did the size, shape and number of the baileys. Another style of fortification was that of the moated castle in which the buildings were erected on an earthen platform which sat within a large water-filled moat. Only a small number of these castles were strengthened with masonry.

Possibly the most magnificent Sussex castle is Arundel. Work may have begun on the building of a defensive work at Arundel as early as 1068 after Roger de Montgomery had been created Earl of Arundel and granted both the Rapes of Chichester and Arundel, amounting to around one-third of the county. De Montgomery had not fought at Hastings but was rewarded by William for his careful stewardship of Normandy whilst the Duke was winning the English crown. De Montgomery was obviously someone William could trust. Like most of the county's castles, it is of a motte and bailey construction and it was well-placed at what was, in medieval times, the estuary of the River Arun.

In the case of Arundel the large central motte has not one, but two adjoining baileys. The original wooded structure was gradually replaced with stone, beginning with the inner gatehouse and curtain wall in around 1070.

Roger de Montgomery also built a castle at Chichester at the north-eastern quadrant of the city close to, and possibly incorporating, the existing Roman walls. It is known to have been a typical motte and bailey, with circular inner and outer baileys extending southwards from the motte. Both baileys were surrounded by dry moats. The entire Norman structure was made of wood, though there is some evidence to suggest that the keep was rebuilt in stone. There is nothing, however, to suggest that the bailey walls received the same treatment. Chichester Castle had a short, but controversial history. It is thought that the castle was besieged by King John's forces during the turbulent period in 1194 when Richard the Lionheart was a captive in France. Little more than two decades later, Chichester Castle was attacked and occupied in 1216 by Louis of France (see chapter six) which lead to it being dismantled.

Travelling eastwards, the Rape next to Arundel was that of Bramber which was granted to William de Braose. Like de Montgomery, William de Braose built his principal castle to command a river. This was the River Adur and the site chosen was at Bramber up to which point the river was still navigable at that time. Built before the end of the eleventh century, the castle had a motte in the centre of the bailey which was formed on top of a natural knoll above the river. Excavations carried out in 1966–7 indicate how the castle evolved from a motte and bailey to an "enclosure" type in the twelfth century, with a stone keep, gatehouse and curtain wall. Though now in ruins, its original size and structure can be gauged from the single wall of the gate-tower, seventy-six feet high, which is still visible from a considerable distance.

Bramber was held by the Braose family until it was confiscated by King John in 1208 who suspected the Braoses of treachery. Eventually the Braose family regained Bramber but the line died out in 1326 and the castle passed to the Mowbray family who had little use for it and it gradually decayed.[1]

The next Rape is that of Lewes which was granted to William de Warenne (from Varenne in Normandy). Lewes was an obvious site for a castle as here was a port and crossing over the River Ouse and the bustling market town stood at the end of the broad Ouse valley which runs to the sea.

The castle at Lewes is unusual in that it was built with two mottes, one on the south-west and the other on the north-east of the castle site on what may be natural chalk mounds built up by large chalk blocks. The mottes were defended by a bank and a dry moat except to the north where the hill is steep enough to act as a barrier. The mottes are linked by a broad oval bailey or courtyard which measured approximately 450 feet by 380 feet.

Two drum towers and a section of the walls of the medieval castle at Pevensey.

At first a simple, single motte was built on the north-eastern mound, called the Brack Mount. Beyond this was a palisaded bailey, later replaced with a stone curtain wall. This castle dominated the town and was ideally placed to control the passage of the River Ouse. But in 1087 William I died and after his first son William Rufus was killed in a hunting accident, the Conqueror's youngest son, William, assumed the English crown which his elder brother, Robert Duke of Normandy, disputed. William de Warenne pledged his loyalty to William which meant that the greatest threat de Warenne was now likely to face was not from the local population but from across the Channel. The result of this was the occupation of the south-eastern mound (Bray Mount) with the large shell keep, the remains of which still stand, and from where the coast can be seen.

The de Warenne family died out in the middle of the fourteenth century, with the family estates passing to the Earl of Arundel. The castle was abandoned and much of the stone removed for other buildings in the area.

Adjacent to the Rape of Lewes was that of Pevensey which was given to William's half-brother, Count Robert of Mortain. Unlike the Rapes to the west, Robert of Mortain built his castle on the coast at Pevensey – the place where the Normans had first landed in 1066. The Conqueror had initially erected his portable wooden castle within the confines of the old Roman fort and Robert of Mortain chose the same place to build his fine stone keep with the walls of the Roman fort becoming the curtain walls of what was, in effect, a large bailey.

The most easterly of the Sussex Rapes was that of Hastings. This was granted to Count Robert of Eu. It is thought that the castle erected by the Normans in 1066 was still at Hastings and that Robert of Eu moved this to its second site on the cliff-sided promontory which in the eleventh century protruded into the sea.

As usual the wood was replaced with stone. This, of course, included the keep, though there is some doubt whether or not the stone keep, which was planned to be built in 1172, was ever completed. From the thirteenth century onwards the castle site was used more for religious than defensive purposes.[2]

* * * *

These then were the great castles from which the Normans ruled their new realm. Yet the principle of feudalism was that of decentralisation and the great landholders relied upon the more numerous lesser nobility to exercise control at a local level.

Amongst the more important of these lesser individuals was the most senior ecclesiastical figure in Sussex, the Bishop of Chichester. The clergy needed the protection of fortified buildings just as much as the knights and the incumbents of that position built numerous castles and fortified residences through the county.

Amongst these was the palace at Aldingbourne (SU922050) for which King Henry VI gave permission to Bishop Moleynes to "crenellate" in 1447. Before anyone could build a castle they had to seek permission from the king to crenellate their property, i.e. to create crenellated walls around their residence. This was to ensure that only those who were loyal to the king possessed military fortifications. Close by this palace is Tote Copse Castle (SU 92270477), also a former property of the bishopric. Tote, or toot, is known to mean look-out, so its original name, as recorded in the Doomsday Book, of Totehal clearly indicates the nature, and purpose of this "look-out hall". When first erected, the flint look-out keep was free-standing and measured approximately thirty-nine feet square. Later curtain walls were added to enclose a bailey with an oval moat surrounding the walls which measured 352 feet east-to-west and 336 feet north-to-south. The ditch was between twelve and eighteen feet deep. The moat may have been fed from either a nearby stream called the Ripe, or from the Aldingbourne millstream. With its deep moat, curtain walls, motte and stone keep, Tote Copse would have been a powerful fortification in medieval times.

Sadly, on the only recorded occasion that it was assaulted – during the English Civil War – the castle fell without a fight (see chapter seven).[3]

Another building which Bishop Moleynes was granted a license to crenellate was the fortified manor house at Bexhill (TQ 74640799). This ambitious clergyman also sought permission to fortify his manor house at Broyle. Though the site of this is not certain, it seems more than likely that it is the place currently known as Broyle Place (TQ47701282). The original house here dated from 1138 but nothing is known of its dimensions, nor of the improvements made by Bishop Moleynes other than the addition of a wet moat which can still be seen.[4]

From the thirteenth century to the sixteenth century the bishops of Chichester also had a manor house at Cakeham. The early house had fallen into ruins by 1363, remnants of which are still present in the current house which was rebuilt in the sixteenth century. The most prominent feature of the building is the hexagonal tower and adjoining stair turret built by Bishop Sherborn in approximately 1519. Another of the bishop's fortified residences was that at Bishopstone (TQ47270094) and another is that at Ferring (TQ 0902), the latter being yet another of those included in Bishop Moleynes 1447 list.[5]

The western River Rother was controlled by a number of castles. Possibly the most important of these was at Midhurst where, on St Ann's Hill overlooking the Rother, stand the partially re-built walls of Midhurst Castle. This was one of the subsidiary castles of Arundel Rape erected by Roger de Montgomery. Built on a Lower Greensand outcrop, the castle had a stone keep with an inner bailey on top of the hill and a further bailey on the westward slopes of the hill. In 1102 Roger's son rebelled unsuccessfully against Henry I which resulted in Montgomery forfeiting his estates and Midhurst passed into the hands of Savaric Fitzcane. When the Fitzcanes acquired the Bohun estates in Normandy they changed their names to de Bohun. The castle was abandoned by the fourteenth century in favour of the once-magnificent la Coudraye (Cowdray House).

The second castle on the Rother can be found at Lodsworth Castle, Selham (SU 93362104), distinguished by its large, prominent motte. This mound is eighteen feet high and completely dominates the River Rother. Initially a small motte was erected here in the thirteenth century. After temporary occupation the top was raised and a palisade placed around it. The footings of a timber structure had been found on the top and this may have been a keep. There is no evidence of any masonry.[6]

Near Harting Church is a moated site which also overlooks the River Rother (SU 78411939). In 1266 Henry Hussey was granted a license by Henry III to enclose and fortify "a certain place in his manor of Hertinge ... with a foss and wall of stone and lime, and to krenellate it at [his] pleasure, and hold the place so fortified and krenellated for ever without penalty or impediment."[7]

The ruins of the Collegiate Church and the north wall of Hastings Castle. (By kind permission of the Director, Hastings Castle.)

Where the Rother meets the River Arun at Pulborough Park Mount are the identifiable remains of a large and strong motte and bailey castle (TQ 03731894). The motte is enclosed by a wide ditch with a counterscarp bank, and to the south, commanding the steep drop to the Arun, is a bailey platform, also enclosed by a wide ditch.

Stane Street, the great Roman road that ran from Chichester to London, also ran close by Pulborough Castle and another castle at Dedisham. It was in 1328 that Edward III gave permission for Thomas Tregoz to fortify his manor house of Dachesam, and it is this which is known to us as Dedisham near Slinfold (TQ 11123287). Here a house is enclosed by a semi-circular moat which joins the River Adur to form the site's north side and to the south-east is a medieval fishpond, so this would seem to have been a moated castle.[8]

As well as Bramber, the upper reaches of the River Adur was defended by Knepp

Old Castle which was built by William de Braose in the eleventh century, and fortified in 1214. The motte, situated upon the flood plain of the River Adur (TQ 16352089) is modelled out of a natural mound. It measures 240 to 300 feet in diameter and is fourteen feet in height and was surrounded by a wide ditch. The castle was largely demolished in 1726 and material used to make part of the Steyning – Horsham road. However, a corner of the keep still stands and is a well-known sight to drivers along the A24 near West Grinstead.[9]

There was a castle at Arlington (TQ 52810397), which is thought to have been a timber and masonry castle which was built at the narrowest point of the River Cuckmere. Also known as the Rookery and as Milton Castle, there is evidence of a motte built close to the river (which was navigable as far as Arlington itself) that appears to have had some stonework added at some point. As well as documentary evidence, the names of local features indicate the nature of the building. Thus, a nearby field is known as Running Field – indicating a place where soldiers could exercise – and just to the east is Butt Lane where archers must have honed their skills on the butts.[10]

To the north-east of Lewes and a little more than one mile from the village of Ringmer is the isolated motte of an early Norman ringwork (TQ 44901433). Situated on farmland adjacent to Clay Hill House, recent excavations have dated the work to approximately 1140. At this period there was an internal struggle for the English throne between King Stephen and Matilda, the daughter of Henry I, and during this time many castles were thrown up without royal consent. Clay Hill would appear to be one such "adulterine" castle which was abandoned shortly after the end of the conflict. The motte now appears as a horseshoe-shaped, irregular mound, which sits near the bottom of a gentle north-facing slope with fine views over the Weald. It is surrounded by an almost circular ditch, ten feet wide, the whole structure being roughly 130 feet in diameter.[11]

Not far away from Clay Hill at Isfield (TQ 44251800), positioned along what was the old Roman road from Lewes to London, are the remains of a motte and bailey at the confluence of the Uckfield Mill Stream and the River Ouse. The inner bailey is protected by the motte and by a short cross-ditch. The outer bailey has its own ditch on the north and a higher outer bank for two-thirds of the way stretching across the alluvium. The whole area comprises some four acres. It would appear that at some later date the motte-ditch was extended into the outer bailey. There is no evidence of walls having been built around the bailey. It is known that in 1171 Isfield was held by Hugh de Folkington from the manor of South Malling. It seems likely that the site was abandoned in the middle of the thirteenth century in favour of a new manor house built where Isfield Place now stands.[12]

A license to crenellate Drungewick Manor at Loxwood (TQ 06183065) was granted in 1447. Most of the moat of the old fortified building survives but the oldest part of the building that can now be seen is the east gable which bears the date 1559.[13]

Another knight who was granted permission to fortify his manor house was Mathew de Mount Martin. He received a licence to crenellate his manse of Burn (now Westbourne). The site has not been located.[14] Another of the Sussex castles which is generally considered to be "lost" is that of Castrum Dheriam. It was mentioned in 1216 when it was held on behalf of Henry III and was defended by Philip d'Albini and William de Wawz against the incursions of Louis of France. Though most writers declare that the site of Castrum Dheriam is not known, it is possible that its name has been misinterpreted over time. It is most probably the castle of Rye – castrum de Ria.[15]

At Chennells Brook Farm, on the northern edge of Horsham was a moated motte and bailey castle (TQ 18803335). This was a late eleventh century castle which was later developed to incorporate water defences. The hillside to the south and west of the motte was excavated and a dam constructed to form a pool into which a stream has been diverted to skirt the defences on the uphill side of the motte.[16]

The distinctive remains of a motte and bailey work known as the Edburton Castle Ring can be found at Fulking (TQ 23781100). It is situated at the edge of the north-facing slopes of the Downs which commands a view north over the Weald and what is known as the "Greensand Way" which runs north of the scarp of the Downs. The motte is around ninety feet in diameter and six feet high, enclosed by an eighteen feet-wide ditch. The bailey is rectangular in shape, being some 105 feet east to west and ninety feet north to south.[17]

Also at Fulking is Perching Manor House (TQ 24101157) where there are earthwork remains of a medieval moated manor house. Royal licenses to fortify Perching Manor were granted in 1262, 1264, 1268 and 1329.[18]

The scant remains of a motte can be found at Castle Field at Hartfield (TQ 48113604), documents relating to which indicate a date for the motte of 1307.[19]

A castle was built at Ford in around 1102 (TQ 00180370) possibly by a Savaric Fitzsavaric. The foundations of a substantial building, including a ditch (which was fed by the influx of the tide) were discovered during the digging of a canal in 1818, close to the church.[20]

Glottenham Castle at Mountfield near Robertsbridge (TQ 726221) is a thirteenth-century building with a gatehouse, with two square towers. The rest of the site consists of a flat rectangular mound surrounded by a ditch.[21]

At Pims Lock at Lindfield (TQ 35642610) is a small motte and bailey. It seems that at an early date this site was taken over as a nunnery.[22]

Records for the Manor of Dixter, or Dixsterve, began in 1340 when an individual called Hamo at Gate was assessed as being liable to find one man-at-arms at a value of forty shillings. In 1464 work was started on the present house of Great Dixter. This building lies on sloping ground in front of what was a moat-enclosed "island" which measured about 140 feet by 160 feet. Upon this piece of land was, most likely, a rectangular timber manor house surrounding a small courtyard. The area of land enclosed is similar in size to nearby Bodiam Castle.[23]

Other fortified manor houses include Boarzell House, Ticehurst (TQ71662849) which consisted of a rectangular moated house and other buildings of possible late-thirteenth century origins. The buildings were demolished in 1859. At Halnaker House, Boxgrove (SU 90830886) was a fortified manor house originally built by Roger de Haye in the twelfth century. The remains of this defensible work survive mainly as ruins incorporated into a modern garden range around a quadrangular walled courtyard. The courtyard was entered by means of a fourteenth century gatehouse.

Permission to crenellate Court Lodge at Udimore (TQ 08920974) was granted in 1479. All that can now be learnt about this property is that a moat once enclosed the church and Court Lodge which still exist.[24]

More substantial remains exist at Crowhurst (TQ 75711231), where the walls of a small medieval manor house built by Walter de Scotncy in 1250 stand on private land on the edge of the village. The ruins consist of a gable end with two trefoil-headed window openings, a pointed doorway and large pointed windows above this. There are other smaller pieces around the site. Crowhurst was held by Harold Godwinson before the calamitous events of 1066 and it seems that it was devastated by the Norman army as the Doomsday Book records the place as having no value ("wasted").

There are some masonry remains of Sedgwick Castle some two-and-a-half miles to the east of Horsham (TQ 18012698). It was of an unusual design, being built with two moats and a stone bailey wall and stone keep. The Doomsday Book records that the manor of Sedgwick was held by Robert Sauvage from his overlord William de Braose of Bramber. In the middle of the thirteenth century, the property being taken over by John Maunsell who was granted a license to "strengthen his house of Seggewick". After Maunsell's death, the Sauvage family re-occupied Sedgwick. However, the Sauvages found themselves on the losing side during the barons' revolt (see chapter 5) and following the Battle of Lewes in 1264, Sedgwick castle was handed to Robert, the son of Simon de Montfort. The Battle of Evesham re-established the old order and John le Sauvage (or Savage) repossessed his family's former lands. In 1272 le Savage exchanged his Sedgwick estate for other lands held by William de Braose. The Barose family held Sedgwick Castle until 1395 but as Bramber Castle was their principle residence, Sedgwick was little used during their years of ownership.

The remains of the gate-tower of Bramber Castle. The castle is located near the roundabout on the A283 at Bramber (TQ 184107).

At Shermanbury is Ewhurst Manor (TQ 211190). A certain Thomas Peverel built a moated manor house here in the reign of Edward I. The moat remains but of the building itself the only survivor is the gateway with an adjoining lodge. The house now on the site is part of a sixteenth century house, originally of larger proportions.[25]

Edward III granted Edmund de Passeleye permission to crenellate his "manse" of La Mote at Iden on 10 December 1318 with a wall of stone and lime. La Mote (TQ 90012393) is considered to be similar in design to Bodiam Castle with its buildings set within a large rectangular moat. Access to the castle would have been via a wooden bridge. The not inconsiderable moat and earthen platform upon which the buildings stood can be freely visited. One of La Mote's most notable residents was Alexander Iden who captured Jack Cade, the leader of the 1450 Kent revolt. Iden, who was at the time the Sheriff of Kent, pursued Cade until he reached a small hamlet near Heathfield, now called Cade Street. In the ensuing skirmish Cade was mortally wounded.[26]

Middle Wood Moat at Waldron (TQ 54461920) is a Norman ringwork, comprising a deep circular ditch with strong inner and outer banks. Even today, in our much drier weather conditions, the moat is damp in parts, which is why this was originally thought to be a moated site.[27]

Set amongst the trees of Fordly Coppice in Verdley Wood, lie the remains of a small fortified manor house. Measuring some sixty-eight feet by thirty-three feet, with walls five-and-a-half feet thick, this rectangular building was constructed in the mid-to-late thirteenth century. Considered to have been a hunting lodge built by the Bohuns of Midhurst Castle, Verdley's defences were never supplemented by a moat or bailey.[28]

*   *   *   *

Over time the Normans integrated with the English and a secure and comparatively peaceful nation arose. As the need for the protection of castles diminished the great landowners built fine modern (and more comfortable) mansions and in most cases their once-formidable fortifications were abandoned. Where the abandoned castles had been strengthened with masonry, the stone was often taken to build other properties or to help with the construction of roads, so that now all that remains of many castles are earthen mounds upon which mighty structures once stood.

The medieval period came to a close by the end of the fifteenth century. Those castles built after that time are considered to be "mock" castles because military defence was not a major factor in their design, the castellated walls and tall turrets being little more than elaborate decoration. There are a number of fine such residences to be found around the county but, with a few notable exceptions, they do not feature in the military history of Sussex.

CHAPTER 5

Democracy's Dawn:
The Battle of Lewes

On his death William the Conqueror bequeathed England to his first son William Rufus, and Normandy to his second son Robert. This division of territory led to much dissatisfaction as many of the English barons also held property in Normandy and in 1088 there was an attempt to install Robert on the English throne. Supporters of Robert occupied Pevensey Castle as a base for another invasion from Normandy. William Rufus responded by laying siege to the castle. Pevensey's strong walls resisted every assault but, after six weeks, the defenders were starved into surrender.

When William Rufus was mysteriously killed whilst hunting in the New Forest, the Conqueror's youngest son Henry – who had not inherited any land from his father – ascended to the English throne. Again Robert threatened to assert his claim to the English crown and Henry I spent the summer of 1101 at Pevensey Castle in anticipation of an attack from across the Channel.

The tussle for the English crown was revived after the death of Henry and Pevensey was drawn into the conflict between King Stephen and Henry's daughter, Matilda. Gilbert de Clare, Earl of Pembroke, possessed Pevensey at this time and in 1147 he declared for Matilda. Pevensey Castle found itself under siege yet again. As in 1088 the castle was blockaded from both land and sea but it could not be taken by assault. Eventually, the garrison was compelled to give up the castle to the king and it remained in royal hands until 1230. Stephen also blockaded Arundel Castle in 1139 where Matilda had taken refuge but the strength of its walls deterred him from an attack and the castle was not taken.

Following Stephen's death the English and Norman territories again became united under Henry II and when the young King married Eleanor of Aquitaine, the Anglo-Norman empire extended from the Irish Sea to the Pyrennees. Though rebellion flared in Henry's Continental possessions, England enjoyed a period of relative stability during both his reign and that of his son, Richard the Lionheart.

Internal conflict, however, returned to England in the reign of Richard's brother, John. These struggles were not for possession of the throne but for political influence. The great barons wanted to restrict the power of the king and to establish the rule of law. The result was the Magna Carta.

If the king was to exceed his authority and flaunt the laws of the land, the charter allowed the barons "to distraut and distress him in every possible way."[1] In the civil war of the thirteenth century this is exactly what the barons were to do.

Any leader who is weak, ineffective or unjust, is likely to face a challenge to his authority. Henry III, to some extent, was all of these. He had failed to fulfil his responsibilities, he had completely mismanaged the economy and he had attempted to rule without the required consultations with his barons. Had he ruled well, there would have been no Battle of Lewes.[2]

A Second World War pillbox built into the ruins of the keep of Pevensey Castle. On the grass below sits a pyramid of catapult stones which may have been used in the many sieges which the castle endured. (By kind permission of the Director, Pevensey Castle.)

Money was in short supply throughout the medieval world and many rents, obligations and debts were paid in kind. Royal grants of land or positions which yielded an income were therefore highly valued. They were also in limited supply. Instead of ensuring that such grants and the income from them were kept circulating within the realm, Henry spent vast sums on military campaigns on the Continent in futile efforts to re-establish his authority over his hereditary lands in France. He also gave away many important posts and a great deal of property in England to his numerous French relations and those of his wife, Eleanor of Provence.

The loss of so much money from general circulation, and the excessive influence that the Provencal "foreigners" were able to exert upon Henry, angered and frustrated the leading figures in England. Though the civil war of the thirteenth century may have worn the gloss of high ideals, in reality it was a conflict driven by jealousy and greed.

Only the great baronial landholders had the strength to challenge the King. His two disastrous military campaigns in France, and the virtual bankruptcy of the Crown, forced the barons to act. Ironically, the man who was to emerge as the leader of the English barons in their dispute with King Henry was himself a Frenchman.

Simon de Montfort was the younger son of Simon the Crusader who, like so many Anglo-Norman nobles, owned land in both France and England. From the early years of the thirteenth century the holders of property on both sides of the Channel had been persuaded into choosing just one overlord – be it either the King of England or the King of France. Simon the Crusader's eldest son inherited the family lands in France, leaving Simon de Montfort to try to claim the English half of the de Montfort estate.

Though he arrived in England with nothing but ambition, Simon de Montfort managed to secure the title of Earl of Leicester which brought with it the position of Steward of England. In this ceremonial role he waited upon the King at important state functions and he soon became a royal favourite – especially with Eleanor, the King's sister. When Eleanor and Simon married, de Montfort became one of the most powerful men in England.

As his military ventures in France had achieved so little, Henry, for once wisely, sought a negotiated peace with King Louis IX. However, Henry, urged on by the Pope who had a vested interest in Italian affairs, became embroiled in an attempt to secure the vacant throne of Sicily for his younger son Edmund. Henry promised arms and money for what was, in effect, the Pope's attempt to bring Sicily under papal control.

The enterprise was doomed to failure from the outset and with the Pope threatening to excommunicate Henry if he did not fulfil his promises, the King turned to the barons for financial aid. He had undertaken this hopeless venture without consulting the great lords of the realm and they were justifiably determined not to allow Henry to drag England into any more unnecessary conflicts.

Forced into a corner, Henry agreed to a series of reforms which became known as the Provisions of Oxford which were promulgated in 1258. The Provisions laid down that the King should rule through a "Council of Fifteen" chosen from the barons and the clergy. The fifteen were required to report to a parliament which was to be held regularly three times a year. In the Provisions, Henry was bound not to grant land or important positions without the consent of the council, and many of Henry's French relations were driven into exile.

At the beginning of 1261 Henry decided that he had had enough of the restrictions imposed upon him by the hated council. Shutting himself up in the Tower of London, he appointed his own advisors and sent an envoy to the Pope to seek absolution from the Provisions. In April Henry's envoy returned from Rome with a papal bull that released Henry from his oath. Free at last from the control of the barons Henry left London with a body of mercenary knights hired from France and marched south. He took Rochester and Dover, after which he moved into Sussex securing reluctant promises of allegiance from the men of the Cinque Ports.

In response the barons called a parliament without the consent of the King. Both sides gathered together their forces and prepared for war. But a few of the leading barons backed down at the last minute. This infuriated de Montfort who then left England to pursue his wife's claims to property in France.

The Earl of Leicester returned to England in the spring of 1263 to become the leader of the reformers, after many of the original group that had promoted the Provisions of Oxford had died or defected to the King. Many of the barons were unwilling to push the issue of reform any further.

The King had, in fact, undertaken some reforms in local government and because of the strong opposition he had faced it seemed unlikely that he would undertake any more extravagant wars or appoint any more foreigners to important positions in England. It was clear that Henry would not accept any other changes unless forced to do so at the point of a sword and few of the barons were prepared to actually fight the King.

Despite the weakness of their position a renewed effort was made to enforce the Provisions and the barons declared that all who resisted the reforms were enemies of the state. With their supporters under arms, the barons attacked and captured a number of the leading, and least liked, Frenchmen. This prompted uprisings against the established order across the country. In most cases it was the foreign clergy or landholders who were the targets of these attacks.

The King was in London, safe behind the massive walls of the Tower. But he could not remain passively in his capital whilst de Montfort's men took control of the country. Henry's first thought was for the safety of his communications with France and he sent his son Edward to secure Dover. This was accomplished but Henry was penniless and the London merchants were not prepared to forward any kind of loan.

This led Edward to break into the New Temple (London), which in those days was used as a safe-deposit vault, from where he stole around £1,000 worth of treasure. Though Edward escaped with the loot to Windsor Castle, many Londoners had now been pushed into the arms of the barons.

Henry's position was not good and de Montfort hoped to bring the King to terms without having to cross swords with his monarch. Whilst de Montfort's emissaries – in the form of a committee of bishops – negotiated with Henry in London, the Earl's army swept round the capital and marched to the south coast. The men of Dover and the Cinque Ports (see chapter five) readily abandoned their loyalty to the King. With the London mob baying for blood and his communications with the Continent now severed, Henry was trapped.

The King was prepared to accept the demands of the reformers but not so the Queen. Eleanor left the Tower to join Edward at Windsor from where she intended to continue the struggle against the barons. But she was spotted by the mob as she tried to escape and was pelted with mud and stones, being saved from harm by the Mayor of London.

Though Henry and Simon de Montfort finally agreed upon the terms of a settlement, the two parties later decided to take their dispute to arbitration. King Louis IX agreed to be the arbiter and Henry and Simon set off for France shortly after Christmas. Henry arrived safely in Paris but de Montfort was thrown from his horse and broke his leg just twenty miles into his journey. Others had to represent the reformers' cause when the two sides met at the court of the King of France.

Henry's main complaint was that the Oxford Provisions denied him the right to choose his own officials or even his own household. The reformers argued that because of Henry's previous mismanagement of state affairs, he could not be allowed unlimited powers. Though the lists of complaints brought by both sides were long and detailed, the principle points of contention were still those of 1258.

Unsurprisingly, Louis, himself an absolute monarch, pronounced in favour of Henry. Louis' decision, enshrined within the Mise of Amiens, solved nothing and when Henry returned to England he found his realm divided in conflict. Along the Welsh Marches and as far south as Gloucester, the private armies of the great barons were openly at war with each other. Though many must have believed in their cause, be they reformers or reactionaries, others saw the conflict as a way to increase their personal power and to avenge earlier wrongs.

On 5 April, Henry's son, the young Prince Edward, attacked Northampton where

The image of Simon de Montfort on the memorial to the Battle of Lewes in the grounds of Lewes Priory. Access to the Priory can be gained from the car park on Mountfield Road, south of Lewes Railway Station (TQ 414095). (By kind permission of Lewes Town Council.)

a number of barons were gathering for a conference which had been called by the Earl of Leicester. Edward captured both the town and the barons before the baronial army, led by de Montfort, could intervene.

When he learnt of the capture of Northampton, de Montfort changed direction and moved upon Rochester. This strategically important town had been occupied and garrisoned on 16 April by two of Henry's supporters, Earl de Warrenne of Lewes and William de Braose of Bramber. The rebel army reached Rochester the day following the fall of Northampton and de Montfort's force surrounded the town. The first attack upon Rochester by the rebels was halted by the defenders setting fire to the southern suburbs of the town. The next day, 18 April, de Montfort drove the garrison from the bailey and into the keep. For the next five days, the baronial army laid siege to the castle but it could not penetrate the great tower.

Edward, meanwhile, had left Northampton with the intention of entering London. When de Montfort was informed of the Royalist threat to the capital he abandoned the siege and returned to London. With the capital held by the rebels

Edward crossed the Thames at Kingston and marched round to Rochester where, on 27 April, he relieved the garrison.

In support of Edward's manoeuvres in the south-east, Henry, with a large body of infantry, captured the Earl of Gloucester's castle at Tonbridge on 1 May. The two Royalist contingents then joined forces and followed in the footsteps of Harold's army 200 years before across the Weald to Senlac Hill. Henry had two reasons for wishing to establish a base in Sussex.

Firstly, the great castles at Hastings, Pevensey, Lewes and Arundel were held by the King's adherents. Secondly, Sussex remained the gateway to Normandy where the Queen had already fled to urge the King of France to help support the absolutist cause.

The monks of Battle Abbey wisely welcomed the Royal army but were forced, nevertheless, to hand over a large amount of money for the army's military chest. From Battle the King continued towards the coast, reaching Winchelsea on 3 May.

Here Henry appealed for help from the Cinque Ports. He wanted them to send a naval force through the Thames to attack London. The leaders of the Cinque Ports had always supported the baronial cause and they refused to assist the King and they sent their ships out to sea so that they could not be taken by the Royalists. In response Henry took hostages to ensure that the Cinque Ports did not participate actively on behalf of the rebels and he left Winchelsea just two days after his arrival.

This time Henry made for a town held by one of his main allies – Lewes. Marching back through Battle, the Royal army bivouacked at Herstmonceux that night and entered Lewes the following day. Henry, accompanied by his brother Richard, established himself in the Priory of St Pancras which was just beyond the town walls. Edward joined John de Warenne in the castle.

It was that same day, 6 May, that the baronial army set off from London intent upon tracking down the Royalists and bring them to battle as de Montfort now accepted that the only way to resolve the dispute was by force of arms. The Earl of Leicester seems to have been well-informed and he was aware of Henry's intention of moving to Lewes before the King left Winchelsea.

De Montfort reached the Sussex village of Fletching, covering the forty miles from London in a single day. Like Harold before the Battle of Hastings, the Earl of Leicester had placed his army just a few miles from the encampment of the enemy. His men could now rest and recuperate, knowing that only a short march would place them opposite their opponents. In those days Fletching was still sheltered by the Wealden forest and the village lay adjacent to de Montfort's estate of Sheffield Park.[3] De Montfort must have known the area well and, as an experienced soldier, it is likely that he had the prospective battlefield fixed in his mind long before he marched upon Lewes.

There was now an inexplicable pause in hostilities. For a full week the two armies remained just eight miles apart. On 12 May, de Montfort despatched the Bishop of Chichester to Lewes to negotiate a peace treaty based upon the King's acceptance of the Provisions of Oxford. The offer was rejected. The following day the rebels moved closer to Lewes, but how much closer is not known.[4]

It is certain that the army bivouacked in a wood and, as it was to take the Royal army by surprise the next day, it is obvious that the rebels were still far enough away as to be out of visual range from Offham Hill where Henry had posted a lookout. From this "wood by Lewes"[5], de Montfort sent a letter to Henry stating that the barons were not in arms against the King but against his French advisors. Henry's reply was that the barons were rebels and traitors. Battle was now inevitable.

The Earl of Leicester did make good use of some of the time spent at Fletching. He ordered his men to sew white crosses on the fronts and backs of their tunics and hauberks. Not only would this aid identification in the fighting to come, it would also reinforce the belief that their cause was more than just a struggle for power – it was a crusade against government without accountability.

It has been calculated that dawn on Wednesday, 14 May 1264, was around 03:00 hours.[6] Within the hour the baronial army would have been on the move and the first units may have reached the foot of Offham Hill, where the Earl planned to make his stand, by 07:00 hours. This is the time given by Professor Powicke based on the assumption that the rebels had marched all the way from Fletching.

As it is known that the barons had moved a little closer to Lewes the day before, it is possible that the first troops may have reached Offham some time earlier. The most likely set of circumstances is that de Montfort achieved his element of surprise by the fact that he had moved to within a few miles of Lewes on the 13th (suggested by David Carpenter as being in the vicinity of Hamsey[7]) allowing him to reach the battlefield soon after sunrise. It is also possible that the rebel army marched through the night and arrived at Mount Harry before dawn.

Surprise was essential to de Montfort's plans. The north-facing slopes of the Downs in this area are very steep and, if the King had chosen to defend the ridge, de Montfort's small army would have been severely disadvantaged. De Montfort needed to gain the high ground and his only chance of doing so was if his march to the battlefield was unopposed.

Element's of de Montfort's cavalry had scouted around Offham two days earlier where they had encountered a Royalist picket and a minor skirmish had ensued at Combe Hollow. There can be no excuse therefore for the Royalist army being unprepared, yet the rebels quite definitely did achieve some degree of surprise. Only one man of the Royalist picket on Offham Hill was at his post that morning, the others having wandered off. This man was caught asleep and so the barons were able to take up their positions upon Offham Hill without interference. The fact that the sentry was still asleep lends weight to the view that the rebels, or at least some of them, reached Offham whilst it was still dark.

There is some doubt as to the route taken by the rebels up Offham Hill. They must have marched from Fletching along the west bank of the River Ouse. This track passed through a marshy defile, just 500 yards wide, between Offham Hill and the river. If the rebel army was caught in column of march in this defile it would have had no room to manoeuvre or be able to find sufficient ground to form line of battle. It would have been destroyed piecemeal by the superior numbers of the enemy.

To the east of Lewes are the steep sides of Malling Hill and to the south and north of the town is the marshy flood plain of the Ouse. The relatively easy south-facing slopes of Offham Hill and the adjoining Mount Harry to the north-west of the town offered de Montfort the only suitable field for battle. As he dare not attempt to force the passage of the Offham defile, de Montfort had to scale the Offham heights from the north.

To reach the top of Offham Hill an ancient sunken track climbs the precipitous northern face of the heights. If the baronial army was to take this track it could do so only in single file. Not only would this mean that, again, the army would be in a highly vulnerable state, it would also take hours for thousands of heavily armed troops to follow one after the other up the track.

Another traditional theory is that the rebel troops marched to the west and took one of the paths which run diagonally up Blackcap Hill above Plumpton Plain. This idea has been dismissed by at least one historian[8] who has indicated that though this move to the west would enable the climb to be made on a broader front, the increased distance that the troops would have to march would result in no saving of time.

It is more likely that many troops climbed directly up Offham Hill but that the rest of the army, some 6,000 or more men, spread out to the west and mounted the hill wherever they could instead of queuing anxiously at the bottom of the track. Some, no doubt, would have gone as far as the pathways up Blackcap Hill. It is possible that this movement towards the west was part of de Montfort's planned deployment, with those troops that were to form the right wing being the ones that climbed the heights near Blackcap.

Other evidence indicates that the rebel army, which might have been stationed at Hamsey throughout 13 May, chose the more circuitous route via Blackcap and Mount Harry to surprise and confuse the Royalist lookouts on Offham Hill. It is stated in the Gilson fragment that "the army of the barons came to Boxholte, which is two leagues distant from Lewes".[9] Boxholte has been placed some 500 yards south-west of Blackcap from where there is an easy ascent to the top of the Downs.[10]

Henry's neglect in failing to post an adequate picket with his enemy so close may seem extraordinary. Yet pitched battles were rare events in medieval England and Henry probably believed that he was in little danger. Lewes Castle was a formidable defensive structure with its two mottes and strong bailey. The town itself was walled and beyond its gates lay an army that was far stronger than de Montfort's band of rebels.

Though de Montfort had marched quickly from London he had shown no aggressive signs since halting at Fletching, almost as if he hoped that the threat of armed revolt would induce Henry to seek a compromise with the barons. It is likely that Henry hoped that he would not have to fight a battle at Lewes and even if de Montfort did try to attack the town his only practicable route was along the west bank of the Ouse. From the top of Offham Hill, with its commanding views across the Ouse valley, a single sentry would suffice to warn of any approach from the north.

It was not, therefore, in a lack of adequate lookouts that Henry showed his weakness as a general, rather it was in allowing de Montfort to choose the time and place of battle. A stronger man, a Harold Godwin or a William of Normandy, would have marched to face the rebels and forced them to fight on his terms.

But the King simply sat (or slept) and waited whilst the Earl of Leicester's men formed line of battle upon the gentle southern slopes of Offham Hill. De Montfort arranged his force in the now traditional three divisions or "wards", but to this he added a reserve ward. The addition of this reserve is considered by historians to have been an innovation in medieval warfare and its introduction into the battle at a crucial stage in the fight was to prove instrumental in securing an unexpected victory for the small rebel army.

Initially, the baronial army took up a position just below the former site of the racecourse grandstand, running north-westwards to the top of what is now the disused chalk pit overlooking the River Ouse. Spanning a distance of 1,000 yards, and taking into account the small force of cavalry and the gaps between the divisions, each ward would possibly have assembled five ranks deep.

Of the three wards, the right wing, composed of de Montfort's best troops, was under the command of his two sons, Henry and Guy. The centre ward was led by Gilbert de Clare, the Earl of Gloucester, and the left, the weakest of the three, was commanded by Nicholas de Segrave. There is no record of who led the reserve and it is probable that this body remained under de Montfort's personal control. The Earl of Leicester was conveyed to the battlefield in a coach, or cart, as his leg, which had been broken on his abortive trip to Paris, had not fully healed.

De Montfort's army has been estimated at around 5,000 to 6,000 men of whom only 500 were mounted. Of this force the left ward (under de Segrave) was made up of volunteers gathered by de Montfort at London. The volunteers owed allegiance to nothing but the cause, whereas the rest of the rebel army was principally composed of vassals of the barons that supported de Montfort. These men, whose lives, property and prosperity were bound up with the fortunes of their baronial overlords, had more at stake than just ideals. They had natural command structures and were well-armed; many would have been armed retainers – trained, disciplined and professional soldiers.

The knights of both armies, including the great barons, would have worn a chain-mail hauberk little different from that used by the Normans in 1066. The hauberk had long sleeves and a hood, or "coif". An elaborate helm, which completely enclosed the head, was worn over the coif. The legs were also protected by chain mail in the form of a stocking (called a chausse). Over the hauberk would be a surcoat of cotton or silk which reached down to the ankles. Usually decorated with heraldic devices, at Lewes the baronial army replaced or covered their surcoats with the white crosses prepared at Fletching. Whilst the fully armoured knight was still in the future, by the time of the Battle of Lewes some of the wealthy knights were already adding plate armour reinforcement to the knees, elbows and shins.

The mounted retainers might have possessed no more than a helmet and a leather jerkin or padded doublet. This was also as much protection as the foot soldiers would have worn. Usually armed with pikes, swords and daggers, the infantry also carried longbows. The bow was to become the pre-eminent battlefield weapon a hundred years later in the great battles of Crecy and Agincourt where they were used en masse and in controlled volleys. Such tactics had not been developed by the middle of the twelfth century despite the known success achieved by William's archers at Hastings.

After they had assembled into their allotted positions de Montfort ordered his men to kneel in prayer. It is said that they flung themselves onto the grass with their arms outstretched to form the shape of a cross.

Much ink has been used to debate the exact location of the battle. Interesting though such scholarly work may be, it is difficult to accept that the battle was fought in any one particular place. Though it seems positive that the baronial forces stood in battle array upon the Offham heights it is far from certain that they remained stationary when the King's army marched into view.

As the skeletons of the unfortunate victims of the slaughter have been found in considerable quantities, as far apart as the site of the Offham chalk pits and Lewes Prison, it appears evident that the battle raged the length and breadth of the southern -facing slopes of the Downs from Offham Hill to the walls of the town.

Offham Hill is clearly visible from the keep of Lewes Castle one and a half miles to the south-east, and it is hard to believe that the movement of large bodies of troops on the hill could have gone unnoticed for long. It is said that the Royalist attack began at 09:45 hours and we have estimated that the latest time the first of the rebel troops climbed Offham Hill was at around 07.00 hours.

It cannot have taken almost three hours for Henry's troops to arm themselves and move the mile or so from the limits of the old town to the start line. So it must be deduced that, as far as was possible, de Montfort's troops formed up on the north-facing slopes of the hill and only marched over the crest and into the (presumably) pre-arranged positions on the southern-facing slopes when they were assembled in battle array.

The Royalist cavalry, numbering some 3,000 men in total, was watering its horses along the banks of the Ouse when the first alarm was given. This body is usually stated as being composed of mounted knights. Yet there were only 1,000 to 2,000 knights in the entire country and not all of them were present nor were they all Royal supporters. At least half of Edward's cavalry must have included paid retainers and other men-at-arms.

The pages and grooms rushed their masters' horses back to the town. The mounts were saddled, the knights pulled on their hauberks, grabbed shields, swords and helmets and trotted out to Landport Bottom. It is stated by some authorities that Edward attacked the rebels without waiting for the rest of the Royal army and it is assumed, though not recorded, that Edward passed a message on to his father that he was going to attack without delay. Other sources indicate that the Royal army was drawn up correctly before the engagement, with the three wards alongside each other in the traditional manner. Edward was a natural warrior and already experienced in warfare and it is extremely unlikely that he would have charged into the baronial forces unsupported. Edward's force, being mounted and therefore highly mobile, probably left the other two wards behind as it advanced up the hill.

Edward's division described as "the flower of the army"[11] included many of the most prominent Royal barons. John de Warenne, William de Valance, Hugh Bigod, Roger Mortimore and the Marcher lords were all numbered amongst the heir to the throne's division and, when formed in line of battle, would have occupied the Royalist right wing.

Leaving the rest of the army to catch up with him, Edward led his magnificent force of heavily armoured knights into battle. Usually in medieval battles the two forces formed up in battle array opposite each other, with care being taken to ensure that the armies did not overlap before battle was joined. By rushing up the hill before the rest of the Royal army was in place, Edward displayed not just his bravery but also his impetuosity. It would cost his father the battle.

Though the slope of the hill from Landport is not severe the horses, with their iron-clad riders, would only have moved up the incline at a walk. Before them, on the left of the baronial army, stood Nicholas de Segrave's ill-equipped band of Londoners. Ahead of the Londoners was a body of high-ranking troops, probably mounted knights which included John Gifford.

When Edward's men were just a short distance from de Segrave's line, the horses

The barbican and gatehouse of Lewes Castle. The castle is on the north side of Lewes High Street (TQ414101). (By kind permission of the Sussex Archaeological Society.)

would have been spurred into a trot. As the two forces closed to within a few yards of each other the infantry would have fired their bows or released their slings as the cavalry urged their mounts into a full gallop.

The Royalists crashed into de Segrave's ward, scattering the Londoners in all directions and John Gifford, in his determination to be the first man to strike a blow for the barons, was captured. With their formation broken the infantrymen stood no chance against the knights.

It seems certain that this clash occurred immediately above the chalk pits as large numbers of skeletons have been discovered during the quarrying of the chalk. The bodies were buried in small pits containing from six to nine bodies in each. The knights pursued the broken infantrymen along the northern face of the Downs towards Blackcap (for bodies have also been recovered from there) whilst others chased the fleeing Londoners down the steep northern slopes of Offham Hill. The pursuit continued along the banks of the Ouse, into which as many as sixty of the rebels may have drowned.

It is said that the pursuit lasted for four miles and Edward, again showing his

The Battle of Lewes, 1264.

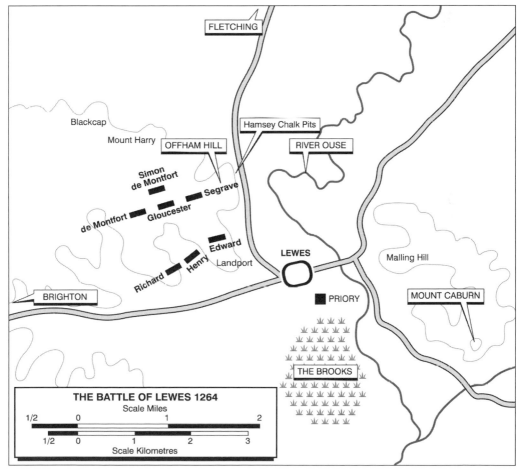

exuberance, allowed his horsemen to get completely out of control. He had utterly destroyed de Montfort's left division. It was never able to re-form and some of the rebels did not stop running until they reached London. But the knights had themselves incurred casualties, with many horses, no doubt, stumbling and falling down the precipitous decline from Offham Hill. Nevertheless, if Edward would have been able to re-form his men and return to the battlefield at this stage of the engagement his achievement would have been considerable. However, this did not happen.

By the time Edward had gathered his scattered horsemen and marched them back up Offham Hill the battle was all but over. De Montfort lost his weakest infantry division. Henry had lost his elite force of cavalry. The odds, which had been decidedly in favour of the Royalists before battle was joined, were now even.

De Montfort and the remainder of the baronial army did not know that the battle was developing to their advantage. They had seen a quarter of their force flee from the battlefield and they knew that it would only be a matter of time before the Royalist cavalry returned. The rest of the Royal army, possibly 6,000 strong, was marching across Landport Bottom towards them. It would not have been surprising if the rebel army had disintegrated. This must have been an anxious time for the Earl of Leicester. But de Montfort and his men stood their ground.

Henry, also, must have been a worried man. Offham Hill cannot be seen from the priory nor from the paths leading out of Lewes, and it is likely that he had not seen Edward's charge. When he arrived at Landport Bottom and looked up the hill he would have seen de Montfort's army posted on the heights and not a sign of his elite cavalry force!

The King, in conventional fashion, had divided his force into three wards. Edward had disappeared with the right-hand ward leaving Henry with his own central ward and the left ward under the command of Edward's brother Richard, Duke of Cornwall.[12] The ground up which the Royalists had to climb starts from where the present-day prison stands with a slope of 1 in 9.[13]

At 600 yards from the prison the incline decreases to just 1 in 30 but the ground slips away to the east to form a shallow hollow. Richard of Cornwall's men would have marched along the higher ground, possibly with some of them moving along the sides of the hollow. Henry's division would have advanced up the hollow where the gradient increases to 1 in 8. Even on level ground it is not easy for a large body of men to maintain formation – up the undulating slopes of Offham Hill it would have been very difficult.

It would seem that the two Royalist divisions attacked simultaneously. Richard's force, opposed by the strongest division – the right ward – of the rebel army, met with a hail of arrows and sling-stones. This, the weakest of the Royalist divisions,

The helm-shaped monument to the Battle of Lewes in the grounds of Lewes Priory. (By kind permission of Lewes Town Council.)

gave way, leaving Henry's men isolated on the hill. It was at this moment that the Earl of Leicester threw his reserve into the action. These fresh troops joined the rest of de Montfort's force, including the cavalry, and drove Henry back down the slope. It is equally possible that de Montfort did not wait to be attacked but instead charged downhill upon the Royalists as soon as they climbed into view.

At the bottom of the hill, somewhere near the prison, Henry rallied his men and made a stand. Here was the scene of the greatest slaughter, for three large pits were unearthed when the turnpike road from Brighton was being improved in 1810. Each pit contained around 500 skeletons and it took many days to remove them all.

Such a concentration of bodies has led many to speculate that the main action of the battle took place at this point rather than on the slopes of Offham Hill. Indeed, it may well be that de Montfort attacked the centre and left Royalist wards as they were forming up outside the walls of the town. Yet casualties occur on a greater scale in battle when one side has broken and turned its back upon the enemy. It may well be that it was here that the retreating Royalists were caught by the pursuing rebels.

Henry fought bravely. Two horses were killed under him and he was wounded and bruised. He and his remaining followers escaped back into the Priory whilst Richard of Cornwall hid in a windmill on the southern part of the battlefield where he was surrounded by his jeering enemies. One historian has suggested that this was a watermill on the marshes by the Ouse.[14] The mill proved an inadequate refuge and Richard was driven out and into the arms of his enemies.

The fighting spread into the town and beyond. Why the Royalists did not escape into the safety of the Castle – the most obvious course of action – remains a mystery. The most likely explanation is that the opposing forces had become so inextricably intermixed that the garrison dare not open the gates for fear of letting the rebels into the Castle.

It was at this stage of the battle that Edward re-appeared on the battlefield. The time that Royalist cavalry returned has been calculated at approximately 14:30 hours. This means that the knights had been absent from the field for at least four hours. Edward's men and their mounts were so exhausted after chasing around for so long that they could barely walk. He found the battlefield deserted apart from the dead and wounded, and the captured Royalists that were in the hands of the rebels. Possibly still unaware of the course of the battle Edward saw the coach with de Montfort's banner flying from it on top of the hill.

The Prince immediately attacked the coach and slaughtered everyone inside. Unfortunately these were Royalist prisoners who were unable to make their identities known before they were killed. It is possible that the placing of de Montfort's carriage on the top of the hill had been a deliberate ploy to mask the Earl's true whereabouts.

In and around Lewes the battle still raged and de Warenne's banner still flew from the Castle keep. All might not be lost. Edward rode down to Lewes still hoping, no doubt, to turn the tide of battle once again in his favour. It seems that he did not fall upon the rear of the rebels but instead he skirted Lewes to combine forces with the Royalists who were still defending the town. He cut his way through to the Priory and joined the King.

The fighting continued in the town, with the Royalists and the rebels still hacking away at each other. The town was in flames, caused by fire-arrows shot from the battlements of the Castle, and the streets were littered with the dead and the dying. Beyond the town the fugitives from the bloodshed tried to escape over the bridge and across the fords.[15] Many of the heavily-clad warriors fell to their deaths in the river and others met a similar fate in the marshes (The Brooks) to the south of the town. Another critical moment in the battle occurred when de Warenne, along with 300 to 400 of Edward's men, gave up the struggle and rode away.

The Priory now came under direct assault from the rebels. Edward gathered his remaining troops in preparation for a counter-attack when de Montfort sent a message into the Priory proposing an armistice. The offer was accepted and the Battle of Lewes came to an end.

Casualties have been estimated at more than 3,000 because, in addition to the

The motte and remains of the keep of Lewes Castle. (By kind permission of the Sussex Archaeological Society.)

burial pits unearthed in 1810, more bodies were found in 1846 when the railway was laid across the grounds of the St Pancras Priory. This means that, as probably only 16,000 men took part in the battle, around 20 per cent of all the combatants were either killed or seriously wounded. We know that few knights were killed so most of the casualties came from the foot soldiers. Some of the Royalists escaped to Pevensey Castle and some fled to France to join the Queen. Others were not so fortunate. It is said that a group of fugitives were cornered and butchered at a point near East Hoathly some six and a half miles to the north-east of Lewes. The place is still known as Terrible Down.[16]

Simon de Montfort had won the battle, now he had to win the peace. Throughout the night and the following day the negotiations to establish a limited form of democratic government began. The battle had destroyed Henry's will to resist and he formally surrendered his sword to de Clare. He allowed himself to be taken prisoner by the barons before negotiations began, even though the Priory was held by a large body of Royal troops, and Edward and Richard's son Henry had managed to establish themselves in the Castle which was still well defended.

During the following day, Thursday, the 15th, the friars from the Priory carried messages between the barons in the Priory and the Royalists in the Castle. From the moment of Henry's capture, however, it was obvious that the negotiations could only have one conclusion – the restoration of the Provisions of Oxford. On the Friday Edward and the young Henry gave themselves up as hostages in place of the King and his brother Richard. By Saturday Henry had succumbed and a letter, in the King's name, went out to his supporters ordering them to hand over their castles to the rebels.

De Montfort's success at Lewes was seen as "miraculous" [17] but it was not the kind of decisive victory won by William at Hastings. Henry had not died where he fought and the Royalist party remained strong. Many northern earls and the powerful Marcher barons had escaped and were certain to oppose de Montfort's authority. Even in Sussex, which had seen enough death and destruction, the Royalists continued to resist. After the Battle of Lewes the Constable of Pevensey had been ordered to hand over the Castle – to which some of the Royalists had fled after the battle – to the barons. He refused and, not for the first or last time, the Castle found itself under siege.

De Montfort seems to have genuinely wished to establish a sound system of elected government based on an agreed, written constitution. It was, after all, the only way that he could justify taking up arms against his King. But so many of the country's leading men had fought for the King and they would never agree to the constitutional reforms de Montfort wished. Too much blood had been shed for there to be any possibility of peace. The conflict was no longer about ideals – if indeed it ever had been – it had now become personal.

The settlement after the battle was termed "The Mise of Lewes". Under the terms of the settlement, Henry was to be advised by a council of nine chosen by three electors, the principal member of which was the Earl of Leicester. In reality the arrangement was little more than a dictatorship controlled by de Montfort. This, the very opposite from the aims of the barons who had supported constitutional change, alienated many of de Montfort's followers.

Though de Montfort did call a parliament, in which representatives of the shires and boroughs as well as the barons and the clergy sat together and discussed the business of the country's affairs, his reactionary enemies were too strong. The King remained a virtual prisoner, often being compelled to follow de Montfort in the Earl's entourage. Edward was under guard at all times and Richard of Cornwall was kept in luxurious captivity at Kenilworth Castle. By keeping the principle royal males under his close control, de Montfort must have hoped to deter the Royalists from direct aggression. It had the opposite effect.

Queen Eleanor, who was still in France, tried to raise an army for the invasion of England and throughout the summer of 1265 de Montfort's troops were stationed along the south-east coast. As the months passed by de Montfort's support declined. His assumption of an almost regal state and the seizure of land and property to add to the de Montfort estates drove many more into the Royalist camp. Finally, his failure to adequately reward the Earl of Gloucester for his part in the great victory at Lewes forced de Montfort's most powerful ally to turn against him.

Simon de Montfort ruled England for less than fifteen months. Towards the end of July 1265, Edward slipped away from his guards and joined Gilbert de Clare. Together, the Earl of Gloucester and the Prince marched upon de Montfort at Evesham. Once again de Montfort faced a Royalist force which greatly exceeded his own. This time, though, the odds were too great even for the Earl of Leicester. De Montfort was killed and his body mutilated by his angry enemies.

Henry was succeeded by his son Edward. Though a strong and successful ruler, Edward I learnt from the conflict with the barons. He maintained regular parliaments and worked through them instead of against them. Though this was forced upon him through financial necessity, it firmly established the principle of rule by democracy which had first occurred in England after Simon de Montfort's great victory at Lewes.

In 1965 a monument was erected at Simon de Montfort's grave at Evesham. It was unveiled by the Speaker of the House of Commons to acknowledge de Montfort's legacy – the English Parliament.

CHAPTER 6

Defence of the Realm: The Wars at Sea

It has long been an axiom that, as an island, Britain's best defence was to attack the enemy at sea and for many centuries the warships and sailors from the Cinque Ports of Sussex formed part of England's coastal defence.

The Cinque Ports were a maritime confederacy whose privileges and duties were legally defined by a Royal Charter of 1278. In return for the defence of the coast against sea-borne incursions and the provision of fifty-seven armed ships and crews for fifteen days each year for the Royal fleet, the confederation was granted certain rights and privileges. These included exemption from many taxes, the rights of wreckage (an important, if irregular, source of income) and Honours at Court. If the ships were required for longer than the fifteen days the king had to pay for their services.

The original five ports were Hastings, Romney, Hythe, Dover and Sandwich with Winchelsea and Rye as attached members of Hastings. The full title of the confederation was the Cinque Ports and Two Ancient Towns. At various times throughout the Middle Ages other towns and ports, from as far as Brightlingsea in Essex to Seaford in Sussex (and including Pevensey and Bulverhythe), were affiliated with the confederation, forming one of the most important naval forces in England. At the height of its power and influence the confederation numbered no less than forty-two towns and villages.[1]

The ports had been active as a confederation long before their position was legally established. It is known that the Cinque Ports' fleet sailed up the eastern coast in support of King Harold's march to York to face Hardrada's Vikings in 1066. Unfortunately for Harold these vessels were still in the north when William sailed from Normandy and the Conqueror found the coast undefended.[2] Ironically it was the loss of Normandy by King John in 1204 which thrust the south coast and the Cinque Ports into the front line defence of England.

Their first recorded large-scale battle occurred early in 1213 when the Cinque Ports' fleet attacked Dieppe and destroyed French ships which had been assembling in the Seine estuary in preparation for an attack upon England. In May of the same year the Cinque Ports' ships formed part of an English naval force which defeated the French at the Battle of Damme where, it was claimed, the Portsmen captured 200 enemy vessels.

In 1216 Rye and Winchelsea opened their gates to the Dauphin of France in his unsuccessful bid to wrest the English throne from the hated King John. The French also occupied Chichester Castle. The following year the Castle was recaptured and the Cinque Ports' fleet, having been bribed to change sides, defeated the French navy in a battle off Sandwich. So that Chichester Castle could never be used again by the French it was pulled down in 1225.

In 1242 the Cinque Ports were granted permission to ravage the French coast but it was during the Hundred Years War (1337–1453) that the men and the ships of the Cinque Ports were most frequently in action. This conflict was a continuation of the confusion that arose after William the Conqueror divided his Anglo-Norman empire between his sons. From that moment on, the leading men in England and France were locked in seemingly endless disputes over the rights to property on both sides of the Channel. Often this took the form of legal debate but sometimes the arguments were decided by the force of arms. So when Phillip VI seized Gascony in 1337 the English king – Edward III – went to war to regain his Gascon possessions and to assert his own claim to the throne of France.

The first battle of the Hundred Years War was at sea. Edward, with a massive fleet of ships, including a large contingent from the Cinque Ports, achieved a great victory off Sluys. French losses were claimed to have reached 25,000 men. The significance of this victory, and of another success by the Cinque Ports' fleet at the Battle of Les Espagnols-sur-Mer off Winchelsea in 1350, was that Edward's army was able to cross the Channel and most of the fighting of the Hundred Years War took place in France.[3]

Inevitably the French fleet felt obliged to retaliate and the Sussex coast, particularly the Cinque Ports, came under attack. Winchelsea was first assaulted in 1337 when around a hundred houses were burnt to the ground. Rye suffered a similar raid in 1339 when fifty of its houses were destroyed.

Twenty years later, on Sunday 15 March 1359, some 3,000 Frenchmen landed whilst the townspeople were in Winchelsea's Church of St Giles celebrating Mass. The French broke into the church killing and raping. Forty of the inhabitants were murdered before help came. In the ensuing conflict some 400 English were drowned in the harbour. When the French sailed away they took with them thirteen well-laden ships.[4]

Exactly one year later, on 15 March 1360, Rye and Winchelsea suffered another raid, with both ports and the surrounding countryside being ravaged and burnt. A retaliatory raid was made by the Cinque Ports' fleet a few months later.

The largest French raid came in the summer of 1377. Rye was overrun by a

Winchelsea's Pipewell Gate which is situated to the north-west of the town (TQ 905174).

considerable force of possibly 4,000 men in 120 ships led by Admiral Jean de Vienne. At the sight of such a large force the inhabitants fled. All the wooden buildings in the town were burnt. Rye's small castle, the Badding's Tower, which had been built in the time of Henry III, proved incapable of defending the town against such attacks and it was clear that Rye would have to be properly fortified. With the help of Royal grants a stone wall was subsequently erected around the town with impressive strong-points in the form of the Land Gate and the Strand Gate. Baddings Tower was sold to a private individual, John de Ypres, in 1430 and has been known as the Ypres Tower ever since.

The French raiders then moved against Winchelsea. But the Abbot of Battle, having learnt of the French incursion, armed his men and sent them to help man the town's defences. The raiders were driven off. Winchelsea's defences were formed

The Strand Gate at the eastern corner of Winchelsea town, overlooking the River Brede.

Rye's Land Gate which is in the north-eastern corner of the old town at the junction of Landgate and Tower Street (TQ 922202).

when the new town was built on its present site at the end of the thirteenth century. The walls were partly wood and earth, with stone only being used at key locations. The whole of the eastern side was surrounded by a wide ditch.

Undeterred by their repulse at Winchelsea, the French continued along the coast, ransacking Hastings and destroying its churches. Hastings was no longer the major port in the region. Hastings heads the list of the Cinque Ports and at its height in the twelfth century it contributed twenty ships to the king's fleet. By the early thirteenth century Hastings' contribution to the confederation was no more than half-a-dozen vessels.[5] Hastings Castle had also declined in importance and as early as 1339 the town and the castle had been ransacked by one of the first raids of the Hundred Years War.

The French attackers continued westwards and, sighting a gap in the cliffs, de Vienne decided to make landfall – they had arrived at Rottingdean. The ships anchored or ran aground and the French troops advanced inland, only to be met by a volley of arrows from the locals. Though outnumbered, the archers were able to delay the French long enough to allow their women and children to escape. One man was sent by horse to alert the people of Lewes.

Meanwhile the rest of the French force made its way ashore. They looted the houses and set fire to the church of St Margaret. As de Vienne prepared to extend his raid further inland one of his scouts reported that an English force of some 500 men was approaching. The French admiral planned an ambush.

The English force was led by John de Caroloco, the Prior of the St Pancras Priory at Lewes. The Prior had no idea that the French were ashore in such large numbers and when he saw the small advance force on the edge of the village, he led the English into the attack. De Vienne, however, had stationed the majority of his troops on the wooded slopes of Beacon Hill, from which vantage point they could watch the English rushing into their trap.

The small French body turned and ran back to the beach, luring the English with them. At a pre-arranged signal, de Vienne unleashed his men who charged down upon the rear of the unsuspecting English. A handful of the English managed to cut their way through the French ranks but Prior de Caroloco was captured and around 100 men were killed.

Having beaten the local militia, de Vienne was now free to plunder the local area and it is possible that the French got as far as Lewes only to find the gates closed and the walls manned. After five days the French took to their ships again, eventually returning to France. It is said that John de Caroloco was taken back to France and ransomed. It has been said that he was released after a ransom of 300 marks had been handed over.

Ecclesiastical establishments of the Middle Ages played an important part in

The Ypres Tower at the south-eastern corner of Rye old town, adjacent to the church. In the foreground is a cannon in the Gun Garden (TQ 922202).

local defence, especially as places of refuge. The great gatehouses of places like Battle Abbey and Michelham Priory, as well as the moats dug around churches, such as that at West Tarring, were genuine defensive structures.[6]

In retaliation for the raid of 1377 the men of Rye and Winchelsea attacked the French coast the following year. They captured all the wealthy people that could be held to ransom and they recovered the church bells of the two towns which had been taken by the French the previous year.

The French attacked the Sussex coast again in 1380. Led by Admiral Jean de Vienne, the Cinque Ports of Rye, Winchelsea and Hastings were once more the main targets of the raiders. The final French raid of the Hundred Years War was against Rye in 1448.

The repeated French attacks prompted a number of important landowners living close to the coast to build castles.

Amongst those was Bishop William Rede who sought a license to crenellate his house at Amberley after the raid of 1377. Though Amberley is more than six miles from the sea,

The medieval gate-tower and moat of Michelham Priory. The Priory is situated to the east of Upper Dicker on the road towards Hailsham (TQ 558093). (By kind permission of Denis Mace.)

it is less than a mile from the Arun which French ships could easily navigate. With curtain walls reaching forty feet in height the castle was protected by a moat along its southern face and the extensive marsh land of the Wild Brooks to the north and west. Its most impressive feature was its twin-towered gatehouse, built with a drawbridge and portcullis. Amberley Castle was attacked only once, in 1643 during the Civil War, when it was captured without a struggle by the Parliamentarians.

Around the same time that Amberley Castle was being fortified, Roger de Ashburnham also received permission to strengthen his manor house at Scotney. Until the nineteenth-century boundary changes Scotney was in Sussex, but is now in Kent. A few years later, on 21 October 1385,[7] Sir Edward Dalngrigge received a licence to crenellate his property at Bodiam. Like Amberley, Bodiam Castle is near to one of Sussex's major rivers. In this instance the Castle overlooks the River Rother, close to an ancient harbour which had been in use since Roman times.

The front view of Bodiam Castle, showing the main gate and barbican. Bodiam Castle is signposted from the B2244 to the north-east of Robertsbridge (TQ 785256). (By kind permission of Denis Mace, and the National Trust.)

Bodiam, one of the most picturesque castles in England, was built within a huge rectangular moat, some eight feet deep, which measures 542 feet by 340 feet. Rising to forty-one feet above the level of the water, the short curtain walls are flanked by four circular drum towers at each corner of this virtually square building. Midway along each of the southern, eastern and western walls is a rectangular tower and the northern wall boasts an impressive gatehouse. The towers stand twenty feet higher

The southern face of Bodiam Castle. (By kind permission of Denis Mace and the National Trust.)

than the walls. Bodiam is classified as a courtyard castle which means that the internal buildings are set around a central courtyard.

The towers of the gatehouse flank the entrance which was built with three portcullises and a drawbridge which led to a barbican gate. A second drawbridge led to a small octagonal island which was reached by a bridge from the western side of the moat. It is also known that the castle was armed with a 15-inch "bombard", one of the earliest types of artillery piece, as one of these guns was found in the moat. This weapon is now on display in the Royal Artillery Museum at Woolwich.

With such defences, the castle would have been virtually unassailable, yet the only occasion that it was attacked – during the Civil War – it appears to have been given up without a fight. Bodiam was also besieged in 1483 but nothing is known about the event.[8]

Herstmonceux Castle was built in the penultimate decade of the Hundred Years War by Roger de Fiennes who made his fortune fighting, and plundering, the French. Though the castle is not near a navigable river it does command the exposed Pevensey Levels. Despite its impressive double-parapeted gatehouse and water-filled moat, Herstmonceux is considered to be more a fortified manor house than a true castle.

Herstmonceux Castle. The castle is signposted from the A271 to the east of Herstmonceux village. (TQ 646104).

During this period of unrest Pevensey Castle was garrisoned with around twenty or thirty men, usually consisting of ten men-at-arms, twenty bowmen and a watchman. However, in 1372 the Castle passed into the hands of John of Gaunt, the Duke of Lancaster, and he refused to defend the Castle against the French raids. His failure to provide troops to garrison the Castle during the 1377 raid (claiming that if the Castle was damaged he could afford to re-build it!) made the Duke an unpopular figure. During the Peasant's Revolt four years later the locals had their revenge and a mob broke into the Castle and burnt the court rolls used for assessing the Poll Tax. A similar attack was made at this time upon Lewes Castle.

In 1394 John of Gaunt went to Ireland and he entrusted the Constableship of Pevensey Castle to Sir John Pelham. When, five years later, John of Gaunt's son, Henry Bolingbroke, clashed with Richard II, Pelham remained loyal to the Gaunt family and Pevensey Castle found itself under siege for the final time in its history. On this occasion the Castle, held by Pelham's wife Joan, was not taken and after Bolingbroke was crowned Henry IV, Pelham received the Castle and Honour of Pevensey as his reward.

With the ending of the Hundred Years War, the military importance of the Cinque Ports faded. Their decline was due in part to the growth of the Royal Navy but also to the silting up of the harbours. Only Dover, with aid from the state, has managed to keep its harbour open. The Cinque Ports were called to defend the realm just one more time when England faced its severest test since 1066. This time, though, it was not from France that the would-be invaders came, but from Spain.

Religion, which has so often whipped up the storm of international conflict, was the wind behind the sails of the magnificent armada of war ships that departed Spain in 1588 intent upon the subjugation of liberal England. Catholic Spain, then the most powerful nation in Europe, numbered the Netherlands (present-day Belgium and Holland) amongst its possessions. The growing Protestant movement in the Low Countries worried the severely orthodox Spanish monarch, Philip II, and he decided to end the advance of the heretics and enforce strict Catholicism upon his wayward Dutch and Flemish subjects.

A strong force of mercenaries from Spain's Italian provinces, led by the Duke of Alva, was despatched to the Netherlands in the summer of 1567. Alva arrested the province's leading figures and instigated a reign of inquisitorial terror against the defenceless Protestants. Many fled the Inquisition by crossing the North Sea. The Low Countries had long been England's commercial inlet into Europe and the Flemish weavers and Dutch merchants received a friendly welcome from their old trading partners in Protestant England.

Tension between England and Spain was heightened the following year with the capture of an English fleet of ships in the Caribbean by the Spaniards, and by the retention of the cargo from a Spanish convoy that had sought shelter in the ports along the south coast. That cargo was gold bullion which had been destined to pay the troops occupying the Netherlands. Firstly Spain and then England responded by placing embargoes on each other's trade with the Low Countries.

Relationships between the two countries deteriorated even further when Mary Queen of Scots attempted to seize the English throne with the assistance of the Spaniards. Mary's Catholic supporters captured Hartlepool to allow Alva's men a secure disembarkation but the Spaniards lacked the naval strength to ensure a safe crossing of the North Sea and the rebellion was quickly quashed.

By contrast, northern Europe continued to experience great civil unrest amidst Reformation and Counter-Reformation. It was, therefore, in England's settled shires that industry could flourish in peace.

In Sussex the Wealden forests glowed with the fires of the gun foundries. Firstly for the ships of the Royal Navy and then for the forts and castles of the shores, the cannon of Sussex armed the nation – and none too soon. For the dare-devil actions of English privateers on the Spanish Main and open support for the Dutch rebels had enraged Philip and he would tolerate England's interference no longer.[9]

Philip planned to crush England with overwhelming force. An armada of transport vessels and warships, led by Medina Sidonia, would sail into the Channel and drive the Royal Navy from its home waters. At the same time the army in the Netherlands, now under the command of the Duke of Parma, would cross the North Sea on flat-bottomed barges taken from the waterways of Flanders.

Elizabeth, and her advisers, were well aware of Philip's preparations and whilst all effort was to be concentrated upon stopping the Spaniards at sea, consideration was also given to the defence of the coast.

Firstly, a chain of fire beacons was established along the entire southern and eastern coastlines. They were formed in pairs. Lighting one beacon was to indicate a small raid which might be repelled by local men; lighting both beacons meant that a full-scale attack was imminent.

In Sussex these were located at: West Wittering, Bracklesham, Selsey, Sidlesham, The Trundle, Pagham, Felpham, Littlehampton, East Preston, Kingston, Ferring, Goring, Worthing (Heene Mill), East Worthing, Lancing, Aldrington, Brighton, Rottingdean, Seaford (Bishopstone), Wilmington, Willingdon, Beachy Head, Cross-in-Hand, Burwash, Cooden Down and Fairlight.[10]

From the coast the alarm could be passed all the way to London with beacons on Highdown Hill, Chanctonbury Ring, Ditchling Beacon, Firle Beacon and Crowborough Beacon transmitting signals to the North Downs and from there to the capital. The maintenance of the beacons, which were pitch-filled iron baskets on top of wooden poles, was the responsibility of the community and five

A modern reproduction of a fire beacon. This example is at West Wittering Beach (SZ 768984).

householders were to oversee each pair. These householders had to ensure that at least two of them were home at all times and no one living on or near the coast was allowed to move home without permission. The beacon system was supplemented by a relay of post-horses which were held in readiness along the coast.[11]

Secondly, batteries were to be built or restored and armed with cannon, especially along the flat, open beaches between Brighton and Selsey. Brighton, a frequent target of raids from the sea, already possessed a gun garden and blockhouse. Situated on what was once a low cliff between the present-day Black Lion Street and Ship Street, the gun garden fronted the sea with the circular blockhouse standing to a height of eighteen feet placed behind it. Initially sixteen guns were housed in the garden and blockhouse but by the time of the Armada this had been reduced to just six. Trenches already existed at Whitehawk Hill and others were planned for Saltdean.

Further to the east, Newhaven, East Blatchington and Cuckmere Haven were to be provided with more substantial earthworks and Birling Gap was to be "rammed up". Alfriston, Eastbourne and Hastings were all to receive defensive works or ordnance. A two-gun battery was formed inside the outer bailey of Pevensey Castle, and Camber Castle was kept in good condition and was well-armed. At Rye, still an important port, the Gun Garden was furnished with artillery as was the Land Gate and the Strand Gate.[12]

One of the two "demi-culverns" that were placed in a battery within the outer bailey of Pevensey Castle at the time of the Spanish Armada. The gun is on display inside the castle, (TQ 664048). (By kind permission of the Director of Pevensey Castle)

At Shoreham a small defensive work for three guns was raised on the east bank estuary of the Adur. Further west, at Littlehampton (then still known as Arundel Haven) it is possible that a fort was erected on the east bank of the Arun to house four medium-calibre cannon. At Kingston (near East Preston), Goring, Worthing and Lancing defensive trenches were dug but they do not appear to have been armed with artillery.

Pagham Harbour was particularly well defended with a battery at, or near, East Beach (East Norton) to accommodate three guns, with another three pieces mounted on the eastern arm of the harbour entrance. The height of the former Norman ringwork at Church Norton overlooking the southern edge of the harbour was raised and used as a lookout post.[13]

Responsibility for the defence of the coast from Kent to Dorset was placed in the hands of "Black" Sir John Norris with the defence of Sussex delegated to Lord

Howard of Effingham – the Lord Admiral of England – who held the title of Lord Lieutenant of Sussex and Surrey. He was assisted by the Queen's cousin Lord Buckhurst.

Lewes, situated in the middle of the county, was selected as the military headquarters and Buckhurst moved into the town. The house where he stayed still stands and is now "Shelley's Hotel" in the High Street. The county's reserve artillery and munitions store was also at Lewes.

It was intended that the Spanish landing would be met only by local forces with the main English armies concentrated further inland. It has been estimated that in the south and south-west the shoreline would have been held by some 21,000 local militia, armed with whatever weapons they might possess. The Elizabethan militia was intended to be a formation of all able-bodied males between the ages of sixteen to sixty. These men had to be prepared to turn out in the defence of their shire at an hour's warning. In each district a number of men were given military training.

These "trained bands" were well-armed and were the backbone of the local defence force. In Sussex there were supposed to have been 2,000 trained men. Of these, 800 were to have carried firearms and the remainder equipped with halberds or pikes. The bow was still considered a weapon of war though its place on the battlefield was being usurped by the matchlock musket.

To protect the south-east and the Thames estuary two small armies, one of 12,000 men and the other of 6,000 men, were to be stationed at Tilbury and Sandwich respectively. Away from these coasts a force of some 27,000 to 34,000 men from the trained bands of the counties would be assembled and another army, 36,000 strong, would be held in reserve to protect the Queen.

This last body would be composed of men from the court, from the City of London and the Home Counties. Sussex was expected to find 260 horse and 4,000 foot of which 2,500 were sent to join the main army in the interior. Against these numbers Philip sent 130 ships with 30,000 men who would join forces with the Duke of Parma's 30,000 troops waiting on the Flemish coast.[14]

The Sussex militia were first assembled in the summer of 1586 when fifty ships were sighted off Brighton. Lord Buckhurst responded immediately by bringing together 1,600 men between Brighton and Rottingdean. They camped out on the edge of the Downs that night and they were joined by more men the next day. It proved to be a false alarm as did a similar scare the following summer when horsemen were placed along the coast after reports that an invasion fleet was approaching through the Channel.

With the prospect of invasion becoming increasingly likely Buckhurst was ordered by the Privy Council to round up all "recusants". A recusant is someone who refuses to attend their parish church which effectively meant, and was intended to mean, all Roman Catholics. They were to be placed in the care of the clergy or other people of rank, but if this was not possible the Catholics were to be jailed.

From the outset the Armada ran into difficulties. Storms delayed its departure and further bad weather struck the great fleet before it had even left Spanish waters. Eventually, on the morning of 19 July 1588, the Armada passed the Lizard to head up the Channel. The warning beacons were lit: "Swift to East and swift to West the ghastly war-flame spread," a contemporary poem ran. "High on St. Michael's Mount it shone: it shone on Beachy Head."[15]

The English fleet put to sea and the following night slipped round the Armada to place itself windward of the Spanish vessels. Though outnumbered, the English could now control the coming battle. Amongst Lord Howard's ships was a vessel from Rye. The 60-ton vessel *William* was hired from a French privateer and was manned by fifty-eight sailors captained by William Coxson. Four cannon from Rye were added to whatever armament the ship already carried.

Another ship, the *Ann Bonaventure* of 70 tons and a crew of forty-nine, was supplied jointly by Hastings and Winchelsea.[16] A third ship from Sussex was provided by Lord Howard with the cost being shared by all six rapes of the county. Hundreds of other sailors were recruited from the Sussex ports to fight with the navy, leaving some parts of the coast dangerously short of defenders.

For the next five days the two fleets fought periodically. The Armada moved in a crescent, or concave, formation, covering a distance of seven miles, with the largest ships at the tips of the crescent. It is often assumed that the battle in the Channel was conducted by an overwhelmingly large number of big Spanish galleons against a weaker force of small, but more manoeuvrable, English warships. The reality was far more complicated.

The disparity in numbers was not very great, with the combined fleets of Howard and Sir Francis Drake producing a total of only twenty to thirty less vessels than the Spaniards. In general the tonnage of the ships of the two nations was also roughly the same but the English vessels were of a far more modern design and carried a heavier weight of cannon.

The success of the Spanish land armies meant that the military predominated over the navy to such an extent that their ships were manned by three soldiers to every sailor. In the English ships there were three sailors to every soldier. The English ships did not dare approach too close to the Spanish vessels packed with soldiers for fear of being boarded but their guns, which far out-distanced the Spanish cannon, could inflict little damage upon the stout hulls of the Armada from long range.

On the 25th the Armada passed Selsey Bill and Buckhurst was ordered to see that the militia was mustered and posted at the chosen places along the coast and at important points of communication throughout the county. But by the 26th, the

A French cannon of a type used in the Battle of Beachy Head. It fired a 5-6 pound ball and was located on the upper decks of the ships. It is on display at the entrance to the Eastbourne Redoubt.

Spaniards had reached Beachy Head and it seemed unlikely that the great fleet would attempt a landfall in Sussex.

With day after day of running battles the English fleet soon became desperately short of powder and shot. Buckhurst was ordered to furnish Lord Howard with as much ammunition and food as the ships required. Gunpowder from the Lewes arsenal was sent down the Ouse to Newhaven and then shipped out to Howard's supply vessels. Hastings, assisted by Pevensey, Winchelsea and Seaford, also helped to keep the fleet supplied.

On the 27th, the Armada sailed past Rye and, four days later, Buckhurst allowed the militia to stand down.

In the fighting the Spaniards lost just three ships, but these were amongst their most important galleons and their loss seriously affected the morale of the fleet. By the 28th, the Armada, damaged but still largely intact, was approaching Dover where the rest of the Royal Navy, under Seymour, was guarding the Strait, waiting for this very moment.

The Armada, its numerical advantage now lost, anchored in the Calais Roads to await news from the Duke of Parma. Despite ample notice of the Armada's approach, the Duke's troops were not ready to embark and Parma declared that it would be two more weeks before his men could join the invasion fleet. Medina Sidonia knew that he could not remain at anchor for such a period of time with the English fleet able to attack the stationary Spanish vessels at will. With the Spanish ships packed close together under the Calais defences they presented an ideal target for fireships.

This was a common naval tactic and a highly effective one. At midnight on 7 August, eight fireships sailed into Calais. Although the Spaniards had been expecting just such an attack, they cut their anchors and put out to sea in utter confusion.

The following day the English fleet attacked the broken and disorganised Armada at the Battle of Gravelines. It was the final battle of the campaign. With little possibility of reaching Parma's men at Dunkirk, and with his ships damaged and his men discouraged, Medina Sidonia turned for the north to round Scotland and return through the North Atlantic to Spain. Of the 130 or so ships that set sail from Corunna in July almost half were lost.[17]

Almost 100 years after the defeat of the great Armada, the "Glorious" Revolution of 1688, which put a Dutch Protestant monarch (William of Orange) on the English throne, led to further trouble with Catholic Europe. On 30 June 1690, a powerful French fleet of seventy-eight men-of-war plus twenty-two fireships, met a combined Anglo-Dutch force off Beachy Head.

Despite the fact that the allied fleet numbered just fifty-six vessels, it was the Dutch and British ships which attacked first. The battle raged all day until the wind dropped late in the afternoon. During the night the allied fleet – commanded by Lord Torrington – decided to retire.

The French gave pursuit the next day and one English ship, *Anne*, was driven onto the shore at Winchelsea where it was attacked by French fire-ships. The fleet escaped eastwards but allied losses amounted to eight ships and hundreds of men. The Battle of Beachy Head was, without question, a defeat for the Royal Navy and Lord Torrington was duly sent to the Tower and court-martialled.[18]

CHAPTER 7

King Against Country:
The English Civil War in Sussex

T he English nation, divided by religion and loyalty, drifted reluctantly into civil war in 1642. It is hard to say whether it was King Charles I or his political opponents that first threw down the gauntlet. Certainly Charles, in trying to raise revenue for his wars against France and Spain, had imposed taxes in defiance of Parliament. His flagrant disregard for the wishes of his subjects, coupled with religious upheaval and mismanagement of the economy, drove many of the most powerful men in the country to oppose him.

Though there were many stated reasons for the Civil War of the seventeenth century, in reality it was a revival of the baronial wars that had halted so abruptly at Evesham. Once again a weak king had tried to over-extend his authority. The democratic principles established after de Montfort's victory at Lewes, limited though they were, had been preserved by Edward I and the great Tudor monarchs that had followed him. Charles I was foolish enough to challenge those principles. His belief in the Divine Right of Kings to rule as they saw fit was the real issue upon which the country went to war. Charles I would not renounce this right, and it cost him his life. Though the monarchy was ultimately restored, the point had been made. Charles II was a constitutional monarch, as would be his successors.

The final descent into war began on 4 January 1642, when Charles tried to arrest five leading Members of Parliament for treason. In response Parliament took control of the Navy and began to raise an army. Though negotiations continued between the King and his opponents for some months, both sides prepared for war. Eventually, on 22 August, the King raised the Royal Standard at Nottingham and hostilities formally commenced.

Sussex saw none of the great battles of the English Civil War and its skirmishes and sieges were small affairs. Yet there was plenty of fighting between Royalist and Roundhead and the occupation of Sussex, with its many cannon foundries, was of considerable importance to both sides.

It is usually stated that Sussex, whilst generally Puritan in its ideology, was divided between a Parliamentary east and a Royalist west. In reality, the picture was far more complicated than this and supporters of both sides could be found throughout the county. Neither was there a distinct class divide. Though it is true that most Royalists tended to be men of rank, many of the wealthiest landowners also supported the Parliamentary cause. At the outbreak of hostilities Sussex had twenty-eight Members of Parliament of which eleven could be considered Royalists and seventeen Parliamentarians.[1]

From the outset both sides tried to seize control of the militia trained bands and the store of weapons and ammunition in each county. The King ordered a "Commissions of Array" to bring the militia under his authority and Parliament did the same through a Militia Ordinance Act. At the county town of Chichester an order from Charles I banning the Militia Ordinance was read by the Mayor. This was soon followed, on 19 August, by the county Recorder, Christopher Lewknor, and other influential men, demanding the city's arsenal for the King's service.

An officer of the trained bands, Captain Chittey, refused to hand over the magazine and he mounted a strong guard of militia over the military stores. Five days later the people of Chichester, organised by William Cawley, one of the Members of Parliament for Midhurst, declared themselves in support of Parliament. This did not stop local Royalist sympathisers from trying to rally support and they raised a body of light cavalry which drilled each day in the Cathedral Close. Despite the tensions within the city the opposing sides did not descend into actual armed conflict.

For the next few months the Puritans' control of Chichester and the rest of Sussex went unchallenged but in October Parliament ordered the leading Sussex MPs to put the county into a state of defence in readiness for a Royalist attack. This was because the King, at the head of a large army, was threatening to march upon London.

A worried Parliament also demanded that all anti-Parliamentarians in Sussex should be disarmed. This pushed the Royalists into action. On 15 November, Royalist forces, led by the Sheriff of Sussex, Edward Ford, gathered in Chichester and took control of the city without a fight. Ford ordered the trained bands to present themselves outside the city the next morning. Ford, accompanied by 100 Royalist horsemen, met the militia half a mile beyond the walls of Chichester and marched them into the city.

Once inside the walls, Ford ordered the trained bands to put down their arms which, surprisingly, they appear to have done without dispute. Captain Chittey was removed from his command and was replaced by the Royalist Sir John Morely. So, despite strong Parliamentary popular support in and around Chichester, the city had become a Royalist stronghold without a shot having been fired in anger.

The Parliamentarians' response was swift and effective. Sir William Waller, one of Parliament's most successful generals, marched upon Chichester at the head of around 6,000 men. Waller had recently captured Portsmouth from the Royalists and his main force approached Chichester along the coast road through Havant.

Despite having been informed of Waller's advance, Ford intended to follow up his success at Chichester with the capture of Lewes Castle. He ordered all men capable of bearing arms to join him under pain of death and of having their houses burnt. With an increased, but reluctant, body of men he moved upon Lewes but was met at Haywards Heath by a smaller Parliamentary force. The Puritans attacked Ford's men, probably on the high ground where the church now stands which was then open heath.[2]

The combat continued for an hour until reinforcements arrived from the east and completely routed the Royalists. Ford's unwilling followers threw down their arms and ran, the Royalists suffering not less than 200 casualties.

Ford and his supporters retreated back to Chichester and prepared to face Waller. As the Parliamentarian army neared the city Waller despatched a small force to capture Arundel. The great Castle, regarded in Tudor times as being the most powerful in the country,[3] was defended by only 100 men and the Earl of Arundel was out of the country at the outbreak of hostilities. If adequately garrisoned and provisioned Arundel Castle could have been rendered virtually impregnable but when the main gate was blown in and the defenders taken by surprise this magnificent Royalist fortification, along with 100 horses and a store of weapons, was seized without the loss of a single man.

Waller's force arrived before Chichester on 21 December 1642, after a clash with a party of Royalists in which it is said that 200 of the King's supporters were killed for the loss of just forty Parliamentary troops. Waller was joined by the Sussex trained bands that were determined to regain their arms and, no doubt, their credibility.

It was soon made clear to Waller, however, that the Royalists were not overawed by the strength of his forces because as soon as the Parliament's army arrived outside the walls of the city the defenders mounted a sortie. The attack was driven back into the city with the loss of one man killed and another taken prisoner.

The city's main fortification was still the old Roman walls and the place could not be expected to withstand a full-scale siege for more than a few days. As soon as the Parliamentarians arrived (known as Roundheads because of the close-cropped hair of their London apprentice-boy soldiers) they began constructing siege batteries on a hill known as The Broyle which overlooked the city walls. The following day, 22 December, Waller summoned the garrison to surrender.

Waller's terms were that Edward Ford and all Catholics were to be handed over as prisoners, the soldiers were to lay down their weapons and leave the city, and the officers were to give a pledge that they would never again take up arms against

Parliament. Though the garrison was prepared to offer up all the "Papists" the rest of Waller's terms were rejected and on the 23rd the siege guns opened fire, though to little effect. The defenders resisted by mounting cannon on top of the former castle motte which were able to fire over the walls at the attackers.

Surprisingly, the walls seem to have withstood the bombardment and it was only against the city's gates that progress was made. The gates could only be approached through the suburbs and on the 24th the besiegers occupied the houses by the west gate. The garrison responded by setting fire to some of the houses next to the gate and the attackers had to withdraw. The same situation developed at the east gate and again fire was used to dislodge the besiegers.

For the next two days the Parliamentarians attacked the city from all sides yet it was not until Boxing Day that the besiegers had cleared the suburbs and had brought their cannon to within 100 yards of the north gate where they could fire into the marketplace.

A reinforcement of troops from Arundel under Colonel Roberts had joined Waller and had taken control of the ground opposite the south gate. It was obvious that the city could not hold back the besiegers for much longer. With the attackers forcing an entry through the postern which opened into the deanery, coupled with clear preparations for simultaneous attacks upon the east and west gates, the garrison offered to surrender on terms. But Waller was no longer willing to negotiate and the garrison was left with the choice of unconditional surrender or a fight to the death. They chose to capitulate.

Chichester had delayed Waller for just eight days. Many of the leading Sussex Royalists were taken prisoner, including Sir Edward Ford, and the county came under Parliament's undisputed control. The Bishop of Chichester's residences were also attacked. At Aldingbourne the Bishop's palace was ransacked and Tote Copse Castle was levelled to the ground.

The Royalist prisoners included seventeen captains, thirteen lieutenants and eight ensigns along with around 400 dragoons and 300 to 400 infantry. The captives were marched off to London, some being conveyed to the capital by ship from Chichester Harbour. Chichester remained a Parliamentary-garrisoned city with Colonel Anthony Stapely as its governor until March 1646 when the guns were removed to Arundel.

There is no doubt that the control of Sussex by Parliament brought considerable benefits to their war effort nationally. At this time there were around twenty-seven furnaces in Sussex, the majority of which made guns and shot – the most important being the Royal Foundries in St Leonard's Forest. In addition there were forty-two forges or iron-mills.[4]

It was in Sussex – at Buxted near Uckfield in 1543 – that the first cannon had been cast as a single piece in England. Before that event cannon had been made by strips of iron bound together by iron hoops. For the subsequent 200 years the gun foundries of the Weald were the most important in the country. The Sussex-made guns were regarded as being the finest and cheapest in Europe and laws were passed to prevent the unlicensed export of these weapons to hostile countries.[5]

The occupation of Sussex and its ports by Parliamentarian troops also meant that one of the potential avenues through which Charles might receive financial and military assistance from France was sealed off. Sussex's position on the coast helped Parliament's cause in July 1644 when a Puritan force under the Earl of Essex needed money to pay his troops but the occupation of intervening counties by Royalists prevented any overland communication. The money, £20,000, was sent from London to Arundel and Chichester from where it was shipped round the coast to Devon.

Since the end of the Hundred Years War, England had known many years of relative peace. In 1642 there was no standing army and few soldiers with any fighting experience. The principle military forces in England at the start of the war were the trained bands of local county militia. However, these were not obliged, nor usually willing, to serve beyond the boundaries of their own county.

Though the trained bands were the best infantry that either side possessed, the localised nature of their enlistment meant that they could not be used in country-wide campaigns and the opposing armies resorted to recruitment and impressment. As a result many men, other than those who were motivated by personal beliefs or convictions, could be induced to change sides, depending on the current fortunes of the opposing armies.

Apart from the trained bands the regiments of foot and horse in both armies were raised for a specific engagement or campaign and were disbanded when hostilities were concluded. This changed with Parliament's creation of the "New Model" Army in which regiments became permanent establishments, laying down the foundations of the modern British Army. In military terms, the decision of 27 January 1645, to create a regular standing army was the most significant of the entire conflict and it won the war for Parliament. At its inception Sussex was directed to supply 600 of their finest men, and a large sum of money, for this service.

The principle infantry weapon of the English Civil War was the matchlock musket. These were large and cumbersome implements with a barrel length of up to four and a half feet. There was no common pattern and no standard calibre. The effective range of a smooth-bore musket was extremely limited but at close quarters a musket volley could be devastating. The bayonet had not been invented at the time of the Civil War and musketeers were easy prey to well-mounted cavalry.

To defend the musketeers from cavalry attacks a proportion of the infantry in each regiment were armed with pikes. These were iron-headed spears mounted on wooden (ash) poles between fifteen and eighteen feet long. Pikes were not only designed to defend the musketeers but were also used offensively and the "push of pikes" could decide the battle. The secondary weapon of both musketeers and pikemen was the sword.

The cavalry were armed with swords and, when they could be procured, pistols and short-barrelled muskets called carbines. In the main the cavalry wore buff leather coats with steel breastplates and back plates, plus an open-faced steel helmet. Some also had a steel gauntlet to protect their bridle hand and steel thigh-guards called tassets. Complete suits of armour were expensive and heavy and were a rare sight on the Civil War battlefields.

A recent development was the dragoon, or mounted infantryman. Armed and equipped as musketeers these highly mobile troops were ideal for scouting and as advance guards or rearguards.

Pikemen usually wore buff coats with breastplates and backplates, helmets and, frequently, tassets. Musketeers were not armoured and usually wore just their buff coats and a wide-brimmed hat. The ubiquitous buff coat was a thick ox-hide sleeveless jacket with a skirt that covered the thighs. It could resist sword cuts and bullets fired from long range.

Artillery of the seventeenth century was of limited value on the battlefield as the cannon were difficult to manoeuvre and could only maintain a very slow rate of fire (eight to ten rounds per hour). It was in siege warfare that artillery was most effective. There were two basic types of ordnance, the cannon and the mortar. Cannon threw solid, iron balls weighing up to sixty-three pounds, in a relatively flat trajectory, and were used to batter down the walls of a castle. Mortars fired explosive shells in a high trajectory over the battlements to fall inside the castle.[6]

For almost twelve months Parliament's hold upon Sussex remained unbroken despite occasional attacks by Royalist forces. A Cavalier raid on Petworth House had captured twenty Parliamentarian cavalry who were taken back to Oxford. South Harting, near the Hampshire border, had also witnessed a skirmish in which 120 men of the Earl of Crawfurd's Regiment drove off some 200 Parliamentarian dragoons. Both sides lost only a handful of men.

Waller was appointed Major-General of the Association of Sussex, Kent and Surrey, with Farnham becoming his base of operations. The departure of Waller's forces to Farnham allowed the Royalists troops in Hampshire to invade Sussex, and in December 1643 the county was drawn into the main theatre of the war. King Charles had planned a combined advance upon London from the north, and from the south through Sussex and Surrey.

The southern attack was to be delivered by Sir Ralph Hopton, who had been the first man to oppose the King with force the previous year but was now an important

Royalist general. Hopton's route through Sussex was by Harting and Marden and then over the Downs to Arundel. To keep open his line of communication Hopton garrisoned Harting Place and Edward Ford's regiment of horse was quartered at his father's house of Uppark to guard the passes through the Downs.

Detachments of cavalry from Hopton's force were sent to capture the great country houses of Petworth, Cowdray and Stanstead. In those days Stanstead was a castellated building with a turreted gateway and the first Royalist assault was driven off. After a sharp fight, however, this fine old house fell to the attackers.

Hopton's advance guard, led by the irrepressible Edward Ford, reached Arundel on 6 December 1643. Ford captured the town and laid siege to the castle. The Parliamentary garrison was strong enough to hold the powerful fortifications against Hopton's force of only 5,500 men. However, Arundel had not expected an attack.

Sussex's best defence was its inaccessibility but heavy frosts had hardened the normally muddy roads and Hopton's rapid march caught the Parliamentarians unprepared. The Castle was not provisioned for a prolonged investment and the garrison's reserves of ammunition were very limited.

News of Hopton's arrival at Arundel spread quickly throughout the county. Measures were immediately taken to garrison Bramber Castle and strengthen its fortifications. Shoreham, whose castle has long since disappeared, was also placed in a state of defence with six large cannon from Rye, and timber and lead from the ruined castle at Camber. But before any help could be offered to Arundel the garrison surrendered.

From Arundel Hopton's forces then moved eastwards and Colonel Morely, with as many men as he could muster, decided to hold the line of the Adur. The Royalists attacked Bramber Castle which was held by a small Puritan unit under the command of Captain James Temple. Unlike Arundel, Bramber held out. A second attempt to force the passage of the Adur by the Royalists at Bramber Bridge was also driven off.[7]

Though Morely had prevented Hopton from moving into eastern Sussex, the county west of the Adur was firmly in Royalist hands including the great houses of Cowdray, Petworth and Stanstead, as well as Arundel Castle. It was time for Waller to intervene.

He set off from Farnham on Sunday 17 December, marching by way of Haslemere and Midhurst. Hoping to take the garrison of Cowdray House by surprise, he sent two regiments of cavalry to block the roads and surround the house. The Royalist garrison, of four troops of horse and 100 foot, learnt of Waller's advance and the men escaped to Arundel. Petworth, where Hopton had his headquarters, was Waller's next target but again the Cavaliers escaped, with Hopton making his way to Winchester and others joining the garrison of Arundel Castle.

Cowdray House. The ruins of this fortified manor house are only open to the public at specified times. They can be viewed from a public footpath that leads off the main A272 road (SU 892217).

The Castle was occupied by around 1,100 men including the troops from Cowdray and Petworth. Waller, with 6,000 men, camped his army within a mile of Arundel on the evening of Tuesday the 19th. At dawn the following morning Waller reconnoitred the town. He found that Hopton had surrounded the place with earthworks which had to be taken before the Parliamentarians could approach the Castle. After a preliminary artillery bombardment Waller delivered simultaneous attacks upon the north and south-west of the town and after about thirty minutes of fighting seized the outworks and captured some eighty men.

Though the Royalist cavalry made a sortie from the Castle, the town was taken by the Parliamentarians, and the Cavaliers were driven back into the Castle. Waller took another sixty prisoners in the town.

On 21 December, Morely's regiment joined the besieging forces as well as a further 600 cavalry which were sent from the Earl of Essex. The weather, which had been fine and frosty for many days, now broke and the town was lashed by violent rainstorms.

Where possible the besieging troops were billeted in the houses of the town but this meant that they were within range of marksmen posted in the upper part of the Castle. In an attempt to counter the marksmen two light field pieces called "saker drakes" were hauled up to the tower of Arundel Church during the night and at first light they, along with a unit of musketeers, poured a heavy fire upon the battlements.

Yet more Roundhead reinforcements were received, this time from Kent, in the form of a regiment of cavalry and another of foot. The odds against the Royalists were becoming greater by the day and many members of the garrison deserted what was clearly a lost cause. The water supply to the Castle came from Swanbourne Lake and the besiegers began draining off the water from the lake. By Saturday 23 December, this had been completed and the garrison had only the water remaining in the Castle wells.

The situation was becoming desperate for the defenders but they were able to keep in communication with Hopton (even though one messenger was caught and hanged on the bridge within sight of the Castle) via a small boat upon which the messengers crossed the Arun. Despite commanding less than 3,000 men, Hopton marched from Winchester to the relief of Arundel on 27 December.

When news of Hopton's approach reached Waller he left just 1,500 men to continue the siege and he moved to meet the Royalists with the rest of his force. The opposing armies met on the 29th at West Dean, four miles north of Chichester. This was the largest gathering of hostile forces on Sussex soil since the Battle of Lewes. But the advantage in numbers was entirely in favour of the Parliamentarians and Hopton, after a brief skirmish, sensibly withdrew.

After Hopton had failed to relieve the garrison, the Royalists offered to surrender on terms. Waller, whose position was now unassailable, would not negotiate. With some heavy guns that he had received from Portsmouth, Waller began to bombard the Castle on 4 January. The garrison was by this time reduced to an allowance of meat and two spoons of wheat per man per day; many inside the walls had fallen ill.

The next day three commissioners were sent out from the Castle to arrange terms of surrender and at approximately 09:00 hours on 6 January 1644, Arundel Castle was surrendered to Parliament. The siege had lasted seventeen days.

Waller took possession of around 200 horses, 2,000 weapons, twenty barrels of gunpowder and some £4,000. More than 1,000 soldiers, including about 100 officers

The beautifully restored castle at Arundel. Note the large, round keep in the centre of the Castle and the bailey on either side, (TQ 017074). (By kind permission of His Grace the Duke of Norfolk.)

and nineteen colours were taken. Edward Ford was treated with surprising leniency by Parliament, merely being branded as "incapable of any employment".

Arundel and its Castle had suffered severely from both Hopton's and Waller's attacks. Shortly after the siege a visitor to Arundel described the place as "a most dismal sight: the town being depopulated, all the windows broken with the great guns, and the soldiers making stables in all the shops".[8]

During the siege many of the besiegers, as well as the besieged, died of a fever, probably typhus. The Castle was "slighted" in 1649 and left roofless and ruined. Never again would this once-mighty fortification challenge the authority of Parliament.

Waller set about securing Sussex. The garrison of Chichester was increased to 800 men and a large magazine, which included 100 barrels of gunpowder, was formed in Arundel Castle. More troops were also raised through an ordinance of 31 March 1644, which called for 3,000 foot, 1,200 horse and 500 dragoons from Hampshire, Surrey, Sussex and Kent.

During the summer of 1644, Colonel Morley with six companies of men from Sussex assisted in the siege of Basing House, the fortified residence of the Marquis of Winchester, in Hampshire. Later in the year Sussex troops also served as far afield as Dorset. But a large body of Royalists under Sir George Goring was active in the eastern areas of Hampshire, and Parliament ordered 500 dragoons from Kent, Sussex and Surrey to join a force of 1,000 foot from Reading which was to defend the Sussex border. At the same time the trained bands were ordered up to garrison Chichester and Arundel.

Meanwhile, the remarkable siege of Basing House continued and Sussex was ordered to find 400 more men to support the besiegers. Muskets and horses were also taken from the Sussex magazines for the siege. The continual drain upon the resources of the ordinary people, the plundering of the troops and the requisitions of Parliament, drove the people of the southern counties into revolt.

Known as the Clubmen because their weapons were clubs and agricultural implements, the movement began in Wiltshire and Dorset and soon spread to Hampshire and Sussex. A thousand Clubmen met at Rowkeshill[9] near Chichester in the middle of September and a call went out for a further meeting at Bury Hill. This was pre-empted by a Major Young who attacked a number of Clubmen at Walberton with some forty infantry and ten horse, killing one man and causing the rest to flee.

This was followed by the capture of the leading Clubmen and the movement lost momentum. However, resistance to Parliament's demands for men and money continued. Taxes went unpaid throughout the county and few men responded to the call for reinforcements to the New Model Army.

Within weeks of the outbreak of hostilities in 1642, Parliament declared that the cost of the war would be borne by those who supported the King and on 15 October the Lords went one step further by announcing that anyone who refused to help the Parliamentary cause with money would be imprisoned and their goods sequestered.

In January 1644, Parliament, in the hope of persuading Royalists to abandon their support for Charles, allowed those that had followed the King to pay a fine and get their property back if they renounced their allegiance to the Crown. Many leading Royalists took this opportunity of saving their estates. The fines, however, were often nothing short of extortionate and in many cases long legal battles followed.

Sir John Goring of Amberley had repeatedly refused to accept Parliament's right to extract money for the war and he encouraged the local people to place their goods and valuables in his castle where they would be safe from the grasp of the Parliamentarians. This was open defiance and could not be ignored by Waller. He marched the five miles from Arundel and attacked Amberley Castle. Though the walls of the Castle show no signs of having suffered heavy bombardment, Waller forced his way into the castle and seized Goring. Waller destroyed the internal buildings of the Castle and rendered it defenceless by pulling down its parapet.

With the eventual fall of Basing House, after the longest siege of the war, the threat of Civil War was removed from the Sussex borders. Elsewhere the King's fortunes continued to ebb and following his defeats at Marston Moor and Naseby, Charles fled to Scotland where he was captured and handed over to his enemies. The First Civil War was over.

What followed was a sordid and unnecessary affair. Charles refused to bend to the popular will and continued to conspire against Parliament, attempting to garner support from across the Channel. Nothing could have incensed the English people more than this and it was to cost Charles his life.

The iron rule of the Parliamentary army led many to agitate for a restoration of the monarchy, albeit with limited powers, and if Charles had not tried to encourage foreigners to invade the country and fight his own subjects he might well have found himself back on the throne.

The discontent felt throughout England, at what was effectively military rule, found an outlet in a petition of May 1648 which called for the disbandment of the New Model Army and the restoration of the King. In Sussex, Horsham emerged as a centre of Royalist activity at this time and men from all over the country converged upon Horsham and Pulborough.

In the east of the county a force of sixty Royalists tried to capture Rye on behalf of the King. Both of these rebellions were put down swiftly by Parliament's forces.

Nevertheless, these and other uprisings around the country prompted many MPs to suggest that there would never be peace until the King was dead.

The trial of Charles I began on 20 January 1649. He was found guilty of subverting the "ancient and fundamental laws and liberties of the nation". He was executed on Tuesday 30 January. Amongst the fifty-nine signatories to the death-warrant were seven Sussex politicians.[10]

For the next few years Sussex was able to concentrate on restoring its prosperity but during this time war broke out between England and Holland. Around Asia, Africa and the Americas, England and Holland competed fiercely for mastery of the seas and control of the sea-borne trade.

The first actual battle between the two maritime nations occurred in May 1652 when Admiral Blake sailed from Rye harbour to intercept the famous Dutch Admiral Tromp (famous, this is, for fixing a broom to the mast of his ship and declaring that he was going to sweep the English from the seas!). The Dutch responded by attacking the south coast.

In one raid they captured a vessel from Hastings and in later attacks the Dutch landed in East Sussex, plundering houses and driving off cattle. It was during this period that the first and largest warship ever built at Shoreham was launched. The *Dover*, a fourth-rate man-of-war, displacing 533 tons and carrying forty-eight guns, was so big that the crew had difficulty finding sufficient depth of water to float it out of the port! The war was a disaster for the Dutch and it marked the beginning of their decline as a world power.

Charles I's son, Charles Stuart, continued the war against Parliament after his father's execution. His incursion into England with a large Scottish army in 1651 prompted Parliament to demand the Sussex militia regiment be sent to the midlands. This left just two troops of horse in the county but, as Sussex was so far from the seat of war, this force was considered sufficient for the defence of the entire county.

Charles' army was beaten but he escaped capture and eventually made his way into Sussex in the hope of escaping to the Continent. Royalist supporters managed to secure a passage for the young Prince on a ship due to leave Shoreham and, in the greatest secrecy, Charles was escorted through Sussex. With his hair cropped in a Roundhead cut and travelling under the name of Will Jackson, Prince Charles rode over the Goodwood Downs, past Arundel, Bramber (where he stayed at St Mary's House), Beeding and arrived safely at the George Inn at Brighthelmstone, as Brighton was then called.

The party stayed at the inn until midnight on 15 October when it rode through the night to Shoreham. At 08:00 hours the coal-brig *Surprise* sailed on the tide and the following day reached Fécamp in Normandy.

With the death of Oliver Cromwell in September 1658, the Royalists hoped for the return of Charles Stuart. Fears of a Royalist uprising in Sussex and rumours that the Prince might land somewhere on the south coast prompted Parliament into action.

Two thousand men were ordered to Arundel and Lewes and throughout the summer of 1659, two warships patrolled the coast between Beachy Head and Chichester. Cowdray House was garrisoned by the militia and a magazine for the use of the East Sussex trained bands was collected at Lewes. A town guard was formed at Rye. These measures evidently proved sufficient to deter the Royalists from taking up arms.

Yet just a few months later General Monk, with the army at his back, dissolved Parliament and set Charles Stuart upon the throne. To celebrate the restoration of the monarchy after years of dull and oppressive Puruitan rule the beacons were lit along the coast and bonfires blazed across the Downs.[11] It must have appeared to many that all the death and destruction of the preceding eighteen years had been for nothing.

Sussex had a final part to play in this great but unfortunate saga. Richard Cromwell, son of Oliver, escaped to the Continent from a Sussex Port (this time Lewes) just as Charles Stuart had done almost a decade earlier.

CHAPTER 8

The Bastion Shore:
Sussex's Coastal Fortifications

Apart from the Saxon Shore forts of the Romans and the isolated burgs of Alfred the Great, there was no other systematic attempt to fortify the south coast until the reign of Henry VIII in the middle of the sixteenth century.

Henry wanted a son to continue the Tudor dynasty but his wife, Catherine of Aragon, had produced only a daughter and was unable to bear any more children. Henry, consequently, sought a papal annulment of his marriage. As Catherine was the aunt of the most powerful Catholic monarch in Europe, Charles V, the Pope dared not offend the Spanish emperor and he refused to agree to a divorce. Henry, therefore, took matters into his own hands. He severed all links with Rome, declared himself head of the church in England, dissolved the monasteries and divorced Catherine.

The Pope responded by urging France and Spain to unite and bring England to heel. Henry took this threat seriously as, earlier in the century, the French – as ever at war with England – had attacked the Sussex coast.

In 1514 a French force had raided Brighton and burnt the town and in 1545 a large French force had landed at Seaford. At this time Sussex was considered to be "the place of danger within the realm"[1] but with the possibility of two major powers combining their forces against England no coast was safe from attack. So between 1538 and the mid-1540s, Henry built a chain of defensive works around the eastern, southern and western coasts. With the Cinque Ports in decline and the Royal Navy still in its infancy, Henry's aim was to have every port and potential landing place from the Humber to Milford Haven commanded by a fortification.

Though this ambition was never fully realised many fine castles and blockhouses were built at Harwich, Brownsea, Tilbury, Gravesend, Deal, Hurst, Walmer, St Mawes, Portland, Pendennis, Sandown, Sandgate, Calshot, Southsea, Dale & Angle in Pembrokeshire and Camber in Sussex.

Henry's castles were unlike any built before in England. They were not the fortified residences of powerful barons, they were exclusively military installations. Unlike the tall keeps and high curtain walls of Norman and medieval castles, Henry's castles were low and squat. This was because artillery was becoming increasingly

An aerial view of Camber Castle, which clearly shows the Tudor rose configuration. The castle can be reached by footpath from Rye Harbour Road (TQ 922185). (By kind permission of English Heritage.)

important in all forms of warfare and the exposed walls of the traditional castles were easily reduced to rubble by the pounding of heavy cannon.

Beautifully symmetrical in their design, Henry's castles took the form of a Tudor Rose with semi-circular bastions surrounding a circular central tower. Each bastion and the higher, dominating central tower, was simply a platform for artillery. The castle at Camber, typically, had a permanent garrison of one captain, six gunners and eight soldiers.

Located by the mouth of the River Camber, the castle was placed to defend the important harbours of Rye and New Winchelsea. At this time Rye itself was furnished with heavy artillery placed in the Gun Garden in front of the Ypres Tower. More guns were sited at the Land Gate and the Strand Gate. As it transpired, Henry VIII's

A view of the north-western front of Camber Castle. The Castle sits on the Winchelsea Beach Nature Reserve.

England was not seriously attacked and the guns of Camber Castle, removed during the Civil War, never fired a shot in anger.

Between 1625 and 1630 England was again at war with France and Spain, during which time Sussex suffered occasional raids including an attack upon Shoreham in which a vessel was captured by three French ships. At this time the beacons, which had last been lit during the passing of the Armada, were re-built as the braziers had rusted and the poles upon which they rested had broken. Many of the wooden gun carriages of the county's gun gardens and batteries had also rotted to the extent that the guns were useless.

The neglect of Sussex's coastal defences continued until the middle of the eighteenth century when Britain found itself once again at odds with France and her allies. Britain's wars with France throughout the eighteenth century, however, were no longer driven by religious differences. This was an era of rapid imperial expansion, and conflict between two such powerful and ambitious nations was inevitable.

The War of the Austrian Succession (1740-48) saw a vast French invasion fleet actually put to sea, only to be forced back to harbour by a severe gale. The renewal of hostilities a few years later, during the Seven Years War of the 1750s, naturally gave rise to fears of another invasion attempt and it led to the partial re-fortification of the south coast.[2]

The Government's assessment of the situation, based on advice from senior admirals and generals, was that the most likely landing ground would be the open beaches of Kent and East Sussex. In 1757 Lieutenant William Roy began a survey of the Sussex coast and, two years later, Sir John Ligonier, the Master General of the Board of Ordnance, undertook a personal reconnaissance of the area from Arundel to Brighton.

Following these inspections, a new battery was raised at Littlehampton (then still known as Arundel Haven) on the east bank of the Arun estuary. It took the form of an open bastion facing the sea with its right flank parallel to the river.

The parapets and ramparts of what became known as the East Bank Battery were both formed of earth sodded with turf to hold the soil in place. There was no ditch around the work but the open rear was secured by a strong, wooden stockade fence. The ordnance of the battery, which was mounted on a wooden platform to fire over the parapet, consisted of seven 18-pounder cannon. The battery was manned by only four regular soldiers and in the event of an attack it was expected that the guns would be served by sailors from ships in the harbour.

During the Napoleonic invasion scare of the 19th century, however, the Duke of York ordered the battery to be fully manned and supported by at least 200 troops. The East Bank Battery remained in service until 1835.

The "blockhouse" and gun garden at Brighton were still standing, though both of these were being undermined by coastal erosion. There was also a small fort at Hastings which mounted eleven 12-pounders, but between Brighton and Hastings there were no significant defences at all. It was in 1759, therefore, that the Board of Ordnance ordered the construction of batteries in Seaford Bay.[3]

At Newhaven a battery was established on Castle Hill overlooking Newhaven harbour. It housed five 12-pounder cannon and included a powder magazine and barracks. To cover the flat ground between the estuary of the Ouse and Seaford Head two further batteries were built. The first was on Blatchington Down and was armed with five 24-pounders. The second, of five 12-pounders, was on Seaford Beach in front of the town. Both of these batteries also had powder magazines and barracks for the gunners.

A gun emplacement and magazine of the 19th century Lower Battery at Newhaven, which is now adjacent to the West Beach car park. (TQ 448001).

In the same year the decaying Brighton defences were replaced by the Great East Street Battery. This work held twenty antique 20-pounder cannon.

Strangely all these batteries were not under the jurisdiction of the military. The Master Gunner, who was the officer in charge of each battery, was a civilian as was his second in command, though he was also a trained gunner. These were both full-time posts paid for by the Government. Until the middle of the eighteenth century the cost of maintaining and manning coastal defences had to be borne locally. At Brighton, for instance, a quarter of the profit from each boat on the beach had to go towards the purchase of powder and shot for the gun batteries.

The rest of the personnel were local volunteers, often old soldiers.

Though France and her allies amassed an armada of flat-bottomed boats along the coast from St Malo to Dunkirk the Royal Navy kept the enemy fleet blockaded in its own harbours. Twice in 1759, however, the French were able to slip through the blockades with the intention of rounding up the invasion craft and escorting them across the Channel. But on both occasions the French were followed and intercepted by the Royal Navy and the French fleets of Brest and Toulon were eventually caught and destroyed in Quiberon Bay.

A little over thirty years after the destruction of the Toulon fleet at Quiberon Bay, France once again threatened to invade southern England. This was the time of the French Revolution and its greatest military leader, Napoleon Bonaparte.

In the summer (i.e. the invasion season) of both 1793 and 1794, huge tented camps were formed at Brighton. Accommodating 10,000-15,000 troops, the 1793 camp was established along the seafront running westwards for over a mile from the present-day Regency Square. The 1794 camp was pitched on Race Hill. Elaborate training exercises and mock battles, with the Prince of Wales happily playing his part as Colonel of the 10th Dragoons, were a frequent spectacle in and around Brighton at this time.[4]

A signal station, more correctly called a telegraph, was also sited on Race Hill. Messages could be sent and received to and from the adjacent stations at Seaford in the east and Shoreham to the west. These telegraphs were part of a network of signal stations which the Admiralty built on the coast to allow communications both out to the ships of the Royal Navy and along the coast. Sixteen of these stations were in Sussex.[5]

Permanent barracks were later built at Brighton with one for infantry being raised opposite the stables of the Royal Pavilion and another for cavalry along the Lewes Road. At Chichester in the Broyle Road, the Roussillion Barracks were built to accommodate 1,500 men, and at nearby Selsey a wooden barracks housed a further 300 soldiers. Shoreham, Southwick, Steyning, Worthing, Littlehampton, Arundel and Bognor Regis all had barracks during the Napoleonic Wars.

The result of further invasion scares beginning in 1795, which reached a climax between 1803 to 1805, was the complete militarisation of the south coast. Not only was there a massive programme of re-fortification but large numbers of troops were stationed in the south and substantial garrisons established at every important position along the coast.

Amongst the earliest of these fortifications were the batteries at Langney Point

Two gun pivots which once formed part of the defensive armament of the Langney Redoubt. These are standing at the end of the sea-front promenade at Langney Point, Eastbourne (TQ 642011).

The scant remains of a gun emplacement from the Langney Redoubt, situated at the end of the promenade at Langney Point.

to the east of Eastbourne. On this flat and exposed beach two substantial forts were erected in 1795.

Each armed with six captured French 24-pounders, the batteries were enclosed at the rear with loopholed walls and a ditch.[6] Altogether there were ten batteries in Sussex, the others being the existing ones at Rye, Hastings, Eastbourne, Seaford, Blatchington, Newhaven, Brighton and Littlehampton. The companies raised locally to serve these batteries were intended to consist of one captain, two lieutenants and sixty men, of whom at least one third were armed with muskets and the rest with pikes.[7]

In 1801, the Commander-in-Chief of the army, the Duke of York, toured the south coast and drew up his "Information and Instructions for Commanding

Generals and Others" detailing his plans for the defence of London and the south. The principle behind his plan was that there would be no attempt to defend the coastline.

There were so many likely landing places, the Duke reckoned, that it would be impossible to predict where the French would attack. He proposed, therefore, to concentrate his forces at selected points. In West Sussex those points were at North Mundham to protect Chichester and Pagham Harbour; at Warningcamp to defend the Arun valley; at Highdown Hill to watch the coast between Worthing and Shoreham and on Hollingbury Hill to cover Brighton.

If the invaders broke through, or outflanked, these concentration points, the defenders would fall back to a second line of rallying posts. These were to be at Shermanbury, Stopham, Houghton and Westbourne near the Hampshire border. If this second line was overrun the troops would retreat to Horsham and Guildford to defend the roads through the North Downs leading to London.

To impede the French advance the countryside was to be abandoned and every-thing that might be useful to the enemy was to be removed or ruined. Livestock and all means of conveyance (carts, horses and boats) were to be driven inland and crops and magazines were to be destroyed.

The low-lying areas of the Romney Marsh and the Pett and Pevensey Levels were to be flooded by opening the sluice gates of the drainage ditches and by breaching the sea wall.[8] Roads would be blocked or broken up whilst the British cavalry harried the flanks of the advancing invaders.

For a brief period of time Britain and France were at peace but with the renewal of hostilities in 1803, the subject of coastal defence was once again thrust onto the Government's agenda. Napoleon saw Britain as the principal obstacle in his attempt at European, and possibly even world, domination. He formed a vast camp at Boulogne where 100,000 men assembled under the optimistic title of "The Army of England". Only the Royal Navy, and the uncertain waters of the Channel, stood between Napoleon and the Kent and Sussex coasts.

In the autumn of 1804 the Government decided to build an entire series of permanent defences along the coast from Dover to Beachy Head. Eventually these defences were extended to run from Suffolk to Sussex and numbered no less than 103 towers and redoubts and included a massive defensive ditch from below Winchelsea to Hythe in Kent.

The area of land encompassed by this defensive ditch, which became known as the Royal Military Canal, was considered to be the most vulnerable point along the entire south coast. The canal was to begin at Shorncliff above Hythe and terminate at Cliff End to the north-east of Hastings, running for a distance of twenty-eight miles and embracing the flat, low-lying regions of Romney Marsh and Pett Level.

A section of the Royal Military Canal at Pett Level, (TQ 894139).

Along the northern bank of the canal a parapet was formed from the earth excavated during the digging of the canal. In the event of an invasion, defending infantry and artillery would be able to fire over the parapet. The canal was built with a profile similar to a nineteenth century fort, incorporating salient angles to allow flanking, or enfilade fire, along the face of the parapet. Behind the protection of the parapet was a road to enable the safe and rapid transfer of troops along the line to any threatened point. Originally it was suggested that the canal should be sixty-two feet wide at the surface, forty-four feet wide at the bottom and nine feet deep. The adjoining parapet was to be thirty-five feet wide and the accompanying road thirty feet.

On 30 October 1804, the first ground was broken at Shorncliffe. The project was under the supervision of a civilian engineer, John Rennie, who had been responsible for the construction of the London and Waterloo bridges. It was intended that the canal would be completed by June of the following year, but by May 1805 only six miles of ditch had been dug. Amid much acrimony the contractors were dismissed, Rennie resigned and the work was taken over by the Army.

The Royal Staff Corps established its headquarters at Hythe and took over responsibility for the building programme. Soldiers were used to construct the parapet but civilian labour was still used to dig the canal, and by August more than 1,500 men were hard at work.

The ditch was dug by hand, the men possessing only picks and shovels, with the earth being removed by wheelbarrow. Because much of the ground was at or below sea level the ditch was prone to flooding and large steam-driven pumps were in almost constant use. The proposed surface width of sixty-two feet was only accomplished at the eastern end of the canal and along most of its length the canal is only half that distance across. In many parts the required depth of nine feet was not achieved. When the canal was opened in August 1806 the threat of invasion had receded thanks to Nelson's great victory over the French fleet at Trafalgar.[9]

Along the coast on either side of the canal ran the long chain of towers. They were constructed to a design similar to a fort built by the French in Mortella Point, Corsica which had withstood considerable bombardment from British guns in 1793. The "Martello" towers were elliptical in shape with an axis of 45ft by 42ft at the base and 39ft by 35ft at the top. They stood nearly thirty-three feet high and some

Martello Tower No.74 on the seafront esplanade at Seaford (TQ 485985).

Martello Tower No.55, at Norman's Bay, which stands between the seafront properties that back onto the minor road from Pevensey Bay (TQ 684053).

were provided with a dry brick-lined ditch some thirty-eight feet wide and sixteen feet deep. The walls were twelve feet thick on the seaward side and seven feet thick on the landward side.[10]

At the bottom of each tower were cisterns to catch rainwater. Above these was the ground floor where the magazine was located. The first floor was the main living area for one officer and twenty-four men. The entrance was also on this level. It was eleven feet above the ground and was reached by a ladder which could be taken up and stored inside the tower. Where the tower had a ditch, access was over a drop-bridge.

An internal stone staircase led from the first floor to the gun roof. The single 24-pounder cannon was mounted on a sliding carriage. This carriage was fixed to a traversing platform which was fitted with wheels that ran along metal rails embedded into the masonry below the parapet. With the aid of a central pivot the cannon could be turned and pointed in any direction. To counter the recoil the gun was angled upon a 1 in 12 slope which also helped to run the gun forward again. The gun fired over a thick, stone parapet which also had a firing step for infantry. If the tower stood at a point where the ground might conceal the approach of the enemy the fortress also mounted two 5.5-inch howitzers. Such places in Sussex were the Wish Tower (No.73) which still stands on the cliffs to the west of Eastbourne and nearby Anthony Hill (No.68).

Along the most accessible stretches of the coast the towers were built just 500 to 600 yards apart, enabling them to be mutually supporting and allowing their guns to form deadly cross-fires. The towers were provided with the resources to withstand a siege and they were utterly impregnable to troops without heavy artillery.

Altogether, 103 towers were built from Aldeburgh in Suffolk to Seaford. The ones on the south coast were numbered from east to west with No.1 at Folkestone to No.74 at Seaford.

Included with the standard towers were three larger forts. At Eastbourne, Dymchurch in Kent and Harwich on the east coast, three circular redoubts were constructed. The Eastbourne Circular Redoubt is 216 feet in diameter and was originally armed with ten 24-pounders and had facilities for a garrison of 400 men. Unlike the Martello Towers it was partially sunk into the ground and was well concealed from the sea.

This was to be the principal work along this vulnerable stretch of coastline, supported by the Langney batteries and Pevensey Levels to the east which could be flooded by the opening of the Pevensey sluices. To the west, of course, are the towering chalk walls of Beachy Head.

The defences of the Sussex coast were under the command of Sir James Pultney, who established his headquarters at Eastbourne. The construction of the Martello Towers was a considerable and lengthy operation and with 130,000 French troops waiting at Boulogne for nothing more than a favourable wind to blow their boats across the Channel, immediate measures had to be taken. So Pultney arranged for the construction of "emergency" batteries to be erected around the coast. Situated about 500 yards apart along vulnerable parts of the coast, Pultney had the batteries built with earthen ramparts seven feet high and armed with 24-pounders. These batteries remained in use until the building of the Martello Towers had been completed. Though it is not certain how many of these batteries were constructed, it is known that no less than eighteen were erected in and around Eastbourne alone. Work on the Martello Towers began in March 1804 but by the time the great chain of forts had been built it was 1812 and the fear of invasion was but a distant memory.

The return of France to a Bonapartist regime under Napoleon III prompted a rush of new defensive works along the south coast. At Littlehampton, Shoreham and Newhaven substantial fortifications were erected in the 1850s.

Caponier and ditch at the Eastbourne Redoubt. The Redoubt is situated on the promenade to the east of Eastbourne town centre (TV 623997).

The remains of the fort at Littlehampton that can be seen today, (TQ 027012). Just visible beneath the undergrowth is the loop-holed Carnot wall and part of a caponier. Access is provided by the Rope Walk along the western bank of the River Arun.

The new fort at Littlehampton was sited on the west bank of the Arun and was completed in 1854. It was built in the form of a lunette with two flanks and two faces but with an enclosed rear protected by earthworks. Around the work was a dry ditch, twenty-seven feet wide, at the base of which was a loopholed, twelve-feet-high, Carnot wall.

Three small, open bastions were formed on the three salient angles of the Carnot wall to provide enfilade fire along the ditch. It was armed with three 68-pounder and two 32-pounder smooth-bore cannon and the garrison comprised two infantry

A 1932 aerial photograph of the Littlehampton West Bank Fort which guarded the estuary of the River Arun. (By kind permission of Mrs. M. Taylor.)

officers, one master gunner, and forty-eight other ranks, including six trained gunners. With its own artesian well and magazines, it was capable of a sustained defence, even if attacked from both the land and the sea.[11]

An even stronger fort was built at Shoreham. Though just three years newer than the Littlehampton fort, the Shoreham work incorporated some of the most recent developments in fortification. Its basic design was very similar to the Littlehampton fort but instead of small, open bastions on the Carnot wall, the Shoreham fort had large, fully enclosed caponiers. The fort mounted six 68-pounders sited on dwarf traversing platforms which enabled the guns to command the harbour entrance and the beaches on either side of the Adur estuary.[12]

Shoreham Redoubt, showing the loopholed Carnot wall and caponier. The Redoubt is at the end of Fort Haven at the eastern extremity of Shoreham Beach (TQ 233045).

At Newhaven a new battery was erected at the foot of Castle Hill to supplement the guns of the 1759 battery on top of the hill. The new Lower Battery was armed with six guns to defend the harbour entrance and the approach to West Beach. The 1759 battery remained in use and was re-named the Upper Battery.

Lord Palmerston, the Prime Minister from 1855 to 1865, authorised a Royal Commission to re-examine the whole question of coastal defence. The Commission reported in 1860 and included amongst its proposals was the construction of the largest defensive structure in Sussex to replace the old Upper Battery at Newhaven. The reason why such a massive fortification was required here was that Newhaven was rapidly becoming one of the most important ports in Sussex following the opening of a direct rail line with London (1847) and the development of a cross-Channel steamboat service to France in 1849.

The fort was dug out of the chalk headland overlooking the harbour with the cliffs themselves forming the glacis and the ramparts. Despite occupying almost sixteen acres of ground, it was virtually unidentifiable as a fortification from the sea. The landward sides of the fort were protected by a wide, dry ditch and access to the fort is over a bridge and through a cut in the chalk glacis. The ditch was defended by counterscarp galleries from which both infantry and artillery could fire the length of the ditch.

One of the most remarkable features of the fort is a large caponier, with sally port, which was built at the foot of the cliffs by the old Lower Battery. Access to the caponier is via a long tunnel and steps cut through the cliff. With barracks for 245 men and originally armed with nine large-calibre guns, Newhaven Fort was the strongest coastal fortification between Dover and Portsmouth – the Eastbourne Circular Redoubt was now considered to be obsolete. The fort was completed in 1871 and was the first major military structure in Britain to use large quantities of concrete in its construction.

Though the improvement in artillery had made the magazines at the Eastbourne Circular Redoubt vulnerable to attack by naval shipping, the redoubt remained in service and was re-armed, in 1859, with 110-pounders, 68-pounders, and 8-inch muzzle-loading guns. By this time the West Fort at Langney Point had become derelict but the East Fort was modernised with caponiers on the rear walls and re-armed with 68-pounders. This fort was re-named the Langney Redoubt.

Throughout the last decades of the nineteenth century the old gun batteries along the coast were abandoned by the military. The Upper Battery at Newhaven had been incorporated into the Newhaven Fort but the Seaford Battery was washed into the sea in 1860 and the Blatchington Battery was sold off ten years later.

The Langney Redoubt survived until the early years of the twentieth century and the Eastbourne Circular Redoubt still stands today. The latter was disposed of by the Army towards the end of the nineteenth century, but was re-occupied by the military during the Second World War.

The improvements in the range and accuracy of ordnance soon made the Littlehampton and Shoreham forts obsolete. Their parapets were too weak and their smooth-bore guns ineffective. Though extensive re-working was proposed, neither fort received any structural improvement.

The Littlehampton West Bank Fort was abandoned by the military in 1891 but the Shoreham Redoubt continued to be maintained as a military establishment until after the First World War. Shoreham's old ordnance was replaced by three 64-pounder and two 80-pounder rifled guns. The latter remained in service until 1921.

CHAPTER 9

The World at War

There was no serious possibility of a German invasion of England during the First World War and few measures were considered necessary for the protection of the coast. The defence of the coastline was left in the hands of the Territorial Army. Initially there was no attempt to line the shore with troops. Instead a "Central Force" of nine TA divisions and two Yeomanry divisions was held back from the coast ready to counter any advance inland by an invader. Later this policy was reversed and the troops were moved closer to the coast to prevent the enemy establishing a foothold on the beaches.[1]

The only place in Sussex to receive any defensive armament was Newhaven Fort which was re-armed with two rapid-firing 6-inch guns to combat fast German torpedo boats. The guns were served by men of the Royal Garrison Artillery, assisted by Territorial Army Engineers who manned searchlights situated on the harbour breakwater. Newhaven became a principle embarkation port for stores and munitions shipped out from England to the Western Front.

Large tented camps were formed in the area to accommodate the troops destined for the trenches. Huge camps were formed at Shoreham, Tide Mills and on Chailey Common. Ashdown Forest was also the scene of much military activity during this period with camps at Forest Row, Kidbrooke Park, King's Standing, Camp Hill, Pippingford and St John's Common. The Forest continued to be used by the military through the Second World War and even to the present day.[2]

Aerodromes, seaplane bases and airship stations of the Royal Flying Corps, (RFC), and the Royal Naval Air Service (RNAS) were located along the coast. Polegate was the site for one of the earliest non-rigid airship stations. From Polegate the first "Submarine Scout" airship began patrols along the Channel on 6 July 1915. A year later these craft were replaced with the larger SS Zero airships which could remain in the air for over seventeen hours.

By September 1917, six Zeros were operating out of Polegate. The Zero had a crew of three – pilot, observer/gunner and an engineer who sat next to the enginc.[3] The airships, known as "Blimps", were used mainly for spotting German submarines which then operated in considerable numbers in the Channel.

Possibly the most important airbase was at Newhaven. Formed on the East Beach, the RNAS flew seaplane patrols along the coast between Dungeness and the Isle of

Wight. Newhaven's four Short 184 seaplanes were armed with a Lewis gun and could carry a maximum bomb load of one 112lb and two 50lb bombs. The other bases in Sussex were at St Anthony's Eastbourne, Middleton, Goring, and East Preston.

To counter the threat of Zeppelin (and later Gotha bomber) raids upon London, 78 Squadron of the RFC was formed. One flight of this squadron, flying Bristol BE2c and B12 fighters, was based at Telscombe Cliffs. Initially the airfield was operational for just one year from September 1917, but was reactivated for a few months in 1918.

Shoreham Airport was designated as a training airfield and, in 1915, 3 Reserve Aeroplane Squadron arrived flying Maurice Farman Longhorns. Tangmere airfield was built in 1917 (using German Prisoner of War labour) and was the base for 92 Squadron which was equipped with SE5As, and 61 Squadron which flew Avro 504s and Bristol F2Bs. Ford airfield was another training station which became operational towards the end of the war. Ford and Tangmere, as well as Southbourne and Rustington, were amongst the sites originally selected as training bases for the United States air force to fly the huge Handley Page night bombers.[4]

The worrying ease with which German submarines could pass through the Channel prompted the construction, in 1917, of one of the most remarkable structures ever built in Sussex. An anti-submarine barrier was to be laid between the Goodwin Sands and Dunkirk. It was to be strengthened by sixteen enormous concrete gun towers. The first pair of towers, which were to be towed out to sea and then sunk into thirty fathoms of water with the towers rising 100 feet above sea level, was built at Shoreham. Only one was completed by the end of the war and this tower was towed out to the Nab sandbanks east of the Isle of Wight. Now known as the Nab Tower lighthouse, it remains there to this day.[5]

The pounding of the guns on the Western Front could be heard in many areas of Sussex and, because of the county's proximity to the Continent, men wounded in the fighting were taken to Sussex for treatment and care, including large numbers of empire troops. Twenty-five "auxiliary" hospitals were established throughout the county to deal with the influx of thousands of badly injured soldiers.[6]

As in the First World War there was little perceived threat of an attack upon Britain at the outbreak of war in 1939 – other than from the air. Such complacency was immediately swept away when the British Army was driven from the Continent, being saved from complete annihilation only by the heroics at Dunkirk (in which many small boats from Sussex played their part). Suddenly Britain, and the southern and eastern coastlines in particular, appeared to be exposed and defenceless.

Hitler's invasion plan, Operation *Sealion*, has since been shown to have been wholly inadequate in both scale and preparation. Yet in the summer of 1940 none of this was known. Most people, including those in the armed forces, expected that

Hitler would succeed in landing a large force somewhere along the eastern or southern coasts.

The first thrust of Operation *Sealion* would see attacks against three areas. The XVI Army, 90,000 strong, would capture Ramsgate with paratroop regiments securing its flanks from Dover to Pevensey. Ninth Army, of 40,000 men, was to take West Sussex with paratroopers occupying the coastal fringe from Brighton to Chichester. Finally, the 30,000 troops of Sixth Army would land at Lyme Bay and move immediately to occupy Bristol.

After consolidating these beachheads, the second stage of the invasion operation would involve a further 260,000 troops, including six Panzer divisions, pushing out to take up a line from Portsmouth to the Thames Estuary. The final phase would be the capture of London and the south-east from Essex to Gloucester.[7]

With every prospect of an imminent invasion the fortification of the coast became a priority. Apart from a few guns mounted on the walls of Newhaven Fort there were no modern defences of any description anywhere along the Sussex shoreline. Everything had to be built from scratch.

Much of the work was undertaken by civil contractors under the supervision of officers of the Royal Engineers. One of the first steps that were taken was the placing of "emergency coast defence batteries" along every part of the threatened coastline.

As so much ordnance had been abandoned in the retreat to Dunkirk, old 6-inch guns taken from decommissioned warships were to be used in the emergency batteries.

It was intended that each battery would house two of these guns which were capable of firing armour-piercing shells a distance of seven miles out to sea.

By the end of the second week of June 1940, batteries at Eastbourne, Hastings and Brighton had been completed with others at Bognor Regis, Angmering-on-Sea, Littlehampton, Worthing and Shoreham. The batteries between Brighton and Bognor were manned by No.553 Coast Artillery Regiment; those between Eastbourne and Winchelsea by No.552 Regiment.

Newhaven Fort was armed with two 12-pounders and five 6-inch guns, two of which were placed on the ramparts of the fort with the other three on the cliff top immediately to the west. Later in the year further batteries were raised at Cooden Beach, Norman's Bay and Pevensey.

Fire-control headquarters for the Sussex batteries between Bognor Regis and Pevensey Bay was sheltered behind the Downs north of Worthing at Washington, with the guns from Newhaven to Pevensey being under the immediate command of Fortress Control Newhaven. Located in a complex of tunnels cut into the hillside at South Heighton four miles north of Newhaven, Fortress Control was under the authority of the Royal Navy.

The gun emplacements for the Emergency Coastal Battery at Newhaven located on the cliff top to the west of Newhaven Fort (TQ 4477001).

A 6-inch gun in its emplacement on the ramparts of Newhaven Fort (By kind permission of Newhaven Fort).

The battery observation tower for the Emergency Coastal Battery raised in 1940 at Pett Level. Access to the battery position is through the Pett Level Nature Reserve (TQ 891135).

Commissioned as HMS *Forward*, this underground labyrinth received, processed and distributed maritime intelligence from Fairlight near Hastings through to Bognor Regis. Its importance can be gauged by the fact that from 1942 to 1945 the commanding officers at South Heighton held the rank of either Admiral or Vice Admiral.

The movement of ships along the coast was monitored by the Chain Home Low radar stations (see Chapter 9) and the information passed through to South Heighton. No gun was allowed to engage an enemy vessel without specific instructions from South Heighton. It had communications links with Commander-in-Chief Portsmouth, Vice Admiral Dover, RAF Uxbridge and all the local coastal bases. Over the years there has been some restoration and repair at the tunnels at South Heighton with the intention of opening them to the public.[8] The guns along the coast from Hastings eastwards were controlled through Combined Headquarters at Dover Castle.

With the emergency batteries established, more defences were added to almost every stretch of the coast. Rifle-posts, pillboxes, mines, anti-tank barriers and thousands of miles of barbed wire were built, dug and laid along the Sussex shore. Equipment to set the sea on fire with petroleum was installed at Camber Sands, Rye and Church Norton. Amongst the most formidable defensive weapons of 1940 were the Railway Guns. A total of twenty-six of these massive 9.2-inch calibre relics of the First World War operated throughout Kent and Sussex on the tracks of the Southern Railway. One of these remarkable weapons was stored at Newington Pit by the side of Glynde Station.

Other defensive measures included the creation of slit trenches for the infantry and sandbag emplacements for heavy machine-guns. Roads were blocked with felled trees and, at Worthing, by beach huts filled with shingle. Old vehicles were also placed as obstructions in large fields that might be used as landing grounds by German gliders. Throughout the summer of 1940, military and civil engineers turned these improvised works into a planned and permanent defensive line, some features of which have survived into the twenty-first century.

All road signs and place names were painted out, the great chalk features of the Long Man at Wilmington and the White Horse near Alfriston were grassed over, and the lights of the important port of Newhaven were replicated at Cuckmere Haven to deceive the German bombers. In other parts of the county, dummy airfields were formed and, to further confuse the *Luftwaffe*, lighting arrays were erected in rural areas to resemble burning towns.[9]

The piers at Bognor Regis, Worthing and Brighton were partially dismantled so that they could not be used as landing jetties by the enemy. Throughout Sussex the beaches were mined and cordoned with barbed wire. Behind this was often a row of concrete anti-tank blocks with pillboxes for rifles or machine-guns positioned so as to cover the approach from the beach.

The old Royal Military Canal, an obvious defensive feature, once again found a military purpose. The canal, and its adjoining road, was requisitioned by the War Department in 1935. In 1940 it was fortified at key points along its length.[10]

Though it was hoped that any enemy landing would be repelled or at least held by these defences, three more lines of defence were constructed further inland. It was recognised that the three major Sussex rivers would, as they have since the Iron Age, play a vital role in the defence of the county.

The most important of these so-called stop lines, therefore, ran west to east from

A Matilda tank of "B" Squadron, 44th Tank Battalion, in the village square at Findon on 31 December 1940 (IWM H7680).

the Arun at Bucks Green, through Horsham, Mannings Heath and Handcross to Slaugham near the Ouse, and then down to Newhaven. The backbone of this line was an anti-tank ditch that ran from Warren Wood on the Arun to Slaugham. Every bridge and ford of these two rivers was defended by pillboxes (either anti-tank or anti-infantry) and the bridges or crossings blocked with anti-tank blocks. Infantry trenches, minefields and barbed wire would complete the bridge defences.[11]

Two stop lines followed the courses of the Arun and the Adur in their passages through the Downs to the sea. The line along the Arun follows the west bank of the river from Littlehampton to Pulborough and along the Adur from Shoreham to Partridge Green and Henfield. Along these two lines the river crossings were covered by concrete 25-pounder field gun emplacements. These lines concluded at the northern end of the Downs as it would have been impossible to prevent the invading forces fanning out across the Weald once they had broken through the hills. Military airfields like Shoreham and Thorney Island were also protected by pillboxes.

Beyond these defences was a vast fortified line protecting London which ran from Scotland, down the eastern side of the country to the Thames estuary and south of the capital to end at the River Severn. Part of this General Headquarters

A Type 24 infantry pillbox. The one shown here can be seen near Wadhurst, at the junction of Partridge Lane and the B2099 (TQ 606336).

Line – known as Ironside's Line after General Ironside, Commander-in-Chief Home Forces – travelled from the Medway, through Tonbridge, along the River Uck (parts of which were deepened and widened to increase its effectiveness as a barrier to vehicles), and then followed the line of the Ouse through Lewes to Newhaven. This part of the GHQ Line was supposed to isolate the traditional Sussex and Kent invasion coasts.[12]

A 12-pounder breech-loading gun in its emplacement on the cliff-top ramparts of Newhaven Fort, (TQ 448004). (By kind permission of Newhaven Fort.)

General Sir Alan Brooke, who became Commander-in-Chief Southern Command in July 1940, believed that reliance upon static defensive lines was unsound as such structures could either be penetrated or turned. Instead of placing the defending forces along such lines, the troops were to be massed in strong bodies of mobile reserves which could move against any threatened area.

Defensive construction was subsequently limited to fortifying important communications centres (called "nodal" points) throughout Sussex and the south, such as crossroads and railway junctions. The nodal points were to be held at all costs until the mobile reserves arrived or until the defenders were overwhelmed by the enemy.[13]

By the end of 1941, with the threat of invasion all but vanished, the building programme was gradually wound down. The South-Eastern Command had built more than 3,000 pillboxes and had spent almost £4,000 000 on defensive works.[14]

Though these defences were never tested, other military installations were in frequent combat. These were the anti-aircraft batteries with their accompanying searchlight towers which were sited along the coast, across the Downs, in and around the ports, and other urban areas. Many of these were armed with rapid-firing 40mm Bofor guns – others had heavy 3.7-inch anti-aircraft guns which could fire a 20-pound shell up to 40,000 feet. [15]

The fear of nuclear attack during the Cold War years prompted the RAF to construct a gas- and nuclear-proof communications bunker deep within the chalk headland of Beachy Head. Completed in 1953, this huge excavation could accommodate up to 200 personnel. It was abandoned in 1957 and its entrance remains sealed. A similar structure was built at Truleigh Hill, to the north of Shoreham, on the site of the former Second World War Chain Home radar station.

Another large bunker complex, to house troops and the South-East Regional Government in the event of a nuclear attack, was built in the Ashdown Forest at Camp Hill. It was completed in 1986 and was still maintained up to 1992.[16]

A Second World War 25-pounder pillbox, located 400 yards north of Betley Bridge, near Henfield. (TQ 197178).

CHAPTER 10

Savage Skies:
The Battle of Britain

In the spring of 1939 the south of England was once again preparing to withstand an invasion. Following the evacuation of the British Expeditionary Force from Dunkirk in June 1940, it was assumed that the next battle of the Second World War would be fought on the beaches of southern England. Almost every generation of Sussex men and women had learnt to live with the threat of attack from across the water. This time, though, the threat came not just from the sea but also from the sky and for the first time in history a battle would be fought, and won, almost exclusively in the air.

A successful landing depended upon the Germans achieving air supremacy over both the Channel and the beaches of the south-east. Since the end of the Great War most major powers had been expanding their air arms and developing new aircraft.

The Treaty of Versailles, which had been forced upon a defeated Germany in 1918, banned the Germans from forming an air force. But Russia had allowed the Germans to use a number of their airfields to train pilots and test machines. The Spanish Civil War allowed the Germans to practice their flying skills in a real combat situation.

By the outbreak of the Second World War the German air force, the *Luftwaffe*, was one of the most powerful weapons in the world but it was organised and equipped for short-range operations in support of the Germans land-based forces, not for a protracted aerial war.[1]

After easy victories against Czechoslovakia, Poland, Belgium and France, in which a combination of aerial bombardment and rapid armoured ground attack – known as the Blitzkrieg – had revolutionised warfare, Britain was the only country still in arms against Nazi Germany. All that stood between Hitler and the subjugation of Western Europe were the Royal Navy and the fighter squadrons of the Royal Air Force.

In contrast to the expansionist policies in the rest of Europe, Britain scaled down its air force after the First World War. By 1922, though the French *Armée de l'Air* possessed 300 bombers and 300 fighters, the RAF had less than forty aircraft for home defence!

It was only in 1936, and only just in time, that ministers authorised an expansion programme that would give Britain an air force capable of defending its shores. This rearmament programme, designed to provide 124 squadrons for home defence, was scheduled for completion on 31 March 1939 – just a few months before Britain would find itself at war with Germany.

On 1 July 1940, Fighter Command, led by Air Chief Marshal Sir Hugh Dowding, could count on only 639 aircraft – having lost more than 450 fighters in the futile battle to save France. Of the former, 545 were front-line Hawker Hurricanes and Supermarine Spitfires; the rest were second-rate Bristol Blenheims and Boulton Paul Defiants.

Against this force the *Luftwaffe* could bring into action 934 Messerschmitt Bf 109 and Bf 110 fighters, 300 Junkers Ju 87 "Stuka" dive-bombers, and 998 Heinkel He 111, Junkers Ju 88 and Dornier Do 17 bombers, plus 157 reconnaissance aircraft – a total of 2,389 aeroplanes.[2] It is hardly surprising that *Reichsmarschall* Hermann Goering predicted that he would achieve superiority in the skies above Britain in just four days. Yet Britain possessed one great technological advantage over its enemy in the form of radar.

Situated all around the south and east coasts the radar stations, which in Sussex were located at Rye, Fairlight, Pevensey, Beachy Head, Truleigh Hill and Poling, could detect the approach of aircraft up to 120 miles away. Known as the "Chain Home" range, the network was later supplemented by the 'Chain Home Low' system which was able to detect low-flying aircraft.

The numerical superiority enjoyed by the *Luftwaffe* was considerably reduced by the radar teams' ability to pinpoint German attacks and direct RAF fighters to intercept the enemy bombers before they reached their targets. At the beginning of the Battle of Britain the Germans had not developed radar and they were unable to determine the true purpose of the chain of tall masts along the coast, though they did realise that they were a communications aid of some description and clearly of great importance to the British defensive system.

In addition to the radar stations Sir Hugh Dowding received information from the RAF's "Y" intelligence listening service which intercepted radio-telephone communications from German aircraft. The main listening station was at Cheadle but the first subsidiary station was at Fairlight in Sussex. Of possibly even greater importance was the Government Code and Cipher School at Bletchley Park. Here, with the aid of the Ultra cipher machine, the German Enigma codes were deciphered and their messages interpreted. A great deal of the *Luftwaffe*'s communications were relayed by Enigma, and Fighter Command was often aware of the enemy's intentions well in advance – sometimes days in advance – of the actual operation.

The final links in the intelligence chain were the posts of the Royal Observer

A photograph of an Emergency Coastal Battery at Shoreham-by-Sea in 1940. The battery was located next to the Shoreham Redoubt on Shoreham Beach (TQ 233045). The searchlight tower can still be seen. (IWM H8226).

Corps, which was formed in 1925 and was originally manned by two groups of Special Constables covering Kent and Sussex (HQ at Horsham). Each of the 1,400 posts was equipped with a triangulation instrument which gave the observer a positional fix on a grid map. This information, along with the height and number of the "bandits", was sent on to Fighter Command's Operations rooms.

Fighter Command disposed almost half of its entire force in an arc from Middle Wallop in Hampshire, through Sussex, Kent and Essex to Debden in Suffolk. This area was 11 Group, with its headquarters based at Hillingdon House at Uxbridge in Middlesex. In command of 11 Group was Air Vice Marshal Keith Park. The rest of its force was divided into three other groups: 10 Group covered the south-west; 12 Group the midlands and the east; 13 Group north-east England and Scotland.

Each Fighter group was sub-divided into as many as four area "Sectors". Overall strategy was determined by Fighter Command based on the information received through the Operations and Filter rooms at RAF Bentley Priory which was at Stanmore in Middlesex. From Bentley Priory the battle plan would be passed down to the respective Group or Groups who would then be responsible for control of the battle in their area.

The actual tactical handling of the battle would then be taken up by the various Sectors, with each Sector Station possessing its own Operations Room. The system was also highly flexible in that the squadrons could be passed from one sector to another through the network of telephone and teleprinter lines that linked all the Ops Rooms with each other.

Situated two-and-a-half miles east of Arundel in West Sussex, the Chain Home station at Poling was one of the first twenty planned before the Second World War. However, it had not been completed when war broke out. This view of three large transmitter towers at Poling was taken from the south side. Poling's receiver towers, which numbered four in total, are just out of the picture to the right. The remains of the radar station are on private land adjacent to Poling Street. (TQ 045052). Some of the defences built to defend the radar station can still be seen to the south of the site. (By kind permission of Mrs M. Taylor.)

The Sector Station for the area between Truleigh Hill above Shoreham to beyond Southampton was at Tangmere airfield near Chichester. Three squadrons of Hurricanes – Nos. 43, 145 and 601 – were stationed at Tangmere from the end of June until the departure of 145 Squadron to nearby Westhampnett at the end of July. Though other squadrons would take their place later in the conflict, it was these two units that operated from Tangmere throughout the early, and most critical, days of the battle. The Fighter Interception Unit, flying Blenheims, was also stationed temporarily at Tangmere. The Kent airfields of Kenley and Biggin Hill were responsible for the sectors from Truleigh to Pevensey and Pevensey to Dover respectively.[3]

Officially classified as a satellite of Tangmere, Westhampnett (now known as Goodwood airfield) was a fighter base in its own right. Equipped with Hurricanes,

145 Squadron was replaced by the Spitfires of 602 Squadron on 13 August after 145 Squadron had lost nine planes in the fighting of the previous two days.

Thorney Island airfield was the base for the Blenheim fighter-bombers of Nos. 235, 236 and 59 squadrons. The Blenheims were ineffective in aerial combat but they carried out successful bombing raids against enemy-held installations in France.

Shoreham Airport, though not originally designated as a fighter station, became the home of the Fighter Interception Unit flying Blenheims and Beaufighters when Tangmere came under heavy attack. These aircraft proved to be too heavy for Shoreham's grass runway and the FIU saw little action. The Beaufighters were later joined by a flight of Hurricanes.

Friston, on the Seven Sisters five miles from Eastbourne, was an Emergency Landing Ground for damaged aircraft returning from bombing raids across the Channel. It was later up-graded to a satellite station which first became operational when the Hurricanes of Nos. 253 and 32 Squadrons arrived in June 1942.

Ford airfield near Littlehampton was occupied by the Fleet Air Arm. Designated as HMS *Peregrine*, it was primarily used as a training base for the aircraft carrier squadrons.

Across the Channel in Normandy and Brittany the *Luftwaffe* had been preparing advanced airfields close to the coast throughout the early weeks of the summer of 1940. Telephone and telex systems were installed and fuel dumps established. *Luftwaffe* Air Fleets, *Luftflotte* 2 and *Luftflotte* 3 were to spearhead the attack supported by *Luftflotte* 5 operating out of Stavanger in Norway.

The old plaque of Ford airfield when it was the Fleet Air Arm base of HMS Peregrine. *The plaque was photographed in one of the accommodation blocks in what is now HMP Ford (SU 998027). (By kind permission of the Governor of HMP Ford.)*

Each of these Air Fleets was a large, self-contained battle group with its own logistical support units. They were divided into operational formations known as *Geschwaders* of around 80 to 100 aircraft. Bomber units were *Kampfgeschwader*, long-range fighter-bomber units were *Zerstörergeschwader*, the dive-bomber units were *Stukageschwader*, and *Jagdgeschwaders* were the fighter units. These units were composed of up to five *Gruppen* which were themselves sub-divided into *Staffeln* which approximated to an RAF squadron. Each *Staffel* was composed of two or three *Schwarm* (or flights) of four aeroplanes each.[4]

Germany did not possess any heavy bombers and in the Battle of Britain it operated four medium to light, twin-engine bombers supported by two types of Messerschmitt fighters. The first of these bombers was the Heinkel He 111. Though its performance was acceptable by the standards of the day, it could only carry 2,134 lbs of bombs with full fuel tanks (compared, for example, with the later British Lancaster bomber which could carry 22,000 lbs). Its 7.9mm machine-guns were manually operated and could not easily be brought to bear upon fast-moving targets. The Dornier Do 17 was also inadequately armed and carried an even lighter bomb-load than the Heinkel, though it was a little faster than that bomber.

The two other German bombers were both made by Junkers – the Ju 87 and Ju 88. The Ju 87 was the famous Stuka. It was renowned for its near-vertical bombing dives accompanied by the screaming of its sirens in which it could drop its bombs with great accuracy. It was, however, a slow, ungainly aircraft and it proved to be an easy target for the pilots of the Royal Air Force Fighter Command.

The Ju 88 was by far the *Luftwaffe*'s finest bomber. It could deliver its pay-load either horizontally or in a Stuka-like dive. For a bomber it was very fast, being only thirty miles per hour slower than a Hurricane's operational fighting speed and it could out-perform a Bristol Blenheim fighter.

The Messerschmitt Bf 109 was a single-seat, high-performance interceptor fighter. It was faster than either the Hurricane or the Spitfire and it was more heavily armed. Whilst the Bf 109 was regarded as being less manoeuvrable than its two main British fighters it did have one great advantage over its rivals in a dog-fight. Because of its fuel injection system the *Luftwaffe* pilots could escape from trouble by pushing the Messerschmitt into a direct nose-dive.

The British planes, with simple float carburettors, had to be thrown into a half-roll to swill petrol into their engines to prevent stalling before they could dive. Those few seconds, won or lost, could prove decisive. The Bf 109, however, was designed as an interceptor, not as a bomber escort, and it could not carry sufficient fuel to operate for long periods of time over England.

Goering's much-vaunted "Destroyer", the Bf 110, was a much larger, twin-engine aircraft. It had a very impressive armament with its four machine-guns and two 20mm cannon in the nose and another gun operated by a rear-gunner. It was also a very fast aircraft for its day. Yet the Bf 110 suffered from one major defect which greatly reduced its effectiveness – it was structurally weak in the tail assembly.

To oppose these aircraft the RAF had the Hawker Hurricane and the Supermarine Spitfire. Both were capable of speeds considerably in excess of 300 miles per hour. They proved to be extremely manoeuvrable and they were armed with eight Vickers-Browning machine-guns situated in the wings. These were specialist interceptor fighters, designed for aerial combat.

Though Fighter Command possessed far fewer aircraft than the *Luftwaffe*, the vast majority of the machines sent across the Channel by the Germans were bombers. The air war over southern England, particularly in the first weeks of the conflict, was predominately a conflict between German bombers and British fighters. Dowding's pilots were specifically instructed to avoid confrontations with enemy fighters and instead to concentrate their efforts, whenever practical, upon the bombers. It is this simple fact that explains the result of the Battle of Britain. In addition to the Hurricane and Spitfire, Fighter Command operated the sluggish fighter variant of the Bristol Blenheim and the out-dated Boulton-Paul Defiant.

Tactically the opposing air forces adopted very different formations at the start of the war. Each RAF squadron of twelve planes was divided into four sections of three. These "flights" flew very close together in either "V" or line astern formations as a section of three or along with other sections of the squadron. When an enemy was located the fighters would peel away one after another, firing short bursts as they dived past the opposing aircraft.

By contrast the German fighters used the *Schwarm* formation, which the British pilots called the "finger-four". Developed during the Spanish Civil War, the *Schwarm* involved two pairs of widely spread aircraft each flying at different heights and in staggered positions. The superiority of the *Schwarm* soon became apparent and the British pilots eventually abandoned their close-order flying and embraced the principles of fighting in pairs in looser formations.[5]

The *Luftwaffe* had been flying reconnaissance and combat patrols across the Channel since June 1940. British ships had been sunk and aircraft on both sides had been shot down. Most of these raids were at night with fourteen ports, sixteen industrial plants and thirteen airfields becoming targets. The *Luftwaffe* achieved little in strategic terms during this period and it gave the RAF time to build up its fighter aircraft strength.

Hundreds of Spitfires and Hurricanes were being turned out of the factories which, on 14 May, had come under the authority of Lord Beaverbrook. As Minister of Aircraft Production, Beaverbrook reorganised production schedules and concentrated the work upon building and repairing fighters, leaving only limited capacity for other aircraft. The result was a doubling of fighter production to almost 500 aircraft a month by September.

In July the attacks intensified with 10 July 1940 now being considered the first day of the Battle of Britain. On that day the target selected by the *Luftwaffe* was a convoy of ships passing through the Dover straits. The Home Chain system detected an unusually large number of aircraft in the sky above Calais. Park waited cautiously. If this was the start of the anticipated invasion he had to deploy his slender resources carefully. When it became apparent that the Germans were only attacking the convoy, Park despatched just twenty-six fighters to help the ships.

Against some seventy Do 17s, Bf 109s and 110s, the Hurricanes and Spitfires claimed four kills for the loss of three of their own fighters.[6]

The following day – 11 July – a large formation of Stukas escorted by Bf 110s flew along the Sussex coast heading for Portland. Tangmere's 601 Squadron was sent to intercept. Diving out of the sun the Hurricanes broke the formation, claiming two Ju 87s. Later that day 601 was again in action, this time as the Heinkels of *Kampfgeschwader* 55 attacked Portsmouth. Also scrambled was 145 Squadron, which caught the German bombers as they headed for home across the Channel. The raid had cost the *Luftwaffe* dearly. The German air force lost twenty-five planes, having dropped just 168 bombs.

Successful attacks against British shipping, including Royal Navy destroyers, had stopped almost all traffic through the Channel. Yet Dowding and Park were using their fighter squadrons only sparingly, knowing that the big battles for mastery of the skies over Britain were still to come.

Over the course of the next month the Tangmere squadrons were in frequent action over the Kent, Sussex and Hampshire coasts and along the Channel as the *Luftwaffe* attempted to weaken Fighter Command in preparation for the great series of raids that Hitler hoped would drive Britain to the negotiating table. During this "softening-up" period, which was named *Kanalkampf* by the Germans, Bf 109s prowled along the coastline and attacked Allied shipping hoping to draw the British fighters into action.

These tactics resulted in the destruction of 117 British fighters – one sixth of Fighter Commands original strength – by the end of July. The battle had scarcely begun and, though the *Luftwaffe* lost considerably more aircraft during this period, Dowding could ill afford such losses.

Fortunately for the RAF the responsibility for the next phase of the battle was handed over to the German bombers and they would prove to be less formidable opponents than the Messerschmitts. It was at this time, just two weeks before the crucial weeks of the conflict, that Westhampnett airfield became fully operational with the transfer of 145 Squadron from Tangmere.

Another convoy attempted to slip through the Channel on 8 August. This time the twenty-five merchant ships were escorted by anti-aircraft destroyers and barrage balloon vessels. As the convoy crept past Dover, German torpedo-armed E-boats raced from their bases in Northern France and sank three of the ships and, as it approached the Isle of Wight, the *Luftwaffe* swept in for the kill. A formation of more than eighty Stukas from *Stukageschwaders* 1, 2 and 27, twice bombed the convoy before eleven squadrons from 10 and 11 Groups, including Westhampnett's 145 Squadron, could intervene. Three Stukas were shot down but a further four ships were sunk and others were damaged.

In the afternoon the Stukas returned to the attack. Again 145 Squadron, as well as Tangmere's 43 Squadron, was scrambled. The Ju 87s were escorted by a large body of Bf 109s and a major air battle took place over the Isle of Wight. By the end of the day's action the Germans had lost twenty-seven aircraft with 43 Squadron losing six and 145 Squadron five, including the Hurricane of Squadron Leader John Peel. Peel was later rescued from the sea near Bolougne.

Only four ships of the ill-fated convoy reached Swanage harbour. The most successful RAF squadron that day had been 145 Squadron, with two pilots able to claim three enemy aircraft and one pilot, Flight Lieutenant Roy Dutton, having five "kills" to his credit. A congratulatory visit to Westhampnett by Dowding, accompanied by the Secretary of State for Air and the Chief of the Air Staff, was later followed by a visit from the Duke of Gloucester.

On the 11th and 12th the Tangmere and Westhampnett Hurricanes were again in action, defending Portland and Portsmouth from large-scale attacks by Junkers 88s and Heinkels supported by Bf 109s and 110s. Again 145 Squadron suffered heavy casualties, losing eight aircraft in the two days of fighting. The Hurricanes were joined by the Spitfires of 266 Squadron which arrived at Tangmere on 9 August. Though this unit only stayed for three days it was involved in the battle of 12 August and lost two of its Spitfires.

The *Luftwaffe*'s operation to destroy the RAF was labelled *Adlerangriff* or Eagle Attack, the first stage of which was to be the demolition of the radar network. And so early on 12 August, Junkers and Dorniers bombed the radar stations from Dover to the Isle of Wight. Rye radar station was severely damaged but a back-up power supply brought the equipment back on line by lunch time. Pevensey's power main was also hit but the station was able to remain on air. A number of the coastal airfields were also attacked on this day.

The result of the first day of *Adlerangriff* was the loss of twenty-two British fighters whilst the *Luftwaffe* suffered thirty-one aircraft casualties. Importantly the radar network had not been disabled. Day two – *Alder Tag* or Eagle Day – was to be the day that the Fighter Command's airfields were destroyed. It too would be a failure.

On the morning of 13 August a bank of low cloud hung over the Channel and the *Luftwaffe*'s operations had to be postponed until late in the afternoon. Earlier, around midday, the scheduled attack by the Heinkels and Junkers 88s of *Kampfgruppe* 54 had been cancelled but the fighter escort of twenty Bf 110s had not been informed of the cancellation and they, alone, continued their mission against the naval base at Portland.

They were met by a number of RAF squadrons, including 601 from Tangmere. In the ensuing encounter *KG* 54 lost five 110s; 601 Squadron four Hurricanes. Similar confusion led seventy-four Dorniers of *KG* 2, which was already airborne, to continue on to their target although their escort of Bf 110s had been ordered back

A hangar at the former Ford airfield, which was photographed in the grounds of HMP Ford. (By kind permission of the Governor of HMP Ford.)

to base. The Dorniers, however, reached their objective and severely damaged the Coastal Command station at Eastchurch.

The main raids of *Adler Tag* came in the afternoon. Both Tangmere squadrons were scrambled to defend the docks and installations of Portland and Southampton. Waves of Ju 87s, escorted by Bf 109s and 110s, broke through the British fighters to hit Southampton and Andover. Attacks against the Kent airfields by massed Stuka *Staffel* were also delivered, with Detling airfield near Maidstone being badly damaged. By the end of the day the *Luftwaffe* had flown 1,485 sorties to the RAF's 700, with the Germans losing forty-five planes compared with just thirteen of the RAF.

Day three of *Adlerangriff* was far less intense. Limited raids and reconnaissance patrols resulted in nineteen German aircraft being lost against only eight British machines. Middle Wallop was the only airfield to be attacked.

Clear skies on 15 August heralded the *Luftwaffe*'s greatest effort of the conflict. It was to be a huge operation with all three *Luftflotten* attacking the British coast from the Firth of Forth to the West Country.

In the first air raid of the day over Sussex, Stukas knocked out Rye radar station with a direct hit. This was followed by a massive attack against the Portsmouth and Southampton area and 43 Squadron was scrambled to intercept the enemy over the Isle of Wight. Moments later a large formation of Ju 87s from *Stukageschwader* 2 dived out of the bright midday sun above Tangmere. The Stukas screamed down and released their bombs across the exposed airfield.

The runway was bombed, one of the hangars was hit as were parts of the accommodation blocks. Five Blenheims of the Fighter Interception Unit and a Hurricane of 43 Squadron were damaged on the ground before the rest of the squadron turned back to defend their base. The Stuka was no match for the Hurricane and nine German 'planes were shot down with three others damaged. Only one of Tangmere's Hurricanes was lost and three damaged.

The Kent airfields endured similar attacks and an engine factory at Rochester and the Short Brothers factory, where the Stirling bomber was in production, were severely damaged. Two factories at Croydon were also hit – these were the first bombs to land in the London suburbs. *Luftflotten* 5 also attacked the north-east from its base at Stavanger in the mistaken belief that some of 13 Group's squadrons had been sent to the south to help 11 Group. The attack was a disaster for *Luftflotte* 5 which lost sixteen of its total of 123 bombers and seven of its thirty-four fighters. By the end of this crucial day the RAF had flown 974 sorties and had shot seventy-five German planes out of the sky.

On the following day, 16 August, the *Luftwaffe* concentrated their forces upon the airfields of Kent, Hampshire and Sussex. Again Stukas headed in the direction of Tangmere escorted by Bf 109s.

Skipping passed the bomb craters in the grass runway both squadrons of Hurricanes took to the air but they could not prevent some of the dive-bombers reaching the airfield. The six remaining Blenheims of the FIU were destroyed on the ground, along with seven Hurricanes and one Miles Magistar trainer. Pilot Officer William Fisk of 601 Squadron successfully landed his damaged Hurricane only to be strafed by the Germans whilst he was still in the cockpit. He died two days later. Fisk was an American volunteer and he was the first American to be killed in action in the air war over Britain.

Five hangars were struck, two of which were completely wrecked. The workshops, pump-house, stores and sick bay were hit. An air-raid shelter was smashed and the station's power, communications, water and sanitation systems were severed. Over forty vehicles were damaged with thirteen personnel killed and another twenty wounded. Tangmere's Hurricanes drove off the attackers, shooting down four bombers but losing four aircraft of their own.[7]

Other dog-fights had broken out all over Sussex. A Heinkel He 111 of *Kampfgeschwader* 55 was hit by RAF fighters over Brighton, the machine crashing to earth on the Downs above High Salvington. The tail-plane of *Oberleutnant* Ernst Hollekamp's Bf 110 was shot away over Eastbourne and the aircraft broke apart in mid-air. Hollekamp's rear gunner baled out as the machine began to disintegrate but Hollekamp went down with his plane, the wreckage of which was scattered across three-quarters of a mile of Sussex countryside. His body was recovered from the roof of a house in Gaudlick Road in Eastbourne.[8]

The Spitfires of Westhampnett's 602 Squadron also took to the air in defence of Tangmere. Two Spitfires were damaged but both returned to the airfield. Gosport, West Malling, Manston, Lee-on-Solent, and Farnborough airfields were all bombed. At Brize Norton, Ju 88s destroyed forty-six aircraft on the ground, including a number of Hurricanes. Ventnor Chain Home station was again hit and put out of service.

After two days of heavy attacks the main fighter base in Sussex was in a terrible state. Sector Operations was moved to a school in Chichester and what little remained of the Fighter Interceptor Unit was transferred to Shoreham airfield. Fortunately for Tangmere the *Luftwaffe* spent most of 17 August in reconnaissance missions in an attempt to evaluate the extent of the devastation that they had inflicted over the previous days. This allowed the personnel at Tangmere to make a start on repairs to the airfield and its installations.[9]

The *Luftwaffe* estimated that Fighter Command had only 300 serviceable aircraft left and that another intense series of raids on the airfields on 18 August would see the end of the RAF as an effective defensive force. In fact Fighter Command had almost twice that many planes, though it was desperately short of pilots.

Goering's first raids of 18 August were against the Kent airfields. Nine Dorniers from *KG* 76 flew low over Beachy Head and followed the Brighton to London railway to attack Kenley. The Dorniers had been spotted by the Observer Corps and Kenley's Hurricanes were waiting for the German bombers. Only one Dornier returned intact to its base. Biggin Hill was attacked and damaged in a raid by sixty Heinkel He 111s.

It was not until 14:00 hours that Stukas bombed the Chain Home station at Poling. Some ninety bombs were dropped around the radar installation which was very seriously damaged. This success cost the *Luftwaffe* dearly. At the approach of the Stukas, 43, 601 and Westhampnett's 602 Squadron were all scrambled and no less than twelve of the Junkers 87s were shot down.

A second wing of Stukas from *SG* 77, escorted by Bf 109s from *JG* 27, then attacked along the coast. Due to faulty intelligence the Fleet Air Arm bases at Thorney Island and Ford had been classified as fighter bases and it was upon these two airfields that twenty-eight bombers unleashed their deadly cargoes.

With just six Lewis machine-guns to defend the entire airfield the Stuka pilots could pick their targets at will. Ford airfield was destroyed in less than ten minutes. Thirty-nine aircraft were damaged and many installations smashed including the armoury. The fuel dump was also hit, setting it on fire and a dense black cloud engulfed the airfield. Over 100 people were killed or wounded. Ford was so severely damaged that it was abandoned by the Fleet Air Arm and the remaining aircraft and personnel were transferred to other sites.[10]

The *Luftwaffe*'s other objective was Thorney Island. This time the Stukas met some resistance as a number of Thorney Island's Blenheims of 235 Squadron managed to get airborne before the Junkers began their fearsome screeching dives. Two hangars were wrecked (along with the three Avro Ansons inside them) and a fuel dump was hit which ignited with a massive explosion.

As the Stukas circled over the island, 235 Squadron's Blenheims were joined by the Hurricanes and Spitfires of Nos. 43, 601 and 602 Squadrons. Ten Stukas were brought down over Thorney Island with a further three over Ford.

Stukas were never again used against Britain. Though they could bomb with great accuracy they were far slower than the British fighters. Even 235 Squadron's lumbering Blenheims shot down two Ju 87s over Thorney Island. The Stukas were valued and effective bombers and Goering dared not lose any more in air-to-air combat for which they were clearly unsuited. The *Reichsmarschall* also changed tactics, and from 19 August the individual *Kampfgeschwaden* were allowed to select their own targets.

The German aircrews were informed that Fighter Command could not defend Britain for much longer. A few more days of intense endeavour, they were told, would see the *Luftwaffe* as masters of the sky. But the battered airfields, many of which German intelligence believed had been put out of action, were quickly patched up and continued to be operational. Also, where possible, Dowding rotated his tired squadrons to quieter sectors for a few days rest.

Apart from a few isolated raids the *Luftwaffe* was kept grounded for the next four days by poor weather. But on Saturday, 24 August 1940, the onslaught was renewed with raids against Manston, Hornchurch and Portsmouth. *Luftflotten* 3 switched to night attacks with the London suburbs being bombed extensively for the first time in the war. Casualties for the day amounted to thirty-eight German and twenty-two British aircraft.

Late in the afternoon of the 26th, German bombers were detected as they approached Portsmouth. No.43 Squadron was scrambled and engaged the enemy formation over the city. The attackers were driven off at a heavy cost as 43 Squadron lost six planes, though all the pilots survived.

Such losses were repeated across the south-east and Goering's claims that the RAF was nearing defeat were far from exaggerated. Between 8 and 18 August ninety-four of Fighter Command's pilots had been posted killed or missing and the raw recruits that took their place were no match for the *Luftwaffe*'s veterans. The Stukas had been easy meat for the Spitfires and Hurricanes but the Heinkels and Dorniers in their tight formations protected by the fast Bf 109s were a different proposition.

Night raids by *Luftflotte* 3 intensified on the 27th with attacks against airfields and factories across the south and east from Portsmouth to Lincolnshire. By operating at night the *Luftwaffe*'s losses were reduced to single figures, but so were those of the RAF.

If Germany was to invade England the air battle had to be won and this could only be achieved by destroying Fighter Command. This could not be accomplished by night attacks alone. So for the next twelve days the *Luftwaffe* hammered the airfields of the south and east. Each time they were met by Fighter Command. Each time, by sheer weight of numbers, they broke through to their targets. It was a battle of attrition, and the side that suffered the heaviest casualties would lose.

Confirmed kills were meticulously logged on both sides and the totals analysed. Thus on 28 August the *Luftwaffe* lost thirty-one aircraft to the RAF's twenty-eight; on 29 August the score was seventeen to nine. The statistics, however, hid an important fact. Every time a German aeroplane was shot down over Britain the crew would either be killed or captured, whereas many RAF pilots in the same situation were able to parachute to, or crash-land in, safety. Thus on 31 August, for instance, the *Luftwaffe* lost forty-one aircraft and the RAF thirty-nine, and though these were the heaviest losses incurred by Fighter Command in a single day, only fourteen of its pilots were killed.

On the 28th a small two-seater German Gotha 145 biplane set off from France with mail for the troops occupying Jersey. In poor visibility the pilot lost his way and flew over the Sussex coast. The aircraft was spotted by the Observer Corps and two fighters were sent to intercept. The Gotha was forced to land near Lewes racecourse and the pilot was taken to Lewes police station. The captured mail provided military intelligence with some useful information. The Gotha, meanwhile, was taken by the RAF, re-painted, and subsequently used in a communications role.[11]

Sussex was not seriously attacked again until 30 August, when a large force, including Heinkel He 111s, closed in upon Shoreham and Tangmere. No.601 Squadron had been stood down for a period of well-earned rest and 17 Squadron had temporarily taken its place. When the German bombers appeared over Tangmere Nos. 43 and 17 squadrons were in the air defending the Kent airfields and Tangmere was unprotected.

The airfield took another terrible pounding. At the same time Pevensey, Rye and Beachy Head Chain Home stations, along with three others in Kent, were blacked out when their power supplies were severed. No.43 Squadron also lost their Squadron Leader, "Tubby" Badger, who was shot down over Kent. The *Luftwaffe* continued to concentrate its efforts against the Kent airfields and over the next few days personnel at Tangmere were able to repair much of the damage inflicted upon the buildings and installations.

On 1 September 1940, Goering ordered the night attacks to be directed upon Britain's aircraft industry. Despite mounting losses, Britain's war production was gaining pace and it was able to replace its lost aircraft.

The next day, 2 September, Hitler ordered yet another change in strategy. Instead of directing the main strength of the *Luftwaffe* against the airfields of the RAF, the principal target was to be London. It was argued that the RAF would have no choice but to defend London and it would be over the skies of the capital that Fighter Command would finally be destroyed. This was one of the most significant decisions of the Second World War. Though there is no doubt that the RAF suffered major casualties during the Blitz, the fighter bases were given a reprieve at a time when they were on the verge of collapse.

The date set for the start of the Blitz was 7 September. In the days leading up to this date the *Luftwaffe* continued to pound the airfields and aircraft factories. Between 2 September and 6 September the *Luftwaffe* hit eight airfields and the Thameshaven oil tanks. The Vickers factory, where the Wellington bomber was being built, was attacked, injuring some 600 workers and killing a further eighty-four people. During this short period of time the Germans also shot down 107 British aircraft. If the *Luftwaffe* had continued to attack the aircraft factories and Fighter Command's airfields in the south, it is quite possible that they could eventually have achieved their aim of air supremacy over southern England and the Channel.

London was within a few minutes' flying time of 12 Group's southern most airfields. Having spent weeks in comparative idleness whilst 11 Group bore the brunt of the fighting, Leigh-Mallory's men could at last play an effective part in the battle.

Three days earlier, on 30 August, 12 Group's 242 Squadron, led by Squadron Leader Douglas Bader, had been scrambled to intercept a large formation of German raiders to the north of London. Bader achieved a degree of success against the Germans but he was angered by seeing so many enemy aircraft escape unhurt. He later argued, and argued successfully, that if he had led more than just one squadron of twelve planes he would have inflicted far heavier casualties. His reasoning led to the introduction of the famous "Big Wings". Bader was given command over three squadrons of Hurricanes and two of Spitfires – a maximum of sixty aircraft.

The final phase of the Battle of Britain began on 7 September. Throughout the day and night the Heinkels, Dorniers and Junkers 88s ravaged London. During daylight hours the Hurricanes and Spitfires, and during the night the Defiants and other night fighters, flew sortie after sortie. Losses on both sides were immense. The destiny, not only of Britain, but also of Europe, hung in the balance. Little wonder that Churchill declared "Never in the field of human conflict was so much owed by so many to so few".

The battle that raged over London saw 43 Squadron lose another Hurricane before it was at last relieved by 213 Squadron. Tangmere was now the station for Nos. 213 and 607 squadrons, the latter losing seven Hurricanes during the first days of the Blitz.

It is difficult to estimate just how closely Hitler came to destroying Fighter

Command. His decision to attack civilian targets was certainly wrong. Not only did it stiffen Britain's resolve but it also resulted in reprisals against Berlin. Officially, Battle of Britain Day is celebrated on 15 September though the air war over Britain continued for another two months. Realistically, it ended on 7 September when Hitler directed the *Luftwaffe* to exclude the airfields of Fighter Command from their list of objectives.

Apart from the relief given to the fighter stations, Goering's plan possessed another serious flaw. Whilst the principle of compelling the RAF to put every available plane into the air to defend the capital was sound the *Reichsmarschall* overlooked the fact that London was on the very edge of the Bf 109s' effective range.

In raids against the coastal airfields the Messerschmitts could provide the German bombers with protection all the way to their targets, engage the RAF fighters that tried to attack them, and still have enough fuel left to escort the bombers back across the Channel. By the time that the German formations reached London, however, the 109s had only a few minutes air time over the capital before they were obliged to return home. This left the bombers of the *Luftwaffe* fatally vulnerable.[12]

Dowding was also facing difficulties. During August over 300 fighter pilots had been killed or were seriously wounded, whereas the operational training units had turned out only 260 replacement pilots in the same period. These raw recruits were easy targets for the experienced *Luftwaffe* fliers and many became victims themselves within days of joining their squadrons. No.603 Squadron, for example, flew into Hornchurch on 28 August and just eight days later it was withdrawn after losing sixteen aircraft and twelve pilots.

The first great raid on London began in the afternoon of 7 September, when more than 300 bombers and 600 fighters headed directly for the capital, followed that night by another 247 German aircraft. The next day Stukas attacked a large British convoy of ships that was attempting to pass through the Channel. The convoy, which had already been attacked by German E-boats, lost a number of ships before the Ju 87s were intercepted by Hurricanes from Westhampnett's 145 Squadron and Tangmere's 43 Squadron. As usual, when Stukas met British fighters they were severely mauled, but the escorting German Messerschmitts shot down six of the Sussex-based Hurricanes.

Night attacks against London continued with Liverpool also being added to the *Luftwaffe*'s target list. The *Luftwaffe*'s daily losses had reduced significantly due to the virtual abandonment of large daylight operations. Total losses for the 12th, 13th and 14th of September amounted to just thirty aircraft and this led to the belief at *Luftwaffe* headquarters that Fighter Command was in disarray.

So, on 15 September, the German air force mounted huge raids in the morning and afternoon. Both attacks were broken up by the British fighters, with the enemy losing sixty aircraft – the heaviest casualty figures since 18 August. The *Luftwaffe* was stunned at the RAF's continuing ability to resist and it was clear that Fighter Command was far from beaten.

The following day Goering held a meeting with his senior *Luftflotten* commanders. In an attempt to reduce the scale of losses he demanded that they decreased the size of the bomber formations and increased their fighter escorts. Massive raids, such as those of the previous day, would not be undertaken again unless weather conditions were perfect and adequate fighter cover was available.

On the 17th Hitler postponed the invasion of Britain for an indefinite period. His thoughts now turned to his attack upon Russia and the invasion forces along the Channel coast were gradually withdrawn. None of this was yet known in Britain as the nightly raids continued unabated. The most damaging attacks were delivered on 25 and 26 September, when the Bristol Aeroplane Company's works were bombed and the important Spitfire factory at Southampton was completely demolished. An engagement the following day, 27 September 1940, illustrates all too clearly the losses both sides suffering during the battle.

* * * *

By late September of 1940 the inhabitants of south-east England had generally become accustomed to a daily routine of air battles; the staccato clatter of machine-guns, the delicately interwoven vapour trails, banshee howls of aero engines and the not infrequent blossoming of parachutes. The people of the market town of Hailsham were no exception to this familiarity with the ongoing sight and sound of battle, but the sounds reaching them on the morning of Friday, 27 September, were different.

Between 08:45 and 09:05 hours that day no less than 160 Hurricanes and Spitfires had been scrambled to intercept an incoming German bomber force whose target was London. At Mayfield in East Sussex, schoolboy George Tuke, a Home Guard Messenger, stood riveted to the spot in the roadway outside his home, "Newlands" on the Five Ashes Road. A Messerschmitt 110 screamed past the tall trees by his house with a Hurricane in hot pursuit. In George's own words "… it was almost attached to the German's tail".

Whilst the Messerschmitt rear gunner fired continuously at his pursuer the Hurricane also blazed away, returning the fire. Empty .303 cartridge cases pinged off the tarmac road around a stunned George as fired rounds seared through the leafy branches and the tallest treetops swayed in the slipstream of the passing aeroplanes – one either side of the trees. Then, as suddenly as they had burst upon the scene, they were gone.

Now almost out of sight and heading south towards Hailsham both were literally jinking in and out of valleys and curving around buildings and tall obstacles. Vapour streamers curled off wingtips and black smoke trailed from exhausts as both aeroplanes pulled hard in this direction and that. As a display of precision flying George had never seen anything like it.

What he had witnessed was one of the several pursuits that had developed as the German raiders fled for home. In fact, he had watched brief seconds of what would be a duel to the death between the Austrian Commanding Officer of V/*LG* 1, Hauptmann Horst Liensberger (his fellow crewman was Albert Kopge) and South African Flying Officer Percy Burton of 249 Squadron.

Moments later, the pair of aircraft was over Horam, still at rooftop height and still firing. Again, those on the ground were startled by how quickly the battle was upon them and how quickly it then passed. Phyllis Pitcher shouted to her husband Robert who stood atop a pile of hay in their yard at West Street Farm as he stared, mouth open wide, at the amazing spectacle of two battling aircraft flashing by. She called for him to come down to avoid the hail of bullets that lashed the fields around them.

Rooted to the spot, the danger had already passed before he could move from his exposed perch to join his wife behind the safety of farm buildings. Phyllis herself was agape, having clearly seen the faces of the flying-helmeted German airmen looking down at her. Almost matter-of-factly, Robert later recorded in his diary: "Exciting time with planes today. One down at Horam. Two at Hailsham."

Seconds passed between the aeroplanes vanishing from view at Horam and being over the rooftops on the outskirts of Hailsham. Here, the guns of both aircraft finally fell silent and watchers on the ground just heard the roar of engines and had momentary glimpses of wildly manoeuvring aircraft. One of the best views was probably that had by farmer's son Doug Weller as he stood near his father's New Barn Farm in Station Road. Approaching him, head on, he could see both machines plainly as they cleared the town centre, passed over the Railway Station and then the gasometer before curving round towards George Catt's Hamlins Mill. What happened next was so sudden and so unexpected that Doug could scarcely believe what he saw:

> The morning … was bright and clear with only a few clouds in the sky and I was working in a field on New Barn Farm in Station Road. The siren sounded so I stopped the tractor and settled down near a deep ditch (in case bombs started dropping) to have my mid-morning lunch break. The sound of aircraft north of Hailsham alerted me to the fact that they were coming my way. Then I saw a Messerschmitt approaching at great speed over the rooftops of Hailsham with the German insignia clearly visible in the morning sunlight.
>
> At the same time I could see a Hurricane flying out and away in a wide sweep, turning to come into the flight path of the Messerschmitt. I was

expecting there to be a burst of machine-gun fire but nothing happened and he just kept on coming and closing the gap all the time. As he passed slightly below and beneath the Messerschmitt he banked the plane so that the tip of the wing made contact with the tailpiece of the Messerschmitt. The timing of this manoeuvre was perfect and the tail broke off the German 'plane but so too did the Hurricane wing. The Messerschmitt dived straight to the ground ... A huge column of black smoke rose up from the next field where the Hurricane was a blazing inferno with the pilot lying some 20 to 30ft away from the burning wreck. His parachute was extended but not fully opened and this was used to cover his body until the time came to take him away.

The main body of the Messerschmitt had struck the ground at Simmons Field in Mill Road and disintegrated. Its final careering path demolished a sewage pipe mounted on brick piers whilst one of the engines catapulted forward and through a hawthorn hedge into Catt's field behind Hamlin's Mill.

Meanwhile, the out-of-control Hurricane had roared on towards the young Douglas and had slammed into a massive oak tree not many yards from where he stood. The long chase was over. Horst Liensberger, Albert Kopge and Percy Burton all lay dead, their broken bodies just a stones-throw apart.

*　*　*　*

Following the German change in strategy, the final, large-scale, daylight raid over Britain took place on the last day of September. It cost the *Luftwaffe* more than forty aircraft.

Park also announced a change in tactics. The Bf 109s had proven more than a match for the Hurricanes but the slightly faster and more manoeuvrable Spitfires had been successful against the German fighters. The British aircraft were now regularly flying in wings of two or three squadrons composed of the same type of aircraft, so Park ordered his Hurricane wings to concentrate on the bombers whilst the Spitfires engaged the fighters.

Park's new tactics soon became redundant as from the beginning of October the German bombers were used almost exclusively for night-time operations. But Goering wanted to maintain pressure against Fighter Command and he attempted to combine the speed of his Messerschmitt fighters with the destructive power of the bombers by converting some 250 Bf 109s and 110s to fighter-bombers. The 109s were loaded with a single 250kg bomb and the 110s with up to 700kg of ordnance.

The first fighter-bomber raid was mounted on 1 October 1940, against Kent, Portsmouth and Southampton. The fighter-bomber formations, escorted by Bf 109s which had not been converted into bombers, flew at high altitude (around 20,000 feet). This made them difficult to plot and meant a long, hard climb for the Spitfires and Hurricanes in which they were vulnerable to counter-attacks from above by the Messerschmitts.

The consequence was that for the first time RAF daily losses exceeded those of the *Luftwaffe* on a number of occasions during the month of October. The raids, however, were not a huge success. As soon as they were intercepted by the RAF, the pilots of the fighter-bombers jettisoned their bomb load whether they were over their designated target or not. Park also ordered readiness squadrons to patrol the skies above the sector stations at between 20,000 and 25,000 feet so that they could engage the enemy on equal terms.

With autumn approaching and the nights drawing in, the last days of October signalled the end of any invasion threat for that year. The Battle of Britain had cost the RAF 915 aeroplanes and the *Luftwaffe* a staggering 1,733 aircraft. The nightly bombing raids upon industrial centres, docks and cities did not end, however, and to combat this a number of Hurricanes and Spitfire squadrons, including Westhampnett's 602 Squadron, were temporarily switched to night-flying. The RAF also began to deploy the first purpose-built night-fighters.

The Bristol Beaufighters of No.219 Squadron flew into Tangmere on 12 October. Equipped with the recently developed Airborne Interception Radar these fast and powerfully armed fighters were able to locate the enemy's bombers in conjunction with the ground-based radar stations. Ford aerodrome, which had been rebuilt after the heavy punishment it had received in August, was taken over by the RAF and incorporated into No.11 Group Fighter Command, flying the Mk.IF Blenheims of 23 Squadron which were specifically adapted for night interception roles.

With few daylight duties to occupy the Spitfire and Hurricane squadrons these aircraft turned increasingly to the offensive. At Tangmere the Spitfires of Nos. 616 and 145 squadrons undertook attacking patrols, known as *Rodeos* into northern France. With no radar network to warn the Germans of their approach the fighters were able to steal upon the *Luftwaffe*'s forward airfields and catch the enemy aircraft sitting impotently upon the ground.

Though limited and opportunistic, these raids marked a turning point in the war. The RAF was no longer restricted solely to the defensive. The Battle of Britain was over. The Battle for Europe was about to begin.

Between the outbreak of hostilities and the end of 1940, some 180 German and 120 British planes were shot down over Sussex and the seas around its coastline. These incidents claimed the lives of sixty-one British and 143 German airmen with a further 147 Germans captured and taken prisoner. No less than 310 civilians were also killed in Sussex throughout 1940 as a result of enemy action.[13]

CHAPTER 11

Dieppe to D-Day:
The Last Battles

Almost as soon as the British Expeditionary Force had been driven from the beaches of Dunkirk, Churchill had been determined to return to Europe in triumph. It would be many years before Britain could build its military strength to a level capable of challenging Hitler's hold upon the Continent, but meanwhile Britain would not remain cowering on the defensive. The RAF had proven itself against the Germans in the air and it was the RAF that would carry the war into occupied Europe and, ultimately, into the very heart of the Reich.

Leigh-Mallory, who had taken over from Hugh Dowding at the head of Fighter Command, was a proponent of the "Non-stop Offensive" and the airfields of the south were in action over France, and later Belgium and Holland, almost every day. However, Leigh-Mallory's men could not be employed exclusively in missions across the Channel. The *Luftwaffe* continued its night-time attacks against the major British cities and ports and Fighter Command was frequently deployed in defensive roles and escorts for shipping in the Channel. As well as attacks from the air, Sussex also suffered raids from the sea, including an incident in January 1941 when two German E-boats cruised along the Sussex coast firing at troops working on the beaches and another in 1942 when a German submarine sailed up the Cuckmere River and fired several shots at the Exceat Bridge.

Some of the offensive flights over France towards the end of 1940 were patrols undertaken by single fighters or flights of up to six aircraft. The aim of these patrols was to "attack and destroy enemy aircraft, or, if impractical, suitable ground military objectives."[1]

Known by the code name *Rhubarb* these raids proved to be of limited value and they were soon overtaken by operations by Wings of two or three squadrons. In March 1941, Squadron Leader Douglas Bader was offered command of one of these wings with the rank of Wing Commander, his objective being offensive action against German targets across the Channel. He was given the choice of operating from either Biggin Hill in Kent or Tangmere in Sussex. He chose Tangmere. Under his command were three squadrons of Spitfires based at Westhampnett and Merston.

It was expected that these larger formations would tempt the German fighters into the air but as the Spitfires and Hurricanes could do little harm to the *Luftwaffe* on the ground, the Germans simply ignored these patrols. Soon the fighters were accompanied by a few Blenheim or Stirling bombers which the *Luftwaffe* could not ignore. Their effectiveness, however, remained marginal and Allied losses in the missions were comparatively heavy. These operations bore the code name *Circus*. In order to deceive the Germans and convince them that the eventual re-invasion of Europe would take place in the Pas de Calais, twice as many missions were flown into that area than into other parts of France.

Fighter Command was primarily organised and equipped as a defensive weapon. The offensive into Europe demanded a change in both structure and equipment. Towards the end of 1943 Fighter Command became the Second Tactical Air Force and a bomber group was added to the existing fighter wings. Leigh-Mallory remained its commander. The aircraft available to the opposing air forces had changed considerably since the Battle of Britain. In September 1941, the *Luftwaffe* introduced the Focke-Wulf Fw 190 fighter. It was faster than the Spitfire, could reach 26,000 feet in twelve minutes – with an operational ceiling of almost 35,000 feet – and it was highly manoeuvrable. Improved versions of the Messerschmitt Bf 109s were also introduced.

The RAF had also received a new aircraft, the Hawker Typhoon. Though very fast at low and medium altitudes, it soon proved to be no match for the Fw 190s and the later versions of the Bf 109s in aerial combat. Its speed and its powerful armament (which eventually included rockets) made it highly effective as a fighter-bomber and in close support roles for ground troops.

The American Mustang, many powered by Rolls-Royce Merlin engines, was the United States Air Force's principle fighter and a number of RAF squadrons were also equipped with this type. The Mustang was considered to be the best fighter plane of the Second World War. The Hurricane was no longer regarded as a front-line fighter but the Spitfire had continued to be developed and the majority of Leigh-Mallory's squadrons were equipped with the most recent Spitfire marks.

During this time Tangmere had an additional role. It was from there that many secret agents of the Special Operations Executive were flown into France. The agents were housed at nearby Bignor Manor which operated under the guise of a convalescent home for wounded officers. Under conditions of the utmost secrecy the agents were taken from the manor and flown across the Channel at night, usually in Lysanders which were painted black and were without identification markings.[2]

One of the most important pre-requisites for a successful re-invasion of Europe (which was code named Operation *Overlord*) would be the establishment and maintenance of air superiority over the landing beaches and the enemy's interior lines of communication. In order to help achieve the former, attacks were to be

A painting of the control tower at Tangmere airfield. The tower can still be seen on private land to the north of the old runways at the end of a road which runs besides the present-day aviation museum (SU 913066).

delivered against industrial units associated with aircraft construction and against the German fighters, both on the ground and in the air. Of the latter, railway stations became prime targets and this was later extended to include all trains and railway installations. In all of these operations the Sussex airfields were to play a key role.

In preparation for this a number of temporary airfields, known as Advanced Landing Grounds (ALGs), were formed in the south. They were built to a common specification, with each having two metal runways, both fifty yards wide, the principal one being 1,600 yards long and the other 1,400 yards. In conformance with their temporary status no permanent buildings were erected. At each ALG a maximum of four Blister hangars were raised with all personnel being accommodated in tents or local houses.

Funtington, to the north-west of Chichester, was the most westerly of the Sussex ALGs. It became operational in February 1943 with two squadrons of Mustangs. These squadrons, Nos. 4 and 268, flew reconnaissance and deep penetration flights into enemy territory to strike at any available targets. Known as *Ranger* patrols, they were part of the "softening up" process, putting a strain on German resources and undermining morale.

The following year hard standings were laid and in August 1944 three squadrons of Typhoon Mk.IBs replaced the old Mk.I Mustangs. These three Canadian squadrons (Nos. 428, 439 and 440) were tasked to attack V1 flying bomb sites in Northern France and the Typhoons, in their fighter-bomber role, proved effective against such comparatively small targets.

After just three weeks at Funtington another Canadian unit, 144 Wing, flying Spitfire Mk.IXBs, took their place. Led by the man who was to become the Allies' top Ace with thirty-eight accredited kills, "Johnny" Johnson, Nos. 441, 442 and 443 squadrons escorted bombing raids in the build-up to the date of the re-invasion on D-Day.[3]

To the east of Funtington, and a mile or so to the south of Chichester, an ALG was laid at Apuldram. Completed by the end of May 1943, it was firstly the home of 124 Wing with three squadrons of Typhoons. The Typhoons flew sorties against enemy airfields and later against radar stations until 1 July, when the airfield was mothballed until the intensification of aerial operations preceding D-Day.[4]

A further four miles south of Chichester, between the village of Church Norton and Selsey, an ALG was built which became operational in May 1943. 121 Wing, consisting of 65 Squadron, flying Spitfires, and 245 with Typhoons, was based at Selsey until July when the airfield, like many of the ALGs, was closed down to allow improvements to be made in preparation for Operation *Overlord*.[5]

Bognor ALG opened in June 1943, when 122 Wing with Nos. 19, 122 and 602 squadrons of Spitfires arrived and were tasked for ground-attack missions. After just a month of such operations the Spitfires left Bognor and the airfield was not used again until March 1944. During this dormant period the airfield was provided with Blister hangars and hardstanding.[6]

Approximately four miles to the west of Hailsham, an ALG was laid near Deanland Wood with two grass runways. It opened in April 1944 with three Polish squadrons flying Spitfire IXs though it had already been in use as an emergency landing ground.[7]

The largest single offensive operation of this period was the famous, or infamous, Dieppe raid. Under pressure from the Soviets to create a second front to help relieve the strain on the eastern front, the raid was a political, rather than military, necessity and as a consequence was a complete failure. The raid – code-named Operation *Jubilee* – was planned as a "reconnaissance in force" to test Hitler's Channel defences and as a rehearsal for the eventual re-invasion of Europe. Originally devised as a fifteen-hour, two-tide operation to occupy and hold the entire Dieppe area, it was scaled down to a one-tide, six-hour raid with the intention being, in Churchill's own words "to kill as many Germans as possible and to take prisoners."[8]

The men of the Canadian Second Corps, which was stationed across Sussex, formed the main infantry strike force with Newhaven being the principal departure port. Some vessels also left from Shoreham. The Naval support came from Portsmouth. Included in the force were fifty of the new Churchill tanks from the 14th (Calgary) Tank Regiment as well as No.3 and No.4 Royal Marine Commando and a small number of United States Rangers.

The need for air superiority was fully understood and the raid was to be supported by the largest number of RAF aircraft yet employed in a single operation. Altogether sixty-eight squadrons were to fly 3,000 missions in the sixteen hours before and during the attack upon Dieppe.

In the early hours of 19 August 1942, 250 vessels crossed the Channel. The German defenders, however, were alerted before the landing craft even reached the beaches. Not a single tank was able to cross the beach. The large stones, of which the beach surface is composed, got inside the tracks and the tanks ground to a halt. Dieppe's defences were far too strong and only a handful of men managed to fight their way into town. The raid was a disaster.

Of the 4,963 Canadians, only 2,120 returned to Newhaven, many of whom were severely wounded. All fifty tanks had to be abandoned along with thirty-three landing craft. (So much equipment was left behind that Hitler sarcastically thanked Britain for sending the Germans samples of all their weapons!)[9]

The Navy suffered 550 casualties and one destroyer, HMS *Berkeley*, was sunk. Major Pat Porteous of 4 Commando and Major John Foote of the Royal Hamilton Light Infantry both won the Victoria Cross for their bravery at Dieppe.

The Spitfires of 131 Squadron from Merston flew four sorties on the day, three of which were over Dieppe, claiming a number of successes against Fw 190s and Dornier 217s. From Friston the Hurricanes of Nos. 32 and 253 squadrons were used to attack the German gun emplacements supported by the Hurricanes of Nos.3 and 245 squadrons from Shoreham. In total the RAF lost 112 aircraft, though forty-five airmen were rescued from the sea by the RAF's Air–Sea Rescue Service's High Speed Launches which operated out of Newhaven. By comparison, the *Luftwaffe* lost only seventy-two aircraft and the ground troops suffered less than 600 casualties.

It is said that the Dieppe raid taught the Allies many valuable lessons. The first of these was that armoured vehicles capable of destroying pillboxes had to land with the assault troops. This led to the design of floating tanks which were highly successful during the D-Day landings. Secondly, it was realised that a frontal assault upon a fortified harbour was impracticable. The result of this was the development of the Mulberry artificial harbour which could be deployed off a beach away from strongly defended ports.

The districts between the ports of Newhaven and Portsmouth were designated a Concentration Area for the 1st and 30th Corps in preparation for *Overlord*. From February 1944 troops began to pour into Sussex. The 4th Armoured Brigade, consisting of the Royal Scots Greys, the 3rd County of London Yeomanry, the 44th Battalion The Royal Tank Regiment and the King's Royal Rifle Corps, arrived in the county on 10 February, establishing its headquarters at Worthing.

Two months later the 27th Armoured Brigade moved into the Petworth – Ardingly area with Petworth House being taken over by the 13/18th Royal Hussars and the East Riding Yeomanry. Meanwhile, Wakehurst Place was occupied by the Staffordshire Yeomanry. A number of squadrons of this brigade were equipped with specially converted, and highly secret, amphibious Sherman tanks which could make their own way ashore if launched from landing craft into deep water. The elite Guards Armoured Division was stationed in East Sussex.[10]

The cavalry was followed by the infantry in the form of the 15th Scottish Infantry Division which spread its brigades from Hove, through Lancing and Worthing to Ashington and Storrington. Divisional headquarters was at Knepp Castle near West Grinstead. There was also a Commando unit based at Littlehampton. Known as X Troop, it consisted predominantly of anti-Nazi escapees from Germany, including many Jews. Though its activities were highly classified, it is known that they included small-scale, cross-Channel raids and intelligence gathering. Amongst these missions were a series of raids on successive nights between the 15th and 18th of May to investigate the beach defences on the French coast.[11]

Across Sussex, particularly in the designated South Downs Training Area and along the coast, the various regiments practised manoeuvres and beach landings throughout the spring of 1944. The south-facing slopes of the Downs between Clayton and Lewes were used by the Royal Navy for gunnery practice, firing inland from the sea. The Army also practised against the Downs, shooting from Ditchling Common into the nearby hills. Farmhouses in the area served as targets for the Canadian Army and most were damaged. They were rebuilt after the war at the Canadians' expense.[12]

The final large-scale rehearsal for *Overlord*, which took place on 4 May, was called Exercise *Fabius*. It involved the whole of the British 1st Corps, including the tanks of the armoured regiments as well as Royal Engineers and Royal Marine Commandos, "attacking" the beach between Littlehampton and Bognor. Just a few weeks later, on 1 June, the troops were ordered to be ready for the start of the largest sea-borne assault ever undertaken. From that date onwards the invasion would take place as soon as sea and weather conditions were suitable.

During the build-up for D-Day the coast from Pagham Harbour round to the eastern edge of Selsey was subject to the tightest security. Unauthorised civilians were banned from the area and fishing vessels were excluded from the seas around Pagham Harbour. Within this area the component parts of one of the famous Mulberry harbours was assembled. (The other Mulberry assembly area was off Dungeness.)

These unique structures were complete floating harbours comprising quays, jetties and breakwaters. The harbours were to be towed out to lie off the Normandy coast immediately after D-Day which, on 26 May, was scheduled for 5 June. These were massive structures and more than 400 component parts had to be towed across the Channel with a total weight of 1,500,000 tons.[13]

With the date having been decided, all the troops were confined to camp, the Concentration Areas and Marshalling Areas were sealed with barbed wire – many also posted armed guards. During the last days of May the roads of Sussex were filled with convoys of troops and armoured vehicles. The troops in transit were not permitted to speak with civilians.

By 1 June the towns and villages where the troops had spent the previous weeks were empty and quiet as the various regiments were now at their Marshalling Areas near to Newhaven, Shoreham and Portsmouth. The units that were to embark at Newhaven and Shoreham were placed into Marshalling Area J. This stretched from Seaford to Brighton and extended as far inland as Haywards Heath. Within this area were ten major Marshalling Camps, at such places as Firle Park, Stanmer Park and Borde Hill, with a total capacity of 15,000 men and more than 2,000 vehicles. Sussex became a vast car park.

Village greens were used to park military vehicles and dual carriageways were closed off on one side and used as hardstanding for tanks. Each Allied vehicle was painted with a large white star on the sides and roof to aid identification.

By 4 June, the troops had moved down to the ports and some had already embarked upon their landing craft, many of which had been made in Sussex at Littlehampton, Itchenor and Bosham. But the fine, still weather had changed to strong winds and heavy cloud with the possibility of rain storms. It was decided by the planners at Supreme Headquarters to postpone the invasion for one day in the hope that the weather would improve. Fortunately the weather did settle into another period of good conditions and 6 June was declared D-Day.

Throughout the night of 5/6 June the Sussex skies were filled with the dark silhouettes of thousands of Allied aircraft. Along the Sussex coast a series of *Eureka* navigational beacons and lights guided the bombers and transports from their bases in Oxfordshire, Berkshire, Wiltshire and Devon to the aerial rendezvous points above Worthing, Littlehampton and Bognor, before setting out across the Channel. The 6th Airborne Division passed over Worthing but two of its Horsa Gliders, packed with troops, failed to reach France. One landed in Worthing and the other nearby at Sompting.

From Newhaven and Shoreham the ships sailed with their human and armoured cargoes. Through Littlehampton went vessels loaded with ammunition, and from Pagham the Mulberry harbours were towed slowly across the Channel.

It was now time for the Sussex airfields to play their part in Operation *Overlord*. The objective was to form a screen of Allied fighters around the entire invasion area beginning at 04:25 hours on the morning of 6 June. High cover was to be provided by the USAAF and low cover by the RAF. The Allied fighters also supplied escorts for almost every other air activity, from bombing missions to coastal patrols and airborne assault.

From Tangmere the Spitfires of six squadrons of the Royal Canadian Air Force provided air cover for the troops on the landing beaches and they patrolled further inland to prevent German aerial counter-attacks. For D-Day, Ford was also the base for six squadrons of Spitfire Mk.IX LFs. These protected the landing craft as well as the beaches and the surrounding skies. A single squadron of Typhoons at Westhampnett patrolled the skies over the beaches whilst the six squadrons of Typhoons from Thorney Island (including 164 Squadron which was composed partly of Argentinian pilots and 193 Squadron with mostly Brazilian flyers) were given the task of ground attack to prevent enemy reinforcements reaching the invasion coast.

The Free French air force, flying Spitfire Mk.IXBs, based three squadrons at Merston and on D-Day these provided low-level cover for the troop transport vessels. Another Free French squadron was at Shoreham and on 6 June its Spitfire Mk.VBs escorted the gliders of the airborne troops. At Friston was a Belgian squadron (350 Squadron) which, with 501 Squadron, flew sorties over the landing beaches throughout the day of 6 June.

The Advanced Landing Grounds, which had been upgraded for D-Day, were brought into the action. A second Belgian squadron of Spitfires, with a New Zealand and a South African squadron, was stationed at Selsey. Selsey's three squadrons, three Czechoslovakian squadrons from Apuldram and Chailey's Polish squadrons provided low-level cover over the beaches.

Of the three Spitfire squadrons that operated out of Deanland, 611 Squadron patrolled the Normandy beaches, whilst 64 Squadron and 234 Squadron escorted airborne divisions to their drop zones. Coolham's and Funtington's six squadrons of Mustangs formed part of the "Pool of Readiness" which could be drawn upon if the air cover over the landing area was breached. All six squadrons were called into action.

Funtington's Mustangs escorted Beaufighters of Coastal Command on anti-submarine patrols and Coolham's three squadrons were used to escort a formation of tugs and gliders. From Hammerwood, 659 Squadron Air Observation Post flew Auster Mk.IV spotter planes, but their precise duties are not known.[14]

To help avoid mistakes in the crowded skies over Normandy, black and white stripes were painted on the wings and fuselages of the Allied aircraft.

The following is the order of battle for the Sussex-based squadrons in June 1944:[15]

AIRFIELD	SQUADRONS	AIRCRAFT	WING
Thorney Island	198	Typhoon	123
	609	Typhoon	123
	164	Typhoon	136
	183	Typhoon	136
Westhampnett	184	Typhoon	129
Ford	441	Spitfire IX LF	144
	442	Spitfire IX LF	144
	443	Spitfire IX LF	144
	132	Spitfire IX LF	125
	602	Spitfire IX LF	125
	453	Spitfire IX LF	125
	456	Mosquito	85 Group (Night Fighter Force)
Funtington	19	Mustang III	122
	65	Mustang III	122
	122	Mustang III	122
Tangmere	401	Spitfire IX LF	126
	411	Spitfire IX LF	126
	412	Spitfire IX LF	126
	103	Spitfire IX LF	127
	416	Spitfire IX LF	127
	421	Spitfire IX LF	127
Selsey	302	Spitfire IX LF	131
	308	Spitfire IX LF	131
	317	Spitfire IX LF	131
Coolham	129	Mustang III	133
	306	Mustang III	133

	315	Mustang III	133
Chailey	222	Spitfire IX LF	135
	349	Spitfire IX LF	135
	485	Spitfire IX LF	135
Bognor	66	Spitfire IX LF	132
	331	Spitfire IX LF	132
	332	Spitfire IX LF	132
Apuldram	310	Spitfire IX LF	134
	312	Spitfire IX LF	134
	313	Spitfire IX LF	134
Merston	329	Spitfire IX LF	145
	340	Spitfire IX LF	145
	341	Spitfire IX LF	145
Gatwick	2	Mustang II	35
	4	Spitfire PRX1	35
	268	Mustang 1A	35
Shoreham	345	Spitfire V LF	
	277	Walrus (Air Sea Rescue)	
Friston	350	Spitfire V LF	
	501	Spitfire V LF	
Deanland	64	Spitfire V LF	
	234	Spitfire V LF	
	611	Spitfire V LF	

The value of the previous two years of attacks against the German air capacity was clearly demonstrated by the fact that on D-Day the enemy were able to mount less than a hundred sorties. As a consequence D-Day was a success but it was another year before the Germans surrendered. In the days following D-Day the beach-heads were expanded and the Allies drove deeper into France.

The Sussex airfields continued to play a major role in keeping the *Luftwaffe* at bay and in attacking enemy ground troops and supply lines. But gradually, as the war moved away from the coast, airfields were established in France and many of the Sussex-based squadrons transferred across the Channel. Newhaven continued to be a departure point for troops and provisions for many months after D-Day, whilst Littlehampton became an important ammunition supply port.

Sussex now prepared itself to receive casualties from the battle for Normandy. Emergency Medical Service wards were erected at the Royal West Sussex Hospital and the St. Richards Hospital in Chichester (the latter being reserved for wounded German prisoners of war). Two wards were also made available for D-Day casualties at the Graylingwell Mental Hospital. Emergency transport for the wounded was provided by Southdown buses whose vehicles were converted to ambulances by the removal of the seats and the addition of stretcher slings. The hospitals were soon filled to over-capacity and this situation continued until Field Hospitals were set up in France.

A new terror now appeared in the skies over Sussex – the V1. Around a thousand of these flying-bombs fell around the county, causing much damage. Fast fighters, such as the Spitfire and the Typhoon, were able to intercept the V1 and many were shot down. However, the V1 was superseded by the V2 rocket against which there was no defence. Fortunately for the people of Sussex only four of these missiles hit the county.

Throughout the course of the war, more than 103,000 bombs of all descriptions had dropped on Sussex and 4,910 people were killed or injured.[16]

After the war most of the ALGs were returned to agricultural use. Of the principal airfields Westhampnett is now known as Goodwood airfield and is used by civilian light aircraft whilst Shoreham continues to thrive as a small commercial airport.

Tangmere continued to be an important part of the re-formed Fighter Command with two squadrons of Gloster Meteor jet fighters in residence through the 1940s. In the 1950s the Meteors were superseded by Hawker Hunters of Nos.1 and 34 squadrons. In 1958 Tangmere was taken over by Signals Command, with their Canberra and Varsity aircraft. The airfield was closed in 1970.

In 1945 Ford airfield was returned to the Royal Navy, once again adopting the name of HMS *Peregrine*. It remained a training and experimental establishment until 1958. Thorney Island continued after the war as an Air-Sea Warfare Development base before becoming the home of the 47th Regiment of the Royal Artillery.

CHAPTER 12

Witness to War:
On the Home Front in Sussex
1939–1945

Whilst every conflict on Sussex soil involved, directly or indirectly, the people that lived nearby, it was the Second World War that affected almost everyone across the country the most. The following is a selection of dramatic accounts relating to just some of the numerous incidents involving the people of Sussex during the county's most testing time.

To many on the morning of Sunday, 8 October 1944, with life continuing as normal as was possible in wartime Britain, the war must have seemed so far away. But, as they set out for a walk on the South Downs that autumnal morning 15-year-old Peter French and his four friends would soon discover that the effects of this conflict were never far away.

Unsupervised, the five teenagers decided to head up onto the gently rolling slopes of the South Downs above Portslade on a Scout Patrol. Their wanderings took them into Block 5 of the South Downs Training Area – a restricted military area that should have been closed to the public.

Undeterred, the boys continued. At 12:00 hours, they came across a thunder flash lying on the ground. Used during army exercises to simulate exploding grenades or create a diversion, this particular pyrotechnic had previously failed to detonate properly. As a result, it still contained its gunpowder.[1]

One of the boys – probably Peter – removed the powder and having piled it up on the ground put a match to it. The resulting flash caused extensive burns to Peter's forearms; his clothes were also damaged by the explosion. With his friends suffering from shock, all five were taken to hospital.[2] The group had just discovered, at their own cost, that large parts of the South Downs were far from the peaceful chalk grassland they appeared to be; they were part of the Allied war machine.

* * * *

In anticipation of the coming conflict, in 1938 the government's Directorate of

Lands and Accommodation, part of the Ministry of Works, set up a central register to record those areas of land or buildings that would prove of value to the various official departments should war be declared. Little would they have known that in less than twelve months this inventory would be fulfilling its intended role!

No sooner had war broken out, than areas of land listed in the register began to be requisitioned under the Defence (General) Regulations 1939 which had been made under the Emergency Powers (Defence) Act 1939. In Sussex, one of the first tracts of land to fall victim was the area of the South Downs around Cissbury Ring north of Worthing. This Iron Age hill fort, the largest in Sussex and the second largest in England, was requisitioned before the end of September 1939. Overnight, it had become one of the new, wartime, training areas for the British army.[3] Even today, the remains of the rifle range laid out on the southern side of the fort can still be seen.

During the Second World War, a total of 14.5 million acres of land, 25 million square feet of industrial and storage premises and 113,350 holdings of non-industrial premises were requisitioned by the state.[4] The War Office alone requisitioned 580,847 acres between 1939 and 1946. Despite the fact that the requisitioning of land for military purposes often seemed to conflict with another of the government's principal objectives, namely the maximisation of food production, huge areas of the South Downs became closed to all but those serving in the Allied armies.

By the beginning of 1944, the larger training areas on the South Downs had been amalgamated into the South Downs Training Area (SDTA). Not a continuous single stretch of land, the SDTA was divided into nine separate blocks, each of which had its own fixed entry and exit points. A central headquarters unit scheduled and controlled the various activities undertaken in the blocks, and oversaw a staff that maintained them.

Not all the training areas on the South Downs, however, fell within the boundaries of the SDTA. The historic Yew Forest at Kingley Vale, a few miles north-west of Chichester, is one such example. Though heavily used as a range by both the army and RAF during the war, the Vale does not appear on any of the official maps of the SDTA.

With the new use of the South Downs as a training area though, came new risks – risks that increased with the build-up of British and Canadian forces as the war progressed. The biggest problem was that created by unexploded munitions left lying around the training areas. As the preparations for the D-Day landings reached their peak, not just on the Downs but nationally, it was a problem that could no longer be ignored.

At the beginning of April 1944, the Army Council was forced to admit that "during 1943 there were 365 officers and other ranks killed at home stations and

Don't touch! Accompanied by three soldiers, a police officer inspects a 2-inch British mortar bomb that was found lying in the open on the South Downs near Pyecombe north of Brighton.

1,578 injured".[5] All ranks were "urged to exercise greater care in all respects so that the figures for 1943 may be substantially reduced in 1944". After all, "almost every one of these accidents" had been "preventable and unnecessary". Incredibly, in the same period no less than 118 civilians, "including many children" had been killed; a further 390 were seriously injured.[6]

"How would you like your son or your young brother to take home a 'dud' grenade as a souvenir?" continued one set of instructions. "When ordered to search for or mark down or destroy 'blinds' [unexploded ordnance] make a clean job of it. Leave nothing to chance and leave nothing lying about for other men's children to find. Remember that children pay even less attention to warning and out of bounds notices than soldiers do. No fencing and no notices will keep out small boys."

"Do not leave explosive articles lying about where children can get at them," the advice continued. "If you think you have found a 'blind', leave it alone, mark the spot, arrange for a friend to guard it if possible, and report it to an officer at once.

"A 'blind' goes off sooner or later, and if it goes off because a child treads on it or picks it up when birds-nesting or blackberrying or hunting for souvenirs, someone's child is killed." Boys, it would seem, will be boys.

Even the presence of a teacher did not prevent accidents. On the afternoon of 4 November 1943, a schoolmaster took a group of boys on to the slopes of the Downs at Hill Barn. Entering a quarry, and unbeknown to the master, two of the group picked up what is believed to have been an unexploded grenade or spigot mortar round. As they tampered with their "find", it exploded. One youth, a boy named Bedwell, was rushed to hospital suffering from arm and leg injuries and shock. A second received less serious injuries.

Adults would also fall victim to this youthful inquisitiveness. On the afternoon of 3 September 1944, an explosion tore apart a family residence at 4, The Flats, Surrey Street, Worthing. The occupant, Mrs Francis Etherington, was injured. The police soon established the cause; a 2lb anti-tank shell that her husband had found in a field on the South Downs above Findon several months earlier. Returning home, Mr Etherington stored his unexploded souvenir in a cupboard in his sitting room. On the day she had been injured, Mrs Etherington had opened the cupboard door. Out fell the shell, striking the corner of the fender as it fell and exploded.[7]

The tally of casualties on the South Downs would carry on mounting. At 16.00 hours on Saturday, 19 May 1945, eleven days after the war in Europe had ended, another 15-year-old boy, David Weston, sustained injuries to his right thigh and hand after tampering with a 2-inch H.E. mortar bomb he had found at Kingley Vale. Worryingly, the Police report concluded, there had been "no notices or flags, or any indication that Kingley Vale was used as a firing and mortar bombing range".[8]

At about the very same time that Weston was badly injured at Kingley Vale, a train of events was starting to unravel on the South Downs at Findon in West Sussex; events that would clearly illustrate the lethal nature of these incidents.

The group of four boys consisted of cousins Gordon and David Bedson, and friends Leonard Sheppard and Gordon Smith. Intent on poaching rabbits, the group made their way up on to Black Patch Hill. Scouring the west side of the hill, the boys stumbled across a shallow pit covered with galvanised iron sheets. Peering in, Gordon Bedson noticed something lying on the chalky floor. Lifting it out, the boys would probably not have realised that what they had found was an unexploded

British 2-inch High Explosive mortar bomb. Indeed, almost immediately Sheppard found a second bomb lying just four yards away. Waving it at his friends, he proudly declared they had found a pair of "parachute flares".[9]

Taking the two objects with them, the boys continued on their hunt for rabbits. Shortly after, they discovered some peewit eggs and decided to leave their souvenirs on the long grass on the edge of a wheat field on Black Patch Hill and return home.

The following morning the two Gordons called on Leonard. Their intention was to return and collect their finds. Indeed, Leonard took with him a hacksaw, stating that "he was going to cut the fins off the bombs [*sic*] to get the parachutes out".

Having relocated the two "flares", the two Gordons held one whilst Leonard set about it with the hacksaw. The progress was slow – too slow, for Leonard gave up, saying that this "method was too slow and that he was going to break it off". As his friends moved away, Sheppard wedged the "flare" in an iron staple in a post. He then picked up the second mortar bomb, intending to use it to knock the fins off the first.

As his friends momentarily looked away, an explosion ripped through the quiet Sunday morning peace. Gordon Smith was blown forward and thrown to the ground, sustaining injuries to his head and hands. Leonard lay motionless on the ground nearby. Panicking, Gordon Bedson lifted the other Gordon to his feet and the two boys staggered home to summon help. By the time that the village policeman, PC Griffin, returned to the scene, Leonard was dead. Around him were scattered a number of splinters from the exploded bomb.[10]

Aged only thirteen, Leonard Sheppard was as much a victim of the war as those men who had trained on the hills and slopes of the South Downs and who went off to fight around the world and never returned.

For many in Sussex, the biggest dangers brought on by the war came through the German aerial attack on the United Kingdom.

With the Battle of Britain entering its final weeks, the morning of Wednesday, 2 October 1940, heralded a fine day – and another bout of activity by the *Luftwaffe*. As well as targeting London, throughout the day German bombers visited towns along the length of the South Coast – Margate, Dover, Hastings, Eastbourne and Worthing all included.

At about 06:50 hours that morning, Special Constable 195 Harry Etherington was on duty in the town of Eastbourne when he saw a German aircraft release four bombs. Noting that they fell in the area of Upperton Gardens, he immediately ran to the scene. When he reached the rear of 16 Upperton Gardens, he later recorded in his report, "I saw a fire raging, and two persons, a man and a woman, trapped in the flames on a small glass roof above the second floor".

Shouting for a ladder, Special Constable Etherington desperately tried to prevent the couple from jumping down into the basement – though "they were constantly

The letter written by Mr Abel to the Chief Constable of Eastbourne's Police following the events of Wednesday, 2 October 1940. (Courtesy of the Andy Saunders Collection)

licked by the flames from two windows". Eventually a ladder was found, and, through a team effort, the husband and wife, Mr and Mrs Henry Abel, were rescued. One police officer promptly wrapped Mrs Abel in his cape; another rescued the couple's dog which was trapped in a downstairs room.

Once recovered from the shock, three days later Mr Abel wrote to the Chief Constable of Eastbourne's Police. "I wish to record my sincere thanks and appreciation", he said, "for the prompt and efficient way the Police Officers rescued us from the blazing fire ... Without their quick help, and I believe two wardens ... nothing could have saved us as were trapped in the first floor and the flames were right on us." Mr Abel concluded his letter by saying: "I cannot speak too highly of the conduct and welcome encouragement that the quick response for help gave us both."[11]

Acknowledging this gratitude, in his reply the Chief Constable wrote: "Praise of the work of the Police and ARP Services is heard in these days from all parts of the country and it is good to know that the Police and Services are earning their place in the esteem of the population by their devotion to duty in our own town as elsewhere."

Whilst Henry Abel and his wife survived the bombing of their home, many civilians would discover to their cost just how much of a front-line county Sussex actually was.

One of the many killed during the assault on Sussex between 1939 and 1945 was Arthur James Cunningham. A First World War veteran, Cunningham was on duty at Ford airfield at the time of the fateful attack on 18 August 1940. Employed as a constable in the Royal Marines Police – a force which consisted of Royal Marine pensioners, not serving personnel – he was one of those who lost their lives. His family understand that Arthur was covering a colleague's shift to enable that person to take his wife out for the evening to celebrate their wedding anniversary.

Though he was killed on the 18th, Arthur's death was not registered until 20 August 1940. However, two death certificates were issued – one in the district of Littlehampton, the other in Bognor Regis. Whilst they differ slightly in the information listed, it is beyond dispute that he was killed as the result of "war operations". The Littlehampton record notes the fact that Arthur died as a result of "multiple injuries to left leg, arm and eye".

Arthur Cunningham's unusual status as a civilian serving in a military-controlled organisation, led to issues surrounding his commemoration by the Commonwealth War Graves Commission. In fact, it was not until January 2011 that his name was added to this organisation's records, included on the Civilian Roll of Honour for Chichester Rural District.

One of those who witnessed the attack on Ford first-hand was a Fleet Air Arm pilot, known only as "John", who described his experiences in a letter to a friend, Michael Daunt:

"On Sunday ... the old Hun caught us on the hop and sixty Junkers 87s and 88s came down on us without warning out of a blue sky. Never believe anybody who tells you he isn't afraid of dive-bombing. No such man exists. It is the most appalling thing in the world. It is the ultimate horror.

"As soon as I saw the Junkers I began to run to my Action Station; but I was caught in the open and the bloody things seemed to chase me with their guns, and bullets spattered all round. At this stage I was fearfully angry, and I can

The pall of dense black smoke that hung over Ford airfield after the attack on Sunday, 18 August 1940. (Courtesy of the Andy Saunders Collection.)

understand in a way the very foolish action of a Lieutenant Commander whom I saw emptying his revolver at them.12 He got off three rounds before a lot of nasty dark patches appeared in his face.

"I lay down and watched bullets sputtering all round, and then the blast of a 500kg bomb picked me up, removed most of my clothes, and chucked me through a door of a hanger. I lay there, listening to more bombs dropping until I realised that all the machines in the hangar were on fire. So I got out of there and sprinted twenty yards to a little shallow trench where I lay in the most awful helpless terror while huge bits of Ford aerodrome whizzed about the sky and occasionally landed on my bottom.

"I saw the oddest things every time I dared peep up: a big transport vehicle flying, an aeroplane wing doing flock-rolls, a complete corrugated iron roof sailing along as easily as a magic carpet, and a man blown off his bicycle and doing a couple of stall turns while his bicycle did a couple of loops. Well, after what seemed a very long time, but what was actually about five minutes, everything went quiet …"13

Ten minutes after the Germans had first been sighted it was all over. Behind them, the attackers left a scene of utter devastation. Five Blackburn Sharks, five

Fairey Swordfish, two Fairey Albacores and a Percival Proctor were destroyed. A further twenty-six had been damaged.[14]

What struck "John" the most as he began to study his surroundings was a "great roaring noise" which he likened to the sound of the Niagara Falls. This was the sound of 4,000 gallons of fuel burning furiously.

"The next three hours were pretty hectic", he recalled. "The first job was collecting up casualties; and then there was fighting fires, trying to shift ammunition or save aeroplanes and so on, until we were all dead beat. Our water main had a direct hit, our electricity was gone, all our telephone wires were down, our Sick-bay demolished, the Armoury on fire and all the ammunition exploding. It was just bloody awful.

"And yet, in the middle of all this mess, there was comedy and courage to relieve it. Somebody had hung 'Unserviceable' on a burnt out aeroplane; somebody had scribbled 'Closed for Stocktaking' on the empty shell of the parachute store … Then there was our young doctor, a bit white about the gills, driving a car with four flat tyres up and down like a tank over craters and pumping morphia into chaps who were dying.

The memorial to those killed in the raid on Ford airfield on 18 August 1940, which was erected at Clymping Church in 1942 – note the camouflaged hangars in the background and the barbed wire perimeter fence. Arthur Cunningham's name is listed on the right hand panel. The attack resulted in one of the most serious death-tolls from a Luftwaffe *raid on a British airfield during the Second World War. (Courtesy of the Andy Saunders Collection.)*

"Then there was the Captain, everywhere at once and so completely calm that nobody knew he had three bullets in his arm. There were the civilian AFS chaps, some of them badly burned, but still carrying on, and there were the heroic Wrens who had never seen a dead man before, but who didn't turn a hair and made tea in the midst of it all."

Ford was so severely damaged that it was subsequently abandoned by the Fleet Air Arm and its remaining aircraft and personnel were transferred to other sites.

Another who recalled the events of 18 August 1940, the so-called "Hardest Day", was WAAF Corporal Avis J. Hearn.[15] She was based not far from Ford at the Chain Home radar station at Poling:

"When we went on duty that day the Sergeant met us and said 'I want you to change over quickly. We've picked up a mass of aircraft forming on the coast of France'. He said that he wanted one of us to go into the new 'R' Block. We were working in a wooden hut protected by sand-bags and they built a brick hut with a roof that was terribly thick – it would take some bomb to get through that. I'd never been in there before.

"I went in to the hut and took over from another WAAF who was receiving plots from the CHL that was picking up the low-flying aircraft – and that's how I came to be alone in there."[16]

Corporal Hearn, who stood just four feet ten-and-a-half inches high, set about her task. She was manning the telephone switchboard, passing on plots of the enemy aircraft from Poling itself and the neighbouring radar stations along the coast. As the massed Stukas divided into smaller formations to attack their individual targets she passed on the information to the filter room at RAF Stanmore Park.

As Hearn called out the plots an astonishing message came down the wires from Truleigh Hill radar station just ten miles to the east on the South Downs above Shoreham-by-Sea: "Poling, do you realize that last plot we've given you is right above you?"

By then, Hearn could plainly hear the German aircraft diving. "There was a scream as the Stukas dived. It was a hideous sound, and then the noise of the explosions was terrific."[17] Undeterred, she decided that she had to stay at her post, at which point she is credited with the following laconic reply, "The course of the enemy bombers is only too apparent to me because the bombs are almost dropping on my head."

At that moment the Sergeant rushed into Hearn's hut and shouted to her to take cover. But the young WAAF simply replied, "I can't. I've got too much information coming through." Hearn carried on resolutely plotting and transmitting her messages through to Stanmore. "If I'd simply have run and taken cover then that

The site of Poling radar station was decommissioned in 1949 but did not officially close until July 1956. By the late 1960s very few of the original wartime buildings had survived. This receiver block is perhaps the most important exception, though its blast walls have long since been removed and it has been put to use as a workshop and garage. This building, in effect the nerve centre of the site, housed two receivers along with a plotting table. Since this photograph was taken in the 1990s, this structure has been converted to private housing.

information wasn't going through and Fighter Command wouldn't have known about it", she later observed.[18]

The bombs landed so close that they blew out every window of the 'R' Block and one of the main walls was badly cracked. Fully aware of what was happening at Poling, the Stanmore operator again asked "Are you all right Poling?"

Even though the building might collapse at any minute, and the thick, heavy roof fall down upon her, which would almost certainly have killed her, Corporal Hearn continued to work for about twenty minutes until one of the bombs hit the telephone lines and her headphones went dead. It was only then, when there was nothing else she could do, that she finally left the hut to seek shelter.

Outside she could see the ground full of bomb-craters but the damage done to the installations was surprisingly slight, considering the scale of the attack. Though the telephone lines were down, and the long-range Chain Home High radar was damaged, the Chain Home Low radar was still functioning. Within a few days a mobile radar station was erected in woods at nearby Angmering, filling the gap in the radar network's coverage caused by the Stuka attack until Poling was repaired.

Hearn's selfless action that day soon became widely known and it led to the deserved award of one of the highest bravery medals that can be issued: the Military Medal.

"During an enemy air attack, bombs were dropped on buildings of the unit doing very considerable damage", ran the wording of her citation published in *The London Gazette* on 16 January 1941. "Several heavy bombs fell alongside a block where Corporal Hearn was working alone controlling telephones ... doing her work as far as the terrific noise would permit. This airwoman displayed courage and devotion to duty of the highest order."[19]

Throughout the war years, Sussex would suffer air raids and attacks – it had become part of life during the early 1940s. An incident at East Grinstead on Friday, 19 July 1943, however, was unprecedented and resulted in the single greatest loss of life in Sussex since the thirteenth century.

It was one of the first days of the summer holidays for the local schoolchildren, many of whom were in the town's cinema that afternoon. At a little after 17:00 hours a lone Dornier Do 217 slipped out of the hazy clouds, circled the town and dropped eight bombs across East Grinstead's London Road and the High Street.

The devastation was described as "horrendous" as four- and five-storied buildings collapsed into heaps of burning rubble and shops were demolished. Worst of all though was the Whitehall Cinema on London Road. It was known that a minimum of 184 people were in the audience. The usual notice announcing an air raid alert had been displayed, though it is doubtful many people responded. Then there was a terrific crash: "the whole building seemed to collapse like a pack of cards, trapping most of the audience," recalled one survivor.[20]

One of the bombs crashed through the cinema's roof into the front of the auditorium, taking with it the roof dome which fell on the audience. Some people were buried under the falling masonry and killed instantly, others were badly injured, trapped under bricks and girders. Whole families were wiped out and in some cases no tangible trace could be found of the victims. Others, dead or dying, had been blasted into the street outside whilst some bodies had been flung grotesquely into the twisted roof girders. A lucky few staggered into the streets dazed and wounded – many bleeding from injuries sustained from flying glass. The smoking debris and the bodies strewn around was like, one witnessed remarked, "a vision of Hell, and one of sheer and unimaginable horror."[21]

Fires began to spread rapidly from building to building and a cloud of black and yellow sulphurous smoke hung over the town as the rescue work began. No one knows exactly how many were killed that day but 108 bodies were recovered and at least 235 were injured. The precise figures will probably never be known. It was Sussex's worst day of the war.

As well as the deadly cargoes dropped by the *Luftwaffe*'s bombers, a new threat developed as the war continued – the infamous "tip and run" raids.

As the Battle of Britain came to a close, the *Luftwaffe* began arming its single-engine fighters with bombs, using them in preference to twin-engine bombers against many daylight targets. Two units were designated for these *Jagdbomber* (literally fighter-bomber) attacks – 10/*JG* 2 and 10/*JG* 26. Their targets included shipping and coastal installations, railways, gas-holders and selected military and civilian objectives. The detrimental effect on British morale caused by these attacks, delivered by small numbers of aircraft at high speed and low altitude – usually providing little, or worse, no warning to the population – was great.

An early instance of such tactics occurred on 17 September 1942. On this date, two *Luftwaffe* Focke-Wulf Fw 190 fighter-bombers took off from their base at Caen with the intention of attacking Worthing.

Streaking into their target, the two pilots of the 10/*JG* 2, *Leutnant* Leopold Wenger and *Unteroffizier* Hans-Walter Wandschneider, each dropped their 500lb bombs. But they had not fallen on Worthing. In fact the pair had dropped their deadly cargo on the gasworks in Bognor Regis.

One bomb exploded on the rear of the West Parade Hotel in Goodman Drive, killing 68-year-old widow Alice Ford and wounding seven. The other bomb, dropped by Wenger, passed through the gas holder and exploded on a mined bridge at Shripney Road, severing gas, water and electricity services. The water supply was restored almost immediately; the gas supply restored two days later and the road reopened a further eight days later.

The next day, *Leutnant* "Poldi" Wenger wrote the following account of what happened: "Together with my *Rottenflieger* [wingman], a non-commissioned officer, I attacked the gasworks at Worthing. Flying at low-level, I was able to place my bomb between the two gas holders where it detonated. All sorts of things were thrown into the air. My *Rottenflieger* meanwhile bombed the town."

Returning to the day of the attack, as the two Fw 190s fled south back towards France, a pair of Supermarine Spitfires from 412 Squadron, on readiness at RAF Tangmere, was scrambled to intercept the attackers. After a long chase, the British fighters caught up with intruders halfway back to France. Again, Wenger takes up the story:

"Mid-Channel we were completely surprised by Spitfires which attacked immediately. During the course of the dogfight, my Rottenflieger was killed. I saw him diving vertically into the sea. Then they hit my plane, but I succeeded in making my escape. A 20mm shell tore the oil tank open and I lost so much oil that the whole plane looked like a sardine in oil. All was hideous – it went so quickly and I was not able to help ..."

For Bognor Regis, the raid was one of many. During the course of the war, the town's gasworks alone were bombed no less than seven times – in one of these attacks a crippled Dornier actually flew into one of the gas-holders and crashed!

At 12:20 hours on 25 May 1943, twenty-four Focke Wulf Fw 190 fighter-bombers attacked Brighton with devastating success. Making landfall between Roedean School and Rottingdean in line abreast, one section turned west over the town whilst another headed north-west and later acted as fighter escort. Bombs were dropped near the railway and locomotive works and, as the official report states "... others appear to have been aimed, with considerable success, at large buildings ..."

Photographs taken by one of the German pilots involved reveal that one of the main targets was the gasometer that still stands today, despite the best efforts of the *Luftwaffe*, off Bristol Gardens in the city.

Twenty-four civilians were killed in this attack; fifty-eight seriously injured, and a further sixty-nine suffered lesser injuries. British defences claimed to have shot down five enemy aircraft but, in reality, only one was lost. This Fw 190 probably fell victim to a Hawker Typhoon of 486 Squadron flying from nearby Friston. One Typhoon was damaged by friendly fire.

Worthing did not always escape attentions of the "tip and run" raiders. On 9 March 1943, German fighter-bombers again attacked the town with apparent impunity. Despite the best efforts of anti-aircraft gunners, six Focke Wulf Fw 190s of 10/*JG* 2 attacked the gas holders, housing and hotels. A number of properties were badly damaged and the Working Mens' Club received a direct hit and was flattened. At an extremely low level, the German pilots machine-gunned the town's gas-holder before heading south back across Worthing.

A Miss Tilsley had a remarkable escape in this attack. "I was digging in the garden when the machine-gunning started," she later recalled, "and I hurried into the house for cover and just had time to get under the stairs when the bomb fell. When it was over I looked out into the garden again and found a fifteen-foot deep crater where I had been digging".

Others, though, were not so lucky. By the time that the aircraft had done their deadly work and were heading south back across the Channel, nine people lay dead. Four-year-old Edna Mann, whose father Petty Officer Charles Mann RN was away serving at sea, succumbed to her injuries the following day in Worthing hospital. Despite the efforts of Typhoons of 486 Squadron and Spitfires of 610 Squadron, the German aircraft escaped unscathed.

By the end of the war, Eastbourne had earned itself the distinction of being one of the most raided town's on the south coast. Between the summer of 1940 and

Despite the best efforts of anti-aircraft gunners, six Focke Wulf Fw 190s of 10/JG 2 attacked the gas-holder, housing and hotels in Worthing on 9 March 1943. A number of properties were badly damaged and the Working Mens' Club received a direct hit and was flattened. This photograph was taken from the cockpit of one of the attacking aircraft – the photographer's own aircraft is machine-gunning the town's gas-holder at extreme low-level before heading south back across Worthing. Note the flashes caused as his bullet or cannon fire hits the structure. (Courtesy of Chris Goss.)

spring 1944, there had been ninety-eight attacks during which 671 high-explosive bombs and 3,626 incendiaries were dropped. Civilian casualties numbered over 1,100; there were 174 deaths, 443 seriously injured and 489 slightly wounded.[22]

A graphic account of one of these raids, which occurred on 13 April 1943, was provided by Barbara Goacher:

"I was in the shop of Messrs Dale and Kerley with my baby Ian, aged four months ... I left my baby in the perambulator on the ground floor and went up the stairs ... A man's voice shouted 'Take cover!' and I ran downstairs where I had left the baby but found the perambulator empty.

"The sound of exploding bombs and anti-aircraft fire could be heard. I was pushed into the basement of the shop and shouted 'My God, where's my baby?' and a sailor replied 'I have got somebody's baby' and then I saw he had my baby underneath him. He was laying on the floor and it was apparent that he was shielding [Ian] with his body.

"The sailor got up and I saw that he was injured, bleeding profusely from the head. My baby was covered with blood but was only slightly bruised. I thanked the sailor very much for his action and he muttered something about 'one of his own' which I took to mean that he had a child. He tried to get out and I told him to take it easy as he was obviously seriously hurt. He did not say any more and flopped onto the floor in a collapsed state … I found the perambulator had been blown by blast about ten yards from where I had left it and was damaged. Whoever took my baby from the perambulator undoubtedly saved him from serious injury at the very least …"[23]

The German aircraft also took their toll of those at sea. The 5,439ton steamer SS *Barn Hill*, en route from Halifax to London under the command of Captain Michael O'Neil with a cargo of copper and aluminum ingots and other general goods, which included a large quantity of tinned foodstuffs, was one of the very first victims.[24]

The evening of Wednesday, 20 March 1940, was cloudless, allowing the moon and the stars to shine brightly. A freshening westerly wind ensured that the sea was lumpy and full as the *Barn Hill* made her way eastwards through the Channel, entering the final stages of its transatlantic crossing. Everything was peaceful until the *Barn Hill* reached a point some six miles south-south-west of Beachy Head – only hours from its home port and safety. Captain O'Neil himself later described what happened next:

"At about half past ten the look-out shouted 'aircraft overhead!'. We naturally assumed that it was a friendly 'plane, but something about the way in which it circled overhead made me feel uneasy. Then came the first warning of trouble, as the 'plane started a dive towards us. The Barn Hill then shook and began to list, before partly righting herself. A bomb had dropped only a few feet to port! The aircraft then lifted up and dived a second time".[25]

Knocked unconscious in the attack, O'Neil would later be unable to remember the next few minutes. It was subsequently established that in fact a string of bombs had been dropped, straddling the ship. One 550kg bomb hit the stern of the *Barn Hill*, penetrating her deck plating and exploding in the No.4 hold, whilst a second unfortunately fell down her funnel. The contents of the No.4 hold, a mixture of timber and carbide, caught fire.

At the same time the ship's triple-expansion engines ground to a halt. Slowly she began to list to starboard. Four of the crew lay dead and eight more were badly injured (one of whom, 61-year-old Second Engineer Officer Douglas Bertram, died later in hospital). Captain O'Neil had been blown from his feet and rolled under some debris and, hidden from sight, was assumed by the surviving crew members to be dead.[26]

As the *Barn Hill* began to list further, at about eleven o'clock that evening, news of the attack reached the Eastbourne lifeboat station. The lifeboat crew responded quickly, so much so that at 23.15 hours the *Jane Holland* was launched and began to fight her way through the heavy swell to the stricken vessel.

When the *Jane Holland* finally reached the *Barn Hill* at 01:40 hours the next morning she found that a Dutch merchant vessel had already responded to the distress calls. She had picked up eighteen members of the crew, who, having survived the bombing, had taken to a raft. The lifeboat took these eighteen crew members off the Dutch vessel and then went alongside the *Barn Hill*. The steamer was well alight and explosions could be heard within the hull. The bridge had been blown forward and was resting, mangled, on the fore well-deck. Whilst alongside, ten more men were rescued from the *Barn Hill*, joining the eighteen already on the *Jane Holland*. Satisfied that everyone had been rescued, the lifeboat turned about and made its way towards port, arriving just after 03:00 hours.

Drama off the South Coast, 21 March 1940. The Eastbourne lifeboat Jane Holland *pictured alongside the* Barn Hill *as firemen on the tug* Foremost No.22 *play their houses on the still-burning merchant ship. The duties of a lifeboat and its crew were difficult and perilous during peacetime, but the addition of a world at war, and the fact that that the enemy could be just twenty-two miles away, only served to make some situations that much worse. The extent of the damage to the steamer can clearly be seen in this picture. (Courtesy of Beckett Newspapers Ltd.)*

In the hours after the bombing, the badly damaged Barn Hill *gradually drifted north-east, finally running aground near Langney Point. On the Saturday following the attack, the ship finally broke her back, spilling out some of her precious cargo. (Courtesy of the Andy Saunders Collection.)*

The sound of the bombing of the *Barn Hill* and the subsequent explosions had brought the people of Eastbourne out from their homes – despite the fact that is was literally the middle of the night. Sometime after the Eastbourne lifeboat had started to head back to shore, those watching on land began to report that they could hear the ringing of the ship's bell on the *Barn Hill*. It was at 04:45 hours in the morning when this information filtered down to the lifeboat station, though the report had come from the tug that had been sent to stand by the *Barn Hill*. The message read: "Send life-boat at once for injured man on forecastle. Please send doctor with the lifeboat"!

Captain O'Neil later told of how the ship's bell came to be sounding after it was thought all the survivors had supposedly been rescued:

"It was an hour or so after I had been knocked unconscious that I began to come round, to find myself lying on the deck. At first I tried to get up, but could not. My leg was broken, I could not move one of my arms and there was a great big wound in the middle of my chest. The pain was excruciating.

"I was able to piece together why I was there. When the German bomber made its second dive the pilot found the mark with another high explosive bomb. I had been standing on the bridge, which was where this bomb struck. I was hurtled twenty-five feet through the air before I hit the decking and was knocked unconscious. The debris of the bridge had fallen around me, so I must have taken the appearance of a dead person. So it was that when the lifeboat appeared I was assumed to have died in the explosion and left behind.

"For hours I lay on the deck with the ship burning around me. At about 4am I began to come to. The heat from the fires was intense – like the roaring of twenty thousand blowlamps on full blast! I looked about and could just make out the shape of a tug standing nearby. I tried shouting but no one was able to hear me. Then the idea of the ship's bell entered my mind. The only problem that I had was how to get to it, as I was unable to walk."

Getting to the bell would prove no easy task. "I still don't know how I did it," stated O'Neil, "but I managed to roll across the deck to get to the length of rope that hangs on the bell. I lifted myself up by resting on my good arm and gripped the rope in my teeth. I tugged and tugged at the rope causing the bell to start sounding. I was then able to hear shouts from the direction of the tug, but it seems that they were unable to get a man on to the *Barn Hill* to help me."

"After having rung the ship's bell several times I heard shouts and was able to watch as the lifeboat arrived. It was a miracle of seamanship that the lifeboat was able to get so close to the Barn Hill. I then waited as the two lifeboatmen made their way to me. They were taking their lives in their hands doing it, but there is no doubt that I owe my life to those grand fellows. They got me into the lifeboat where I was attended by a doctor."

The culprit is believed to a Heinkel He 111H of *Führungskette des X Fliegerkorps* (Staff Flight X Air Corps), a unit that comprised of just three aircraft. This formation was charged with developing anti-shipping tactics, tactics that would, in a few months time, become a part of the initial phase of the Battle of Britain, the so-called *Kanalkampf* or Battle over the Channel. The German aircraft timed its attacks as being 22:50 hours.

Even today many local people remember with relish the bounty of tinned food, including meat stew and baked beans, which was washed ashore from the ruptured hull of the *Barn Hill*. The news of these rich pickings spread quickly, with people even wading out into the icy sea eager to gather their share. People were not even dissuaded by the fact that the seawater had washed the labels off many of the containers, leaving local residents with the task of guessing the exact nature of a tin's contents! It would seem that many in Eastbourne used the "illicit harvest" from the *Barn Hill* to supplement their meagre wartime rations for many months.

The remains of the *Barn Hill* can still be seen at very low tides near Langney Point. Apart from some sections removed recently to allow access to Eastbourne's Sovereign Harbour, there are parts of the engines, boilers and metal plating strewn around the seabed.[27] These battered remains are testimony to the rescue work of the Eastbourne lifeboat and its crew, without whose efforts it is quite possible that more lives would have been lost as a result of the *Luftwaffe*'s first sinking of a British merchant ship in the English Channel during the Second World War.[28]

Defending the beaches in Sussex that faced the English Channel also presented new and very real dangers in wartime Sussex.

Second Lieutenant Norman F.K. Wilson was posted to the county early in the war as the Officer-in-Charge of one of four sections within 262 Field Company, Royal Engineers to help prepare the anti-invasion defences that would keep Hitler at bay. Such defences included the laying of mines on any stretch of the coast that was considered vulnerable to attack.

The shingle beaches of Sussex were, consequently, heavily mined but these beaches are in almost constant movement, drifting under the influence of tide and wind. Storms could change the depth of the shingle by several feet, causing mines to explode or be thrown up on to the open beach. This meant, for Second Lieutenant Wilson and his team, the hazardous task of recovering the displaced mines.

So frequent had become this problem, Wilson was allocated a trained mine-lifter, Corporal Cox. The corporal and his team successfully cleared several mines during the summer of 1941 until called into action, on 2 June 1941, on Worthing's West Beach.

What exactly happened has never been fully ascertained. What appears may have occurred was that the team had managed to lift the mines they were clearing and were in the process of carrying each of them back up the beach when one was dropped. The explosion happened on the seafront about halfway between the pier and the roundabout at the south end of Sea Lane. All of the three-man team were killed. It was two days before the bodies could be recovered as they lay in a minefield that only Cox and his men could navigate.[29]

Norman Wilson recalls a similar incident at Shoreham-by-Sea which occurred on 25 March 1941, after his Company had demolished almost all of the wooden buildings that once stood at "Bungalow Town" on Shoreham Beach:

"A short time later the Major General, Officer Commanding the 47th (London) Division, arrived in the Bungalow Town with members of his staff to view the progress of the construction of the defences. He was being conducted through the shambles that remained by his local Brigadier ... The Brigadier apparently saw the

173

triple barbed-wire barriers on the far side of the minefield and thought that he was safely on the outside."

"He invited the Major General to follow him around the minefield, but they unwittingly walked through it. The Major General, a few yards behind the Brigadier, stepped onto a 'mushroom mine' and was blown to pieces. The Brigadier had been blown clean through the barbed wire but survived."

Major General Cecil Malden was buried in St Alban's Churchyard, Frant, East Sussex. He was one of just sixty-six major generals, from all the Commonwealth armies, that would be killed in both of the world wars, and was almost certainly the highest ranked casualty to have died in Sussex between 1939 and 1945.

As with landmines, sea mines were also a common problem throughout the war years and beyond. On 22 December 1945, Lieutenant Walter Erskine Prior was despatched from Portsmouth to deal with a floating sea-mine that had been spotted off Bognor Regis pier. When he arrived, Prior discovered that the mine was almost ashore and was moving with the strong waves and currents towards the beach at Aldwick.

From a safe distance, a small crowd of onlookers could only watch as Prior waded out into the breaking surf towards the mine. He was almost within reach of it when it exploded; 600lb of high explosives tore through the air.

A rating who was on the beach with Prior, Wireman Banks, was severely injured; the injuries sustained by his officer would prove fatal. Though treated at the scene, Prior died of his wounds the same day.

Today, a memorial plaque can be found on a wall at the end of Dark Lane in Aldwick. As well as a testimony to one man's bravery and sacrifice, it also serves as a reminder that even after victory the Second World War was still claiming lives in Sussex.

CHAPTER 13

The Sussex Soldier

T he men of Sussex had been defending their communities long before the dawn of history, but it was not until the formation of the militia that the men were organised and trained to act as soldiers in the modern sense of the word. Until the New Model Army set the foundations for a national army, these "trained bands" were England's principle military force.

A remnant of the feudal system of obligatory military duty, every male between the ages of sixteen and sixty was, theoretically, required to serve in the militia. Though dating back as far as the Anglo-Saxon fyrd, service in the militia was not established in law until Edward I's Statute of Windsor in 1285. This item of legislation formulated the Commissions of Array which became the standard method of raising a field army from the shire levies.

This act was repealed in 1558 and each individual's military obligations were re-defined based on their financial status. Thus a man worth only £5 to £10 a year was expected to provide just a coat of plated armour, a pike or halberd, a longbow and a helmet, whereas those worth £1,000 or more were obliged to supply sixteen horses, eighty suits of light armour, forty pikes, thirty bows, twenty bills or halberds, twenty arquebuses and fifty helmets.[1]

Responsibility for the organisation of the militia and the defence of Sussex rested with the Lord Lieutenants of the county. Much of this responsibility was delegated to deputy-lieutenants, who were originally chosen by the Privy Council but, after 1625, were selected by the Lord Lieutenants. It was the duty of the Justices of the Peace to ensure that the constables in their respective rapes mustered the militia, with the assistance of the county muster-master who was an experienced, professional soldier.

Each Sussex rape mustered four companies of foot of 100 men each, plus Chichester had a company of its own. In addition to these twenty-five companies of foot, all of the six rapes also had a company of cavalry, each with a theoretical strength of fifty mounted men. Of the four foot companies of each rape, two were regarded as front-line troops made up of the best men with the best weapons and were known as the "selected" companies. The two non-selected companies were seen as second-rate formations and were poorly armed and usually under-strength.

Companies were commanded by captains, some of whom were JPs, but most of whom were drawn from the local landed gentry. A knight was normally in charge of the cavalry. Captains were chosen by the Lord Lieutenants. In 1626 a pioneer company was raised from each rape from men of gentry status led by a specifically appointed captain of pioneers. There was no financial reward for holding militia appointments (other than for the muster-master which was a paid position) but it allowed ambitious men to make the acquaintance of the most influential people in the county.

The annual muster, the frequency of which could be increased if there was a perceived danger, was usually staged at the same place in each rape, such as Ditchling Common for the Lewes rape and Berwick Common for the Pevensey rape. The horse companies, of which there was just one per rape, mustered together at Bury Hill in West Sussex and Piltdown in the east. Training also took place in local, smaller groups (of no more than twenty), in the weeks preceding the annual muster.

In 1625 the process of selection was abolished and each captain was given a district, or hundred, from which he had to raise his company and this led to an increase in the county's military strength. In 1638, the Sussex trained bands of foot totalled 2,804 men. By this time more men were armed with muskets than with pikes or corslets, whereas twenty years earlier many men were only expected to provide a pike or a half share in a musket.

The cavalry (later to be known as the yeomanry) was composed of men of substance. Those persons with an annual income of at least two hundred pounds were expected to be mounted and armed. However, the deputy-lieutenants were reluctant to force military service upon men who were not only their social equals, but also their friends and neighbours. As a result there were many defaulters at the muster and the county could not raise even 200 cavalrymen. Part of the problem was that there was no actual law which enforced military service as James I had abolished the earlier reforms and reinstated the Statute of Windsor. This was not resolved until the passing of the 1662 Militia Act.

The militia was put on a more standardised basis in 1757 when Parliament ordered each county to recruit a specific number of troops with the men being selected for duty through a compulsory ballot. These men were trained for one month a year and, for the first time, they were paid for their military service through local taxation.

In the absence of a police force one of the principal functions of the militia and the yeomanry was to keep the public peace. This included helping with the control of smuggling, which was endemic along the Sussex coast.

During the Napoleonic Wars the nature of the militia changed. A Supplementary Militia Act in 1796 required a large increase in the militia. Troops were raised in proportion to the population of each area with the larger towns and cities mustering entire battalions. These "regular" militiamen were enlisted for five years. They were continuously under arms and were garrisoned away from their homes, though they were not required to serve overseas. Substitutes were permitted and many who could afford to do so paid others to perform their military service. Service in the militia continued to be a compulsory duty until the middle of the nineteenth century when the Militia Act of 1852 made recruitment voluntary.[2]

Wealthy gentlemen were also encouraged to form their own "volunteer" militia corps. Probably the most famous of these units was the Cinque Ports Volunteers which was formed and led by William Pitt during his period as Warden of the Cinque Ports. Those that joined the volunteers were exempt for service in the militia. Sussex and a part of Kent formed the Southern Military District. The total number of volunteer troops in this district, including the Cinque Ports Volunteers, was counted in January 1804 at 1,521 cavalry and 10,257 infantry.[3]

The Napoleonic Wars also saw a huge number of regular soldiers march into Sussex. During this time Horsham became an important staging post as it was situated at the crossroads of two military routes i.e. between London and the south coast, and between the naval ports of Chatham and Portsmouth.

Large barracks were built in 1797 on the road from Horsham to Worthing but often these could not accommodate all the troops that stopped at Horsham and many regiments had to camp on the common, which was on the northern side of the town. During the nineteen years of its existence the Horsham Barracks saw no less than sixty-nine different regiments pass through its gates. It was at Horsham that one of the most famous regiments of the British Army was first raised.

In 1800, a body of volunteers from fourteen other regiments met at Horsham (later moving to Blatchington Barracks) to make up the Experimental Corps of Riflemen. This unit, the first regular body of rifle-armed troops in the British Army, went on to become the 95th Rifles and then the Rifle Brigade. It continues in existence today as the Royal Greenjackets.[4]

Other barracks were built in towns around Sussex, notably at Arundel, Bognor Regis, Chichester, Petworth, Shoreham, Littlehampton, Pevensey, Hastings, Winchelsea, Lewes, Hailsham, Blatchington, Eastbourne, and East Grinstead.

The barracks at Bexhill-on-Sea became the home of the King's German Legion, (KGL). This body was composed predominately from soldiers of the Hanoverian Army who had escaped to England when Napoleon overran the Electorate in 1803. At that time the King of England was still the Elector of Hanover. Bexhill remained the base for the KGL for ten years during which time close links were established with the community (including 108 local girls who married German soldiers), which continue to this day.

In 1794 the Somerset and Oxford militias were sent to Blatchington Barracks near Seaford. The local shopkeepers took advantage of this influx of new customers by raising prices and selling old produce no longer fit for human consumption. Soon men began to fall ill and, inevitably, the starving troops took matters into their own hands. Some 500 men of the Oxford Militia marched into the town and seized all the bread, flour and meat they could find. Intoxicated with their easy victory over the shopkeepers the mutineers then marched to Tide Mills, stealing more grain and forcing a ship carrying flour to unload its cargo at Newhaven. The following day regular troops marched into Newhaven and, accompanied by the local Seaford Volunteers, restored order. The supposed ringleaders were tried at Horsham assizes and four were later executed.[5]

The largest concentration of troops in Sussex during the Napoleonic Wars was at Brighton. At the 1793 training camp at Brighton were regiments of Volunteer Militia from twelve counties, including Sussex, plus a regiment of artillery and the 10th (Prince of Wales' Own) Regiment of Light Dragoons, making a total of some 10,000 troops.[6]

Later in the nineteenth century even larger encampments were formed at Brighton. In 1861, around 15,000 Volunteer Militia took part in a mock attack upon Ovingdean and the following year almost 20,000 troops entertained large crowds in exercises on Race Hill. Amongst these troops were members of the Sussex Volunteer Rifles and the Sussex Volunteer Artillery.

Regular troops were also posted to Brighton, being accommodated in the infantry barracks in Church Street and the cavalry barracks on the Lewes Road in Preston. Possibly the most famous regiment to have been quartered in the cavalry barracks was the 11th (Prince Albert's) Regiment of Hussars. Led to the Crimean War by their colonel, the Earl of Cardigan (who lived at 45 Brunswick Square), the 11th Hussars charged into the Valley of Death with the other regiments of the Light Brigade at Balaclava in 1854.[7]

The militia, the volunteers and the Army remained separate entities until the reforms of the Secretary of State for War, Edward Cardwell, in the 1870s. The reforms brought the local militia and volunteers together under the administration of the regular Army regiments. To help maintain a strong local identity the regular regiments were provided with a permanent barracks within the county to which they were affiliated.

In Sussex this led to the building of the Roussillion Barracks in Chichester. This became the Regimental Depot of the Royal Sussex Regiment and the headquarters of the Sussex militia and volunteer battalions. Recruitment had always been a problem for the British Army and with these measures Cardwell hoped that the closer ties between the part-time and the full-time troops would encourage more volunteers and militiamen to turn professional.

A tunic of a sergeant of the Royal Sussex Regiment from 1876. On the tunic is the Indian Mutiny campaign medal of 1857–8. The tunic is on display in the Redoubt Fortress and Military Museum, Eastbourne. (By kind permission of Eastbourne Borough Council.)

The last major restructuring of Britain's part-time forces came in April 1908. The militia and the volunteers were abolished and incorporated into a new voluntary body, the Territorial Army. The distinctions between the regulars and the part-timers were swept away with the Territorials being, quite simply, the reserve forces of the British Army, their title later becoming the Territorial Army Volunteer Reserve.

The principle of independent volunteer units was revised in May 1940 when the expectation of a sudden invasion by German forces led to a call for men to form units of "Local Defence Volunteers". The original intention was to encourage men with previous military experience to join the LDV, initially to counter German paratroop landings and one of their early nicknames was the "Parashooters".[8]

Though the age range for acceptance into the LDV was seventeen to sixty-five, it was not uncommon for men in their seventies and boys of fifteen to sign up. Around a third of all recruits were ex-soldiers. At first only British subjects were eligible for the LDV. It was expected that nationally 500,000 men might volunteer yet by the end of June almost one and a half million men had joined up.

Command of the West Sussex forces was handed to a former Grenadier Guard, and the Group Commander of East Sussex was Captain Madden of the Somerset

A photograph of the 1905 camp of the Sussex Yeomanry at Lewes.

Light Infantry. LDV headquarters for the eastern half of the county was at Lewes and at Chichester for West Sussex. Most company and platoon commanders were ex-officers though some were simply men of standing in the local community.

The Sussex LDV, or Home Guard as they were known from 31 July 1940, eventually numbered twenty-six battalions with each battalion being composed of at least four companies of, usually, four platoons. The battalion districts were:

1. Chichester; 2. Petworth; 3. Horsham; 4. Billingshurst; 5. Worthing; 6. Arundel/Amberley; 7. Midhurst; 8. Bognor Regis and Selsey; 9. Shoreham-by-Sea; 10. East Brighton; 13. Haywards Heath; 14. Hove; 15. West Brighton; 16. Lewes; 17. East Grinstead; 18. Crowborough; 19. Burwash; 20. Hailsham; 21. Eastbourne; 22. Rye; 23. Hastings/Bexhill; 24. Uckfield; 26. Worth Forest.

These were the general service battalions, in addition to which there were three specialist Battalions: the 11th (39th GPO) Battalion which was a signals unit, the 12th (2nd Southdown Motor Transport) Battalion, and the 25th (2nd Southern Railway). The last two were, of course, responsible for defending the means of transportation across Sussex and the neighbouring counties.

By 23 June 1940, nearly 17,000 employees of the Southern Railway had volunteered for the LDV throughout Sussex, Kent and Surrey. Sadly they had only

400 rifles between them! Amongst the more unusual Home Guard units was the Lewes Home Guard Cavalry. Composed of former jockeys, huntsmen and landowners, this elite force at one time included more than fifty mounted members. There was also a Sussex Recovery Company formed by Caffyns Garages, with five platoons based around the county. The duties of these platoons included the provision of mechanics and recovery vehicles for the armed forces in the area. The Recovery Company was also responsible for keeping the roads open.[9]

A number of highly secret "Auxiliary" units were created across Sussex. Carefully selected from men with great knowledge of their locality, such as gamekeepers, this was a highly trained corps. In the event of a successful German landing, the Auxiliaries were to disappear into secret hides which had been stocked with food, weapons and ammunition. These men would then slip out of their hides at night to harass the invaders. Their life expectancy was just two weeks after they began their clandestine operations.[10]

Apart from the age restrictions, all that was required of volunteers was that they should be reasonably fit, and men from all walks of life joined up. Schools and church halls were usually taken over as platoon or company headquarters though at Hove, rooms in the County Cricket Ground were used and at Storrington an evacuated monastery was reoccupied by the local Home Guard.

In the early days the poorly-armed Home Guard was not considered to be a fighting force and its duties were limited to observing and reporting enemy incursions, acting as local guides for the regular troops and guarding essential services and installations such as post offices, telephone exchanges, train stations and public utilities. The men were expected to patrol every night for between two and four hours. So from the tops of church towers, water towers, castles and hill tops, the Home Guard maintained a twenty-four hour watch over the towns and villages of Sussex.

As so much equipment had been abandoned at Dunkirk there was a serious shortage of weapons in Britain in 1940. Those rifles that were available were reserved for the regular troops. At first the men of the LDV supplied their own arms but gradually rifles were issued to each platoon, the men sharing the weapons as they took their turns on the nightly patrols. Initially the volunteers received an "LDV" armband with, possibly, a forage cap and those khaki uniforms that were sent to the Home Guard had to be, like the rifles, shared by the men.

The voluntary nature of the force changed in December 1941 when all men between the ages of eighteen and fifty-one became liable for service in the Home Guard. The structure of the Home Guard was also put on a more formal setting with commissions being granted to the senior company and platoon commanders.

Gradually the Home Guard developed into a more sophisticated defensive force. As well as rifles, uniforms and steel helmets, limited numbers of general purpose machine-guns, Bren guns, Spigot mortars, grenades and even 2lb anti-tank guns were issued to the battalions. The Home Guard was also now expected to use this weaponry against the enemy and their role now included that of local defence. This included anti-aircraft duties which at last gave the men a chance to fire their guns in anger. The Home Guard also took over the Coastal Defence batteries, releasing the Royal Artillery gun crews for overseas service. On 31 December 1944, the Home Guard was stood down.

Regular troops also formed part of the defensive forces during the Second World War. In May 1940, the 45th Infantry Division was moved from the West Country to guard the Sussex coast from Rye to Bognor. After the evacuation of the British and Allied armies from Dunkirk the defence of Sussex, Kent and areas of Surrey was undertaken by the recently formed twelve Corps whose headquarters was at Tunbridge Wells.

The 45th Division was incorporated into the 12th Division and was then concentrated between Rye and Newhaven, with the 1st Motorised Machine Gun Brigade posted between Brighton and Shoreham. In reserve was the 7th Corps which was placed between East Grinstead and Reigate. In February 1941, responsibility for the defence of the Sussex coast was entrusted to the First Canadian Corps with 12 Corps now being responsible only for Kent.

The Canadian First Division was stationed in West Sussex, with the Canadian Second Division, comprising the 4th, 5th and 6th Infantry Brigades holding the eastern part of the country. The most easterly of these formations was the 4th Brigade, with the Royal Regiment of Canada occupying the beach defences between Rye and Winchelsea, the Royal Hamilton Light Infantry posted at Hastings, and the Essex Scottish Regiment, along with the 14th Canadian Army Tank Regiment (Calgary), held in reserve at Battle. The 6th Brigade was posted further west, with the Queen's Own Cameron Highlanders of Canada and Les Fusiliers Mont-Royal at Newhaven. The 6th Brigade's reserve was the South Saskatchewan Regiment which was at Lewes.

After the Second World War the coastal defences were abandoned by the army. Newhaven Fort, however, continued under military authority with "B" Troop, 223 Independent Maintenance Battery forming the garrison of just seven men. The fort was taken over by the Battlefield Clearance Unit in 1957 and finally handed to the civilian authorities in 1962.

The principal regular army regiment to bear the name of Sussex was the 35th Regiment of Foot. Raised in Belfast in 1701 by the Earl of Donegal (whose name, coincidentally, was Arthur Chichester) the 35th was granted the unique honour by William III (of Orange) of being allowed to wear orange facings on its uniform. This link with the Dutch Royal house was re-established later in the regiment's history

Bexhill Barracks. Above the door is the badge of the Royal Sussex Regiment. The barracks are on the A259 in the Old Town area of Bexhill (TQ 737080).

when Queen Juliana of the Netherlands was appointed Colonel-in-Chief in 1953. It was not until 1787, however, that the regiment became associated with Sussex.

This happened because the colonel of the regiment was then the Duke of Richmond and he began recruiting men from his estates in Sussex. At this time the 35th was the Dorsetshire Regiment and it was the 25th Regiment that carried the title "Sussex". The Duke was permitted to take the Sussex name for the 35th and from 1804 the 35th became the Sussex Regiment and in 1832 the Royal Sussex Regiment, its facing colours then changing to royal blue.

In those days the regiments were rarely stationed in their affiliated counties when serving in the UK. The troops were moved around Britain to keep the peace, never staying long in one place in case they formed attachments with the locals which might prejudice their policing duties.

Like so many county regiments, the Royal Sussex had a long and distinguished service record. Its campaigns include actions in the capture of Quebec, the American War of Independence, the Napoleonic Wars, the Indian Mutiny, the Boer War, the relief of Khartoum and the two world wars.

During the period of the Indian Mutiny the regiment became associated with the 107th (Bengal Infantry) which was one of the regiments of the East India Company. The East India Company's army was transferred to the British service in 1861 and twelve years later the 107th was brigaded with the 35th at Chichester Barracks which became the Brigade Depot. In 1881, the 35th and 107th were amalgamated to become the 1st and 2nd Battalions, Royal Sussex Regiment.

In the First World War, the regiment was increased to twenty-three battalions, which included the local Territorial battalions. Of these, the 3rd (Militia) Battalion remained at Newhaven throughout the war from where reinforcements were sent to join the other battalions serving overseas.

In the Second World War, the 2nd, 4th and 5th Battalions formed the Royal Sussex Brigade which formed part of the British Expeditionary Force that went to France in 1940 and which was rescued from the beaches at Dunkirk. The 2nd Battalion was later converted into the 10th Parachute Battalion. The 1st Battalion was in Egypt at the outbreak of the war and it fought in the Middle East and the Mediterranean theatres until the end of hostilities. After the war the regiment saw action in the Middle East and Korea.[11]

A Sussex soldier: the monument to the 2nd Battalion Royal Sussex Regiment which can be seen near the pier, off Grand Parade, in Eastbourne. The statue dates from 1906 and commemorates soldiers from the 2nd Royal Sussex Regiment who lost their lives in military operations in Malta, Egypt and India between 1882 and 1902.

The regiment's independent existence came to an end in 1966 when it was amalgamated with the Surrey, Middlesex and two Kent regiments (the Buffs and the Royal Kent) to form the Queen's Regiment. This regiment is now the Princess of Wales's Royal Regiment.[12]

The local volunteers first served abroad when they joined the Sussex Regiment in the Boer War. In 1908 the volunteers formed the new Territorial Army and in Sussex they constituted the 4th Battalion and 5th (Cinque Ports) Battalion of the Royal Sussex Regiment. The 4th Battalion was based in West Sussex and the 5th in East Sussex. In the First World War both these battalions fought on the Western Front, the 4th also serving at Gallipoli and in Palestine.

After the Second World War, the 4th and 5th Battalions joined forces to become the 4/5th (Cinque Ports) Battalion, Territorial Army. This unit was disbanded in 1967 after the Queen's Regiment had been formed. The proud tradition of the Sussex Volunteers lives on, however, in the TA companies of the 3rd Battalion of The Princess of Wales's Royal Regiment which still carry the Sussex name.

A unit of Engineers, the 1st Sussex Royal Engineer Volunteers, was also formed in Sussex. Raised at Eastbourne in 1890, its headquarters was originally at the Eastbourne Redoubt. Over the course of the following few years volunteer companies were formed throughout the county and by the time of the Boer War twelve companies had been established.

The Volunteer Engineers were disbanded on 31 March 1908, and the next day were incorporated into the Territorial Army. As part of the 1st (Home Counties) Division, and later the 8th and 5th Divisions, the Sussex Engineers served in India and the Western Front from 1914 until the end of the First World War.

In the Second World War the Sussex Engineers, then listed as the 44th (Home Counties) Divisional Royal Engineers, with its headquarters at Queen Square in Brighton, fought in France in 1940, being rescued from the Dunkirk beaches with the rest of the British Expeditionary Force. The Engineers were then sent to North Africa where they took part in the Battle of El Alamein and the invasion of Sicily. The unit returned to Britain in 1943 and joined the 30th Corps for D-Day.

In 1947 the Territorial Army was re-formed and the Sussex Engineers formed part of the 119th Field Engineer Regiment. Its headquarters remained at Queen Square, the unit also occupying the former cavalry barracks at Preston. The long existence of the Sussex Engineers ended in March 1967.

The artillery is currently represented in Sussex by the 47th (Hampshire and Sussex) Regiment of Artillery which is based at Baker Barracks on Thorney Island. Prior to 1939 there had been two artillery regiments based in and around Sussex. The first was the 58th (Sussex) Field Regiment RA (TA), with batteries at Hastings and Eastbourne and the 98th (Surrey and Sussex Yeomanry) Field Regiment, with batteries at Brighton and Chichester. In June 1939, the 114th Field Regiment RA (TA) was raised with a cadre of experienced officers and NCOs from the 58th. The 114th was disbanded at the end of the war.

Another Territorial Army unit, the 200 (The Sussex Yeomanry) Field Battery, was formed in 1967 at Brighton.[13] This unit is all that remains of what was The Sussex Yeomanry Regiment which was originally Sussex's volunteer cavalry force. Raised in the closing months of the Boer War as the 1st Sussex Yeomanry, the regiment never saw action as a mounted corps. When the Territorial Army was formed in 1908, the regiment was brigaded with the Royal East Kent Mounted Rifles and the West Kent Yeomanry to form the South-Eastern Mounted Brigade.

This brigade was mobilised in August 1914 at the outbreak of the First World War, but, because of a shortage of horses and a desperate need for infantry, the men were invited to participate in the Gallipoli campaign as dismounted cavalry. From Turkey the regiment went to Egypt and Palestine. At this time the regiment was converted into an infantry battalion, as were other yeomanry regiments. Thus, on 3 January 1917, the 16th (Sussex Yeomanry) Battalion, Royal Sussex Regiment, was created. The battalion was transferred to France in May 1918 where it fought until the end of the war.

In the Second World War the Sussex Yeomanry, having been a cavalry corps and then an infantry regiment, became an artillery battery which, with the Surrey Yeomanry, became the 98th Field Regiment. Remarkably, in 1993, this unit then joined the engineers – becoming the 127 (Sussex Yeomanry) Squadron Royal Engineers TA.

APPENDIX

Sussex's Military Heritage

Sussex has many sites of military interest, though most of these sites are in the southern half of the county – particularly along the coast and across the South Downs. Almost all of these places are readily accessible to the general public.

The Causewayed Enclosures of Neolithic man are now barely discernible though the camp at Coombe Hill, near Willingdon (map reference TQ 575023) can still be accurately traced. Far more rewarding are the Celtic structures of the Iron Age.

The towering ramparts of Cissbury Ring (TQ 140080) are impressive reminders of the importance that our Celtic forebears placed upon defence. Like all the Downland forts, Cissbury is situated on the top of a steep-sided hill with magnificent views along the Downs. All the hill forts offer great walks and breath-taking scenery. Chanctonbury Ring (TQ 139121), Wolstonbury Hill (TQ 284138), Devil's Dyke (TQ 260121), Hollingbury Castle (TQ 322078), Highdown (TQ 093040), Mount Caburn (TQ 445089), Harting Down (SU 807185) and The Trundle (SU 877110) are all worthy of a visit.

Each one displays the same characteristics of a ditch and rampart though some, such as Hollingbury and Harting Down, have suffered severely from the ravages of time. Mount Caburn was also used as a lookout post by the Home Guard in the Second World War and the army built huts on the summit of Highdown Hill in 1940. Many of these sites are preserved by the National Trust and all are free to the general public.

At the coastal hill forts at Seaford Head (TV 495978) and Belle Tout (TV 560958), little is to be seen of the defensive works. Originally a mile or two from the coast, these forts, and the chalk cliffs upon which they sit, are crumbling into the sea. The views along the cliffs, however, are amongst the finest in England.

The most accessible, and certainly the most remarkable, of the Wealden promontory forts is High Rocks. Situated on the border with Kent, near Tunbridge Wells (TQ 561381), the fort was formed on top of a sandstone outcrop which has eroded into a maze of gullies and fissures. The earthen ramparts which secured the rear of the fort were excavated but have now been re-covered and are no longer obvious to the eye. There is a small entry fee to High Rocks.

Another series of Celtic remains which may have had a military purpose are the Chichester Dykes. Although they run intermittently all the way from near Halnaker

(SU 880095) to beyond Mid Lavant (SU 835081) the Dykes are now reduced to a shallow cutting.

The Romans have left us the great castle at Pevensey. Encompassing more than 1,700 years of military history, this is one of the premier sites in Sussex. Much of the old Roman walls, with their D-shaped bastions, still remain and it was within these defences that William of Normandy established his first base camp before passing on to Hastings.

William later built a typically Norman motte and bailey castle here. The visitor today, however, sees an imposing inner bailey of a medieval castle which was besieged four times but never taken by assault. Amongst its attractions are collections of large catapult stones that were found around the site and may have been used in the sieges of the castle in the middle ages.

In the grounds of the inner bailey is one of two demi-culverns that were placed in a battery on the south side of the outer bailey where the sea once lapped up to the foot of the walls. These cannon were listed as the armament of the castle in 1587, the year before the Spanish Armada. The castle was reoccupied in the Second World War by units of the British, Canadian and United States military as well as the local Home Guard. The towers of the castle were converted into barracks and an anti-tank gun embrasure and pillboxes for machine guns, which can still be seen, were integrated into the ruins of the keep.

The other principal military site of Roman times was the fortified city of Chichester. It is possible to walk round the old city walls (restored in the Middle Ages) along the top of an earthen rampart which was formed against the insides of the walls in the eighteenth century. The D-shaped bastions, which were added to the walls at some time during the fourth century, were designed to carry ballistae. Only five of the original bastions are now above ground. All that remains of Chichester Castle is the motte which stands inside the north-eastern quarter of the city. The heights known as The Broyle, where the Parliamentarians established their camp during the siege of 1642, can be seen beyond the walls to the north of the city.

The Saxons have left little to remind us of their military prowess. However, the remains of one of Alfred the Great's "burgs" can be seen at Burpham to the north-east of Arundel (TQ 039085). The burg, now a cricket pitch, commands a bend in the River Arun and its ditch and steep rampart still represent a formidable obstacle.

Saxon England was swept away in the Norman conquest, though the visible remains of their oppressive feudalism can be seen across the county. As well as Pevensey, the castles at Hastings, Lewes, Bramber and Arundel all date from the eleventh century.

There is still something to be seen at Hastings. The castle sits high above the town (TV 822094) and has suffered considerably from the ravages of coastal erosion.

Hastings was a promontory castle, built upon the top of a steep cliff made inaccessible from the landward side by a large ditch cut through the rock. The great tower has disappeared but parts of the main bailey wall still stand as well as the remains of the east gatehouse towers.

Bramber Castle (TQ 184107) is free to the public as most of the stonework was taken to construct roads in the area. The central motte can still be seen with a few scant pieces of the bailey wall. One side of the gate-tower stands high above the bailey indicating just how imposing this structure once was.

Much more remains of Lewes Castle (TQ 414101). With the aid of an audio tour the visitor can examine the remains of the shell keep and part of the bailey. Its most notable feature is the fourteenth century barbican which is still a public thoroughfare. Behind the barbican is the original Norman gatehouse. The larger part of the bailey, which was formerly a tilting-ground for the medieval knights, is now a bowling green and the castle's second motte, the Brack Mount, stands empty and isolated to the north-east. Short sections of the old town walls can still be seen, particularly to the north and west of the castle.

Arundel Castle, ruined in the Civil War, was restored to its present magnificent state in the nineteenth century. The most important remains from its medieval past are a Norman keep and gatehouse and a thirteenth century barbican. These can be viewed from the castle grounds (TQ 017074). Inside the castle is an armoury. Sadly few of the exhibits in the armoury have any connection with Arundel's history, though pikes, bills, swords, muskets, crossbows, suits of armour and Civil War helmets can be seen at close quarters. In one of the other rooms – the South Passage – pole arms and breastplates are also on display. Like Pevensey Castle, the military occupied Arundel Castle in the Second World War. An Observer Corps post was set up on the keep and the east wing of the castle was used for officer accommodation – the troops were under canvas in the grounds.

At Church Norton on the south-western edge of Pagham Harbour (SZ 870959) is a Norman ringwork. It consists of a large mound with a ditch that embraces its front and sides. It may have been topped with a wooden tower. It was used as a lookout post at the time of the Spanish Armada. Access to English Heritage site is denied to the public but it can be viewed from the footpath leading to the harbour.

The battlefield of Hastings, like so many battlefields, is disappointing. Though part of the ground has been preserved and is managed by the English Heritage, the buildings and roads around the site confuse the eye. It is the remains of Battle Abbey (TQ 748157), which sit squarely upon Senlac Hill, that cause the most difficulty.

This is where the English shield wall was formed and where Harold fell and died. Telham Hill (TQ 755138), where William first caught sight of the English positions, can be reached by car or on foot. The view from Telham Hill, however, is partially obscured by the walls and trees of the abbey grounds. A road, Powdermill Lane, now runs across the foot of Senlac Hill where the Normans would have formed up to attack. The hedgerows on the north side of the lane and the perimeter of the English Heritage grounds to the east and west, limit the area of the battlefield which can be examined to just the south-facing slopes of Senlac Hill.

An audio tour is included in the admission price to Battle Abbey and the immediate battlefield. There is a bookshop inside the courtyard of the Abbey and in the grounds are exhibitions and an introductory video. The point where Harold fell is marked by an inscribed stone. On summer weekends Norman re-enactors parade the grounds. Periodically, there is a re-enactment of the battle on the site, with scores of authentically clad mounted knights and hundreds of Housecarls and Norman infantry providing a spectacular display.

Few of the criticisms of Hastings can be levelled at the battlefield of Lewes. A large part of the battlefield remains open downland. It is still possible to walk the old route up the northern slope of Offham Hill known as "Simon's track" (TQ 400120) which de Montfort's army took on the morning of 14 May 1264. This is a steep climb up a narrow footpath and can only be taken in single file. The views over Lewes and the Ouse valley are breathtaking and it is easy to see why Henry III placed his only lookout here. The top of the path skirts the disused chalkpit where many burial pits have been discovered.

An alternative route to the battlefield is via Blackcap Hill (TQ 375125) which can be reached along a bridleway from the B2116. It is likely that some men of the baron's army reached the battlefield from Blackcap Hill. A public footpath/bridleway runs across the top of Blackcap Hill and Mount Harry directly onto the battlefield as does Simon's track.

De Montfort's army was drawn up in a position that ran approximately south-west to north-west in line with the present-day horse stables to the upper slopes of Offham Hill. The entire position can be walked, allowing the visitor almost the same view of the battlefield as Simon de Montfort. Though Lewes has grown far beyond its town walls, the keep of the castle can still be seen from Offham Hill. A public byway joins the stables (where the grandstand of the long-abandoned Lewes Racecourse was once located) with the Offham Road (the A275). Approximately half-way down this byway is a public footpath across the fields to the houses of Landport Bottom. By following this footpath the visitor can walk across the lower slopes up which Henry's and Edward's forces advanced, and the gradient of the ascent can be fully appreciated.

By returning to the stables the visitor can follow the bridleway towards HM Prison Lewes. This is the route taken by the Royalists, both in their attack and their retreat. Because of the lie of the land Offham Hill is not visible from this track. At some point is the site of "King Harry's Mill" where Richard of Cornwall sought refuge. The circular mound, which comprised the only remains of the windmill, was reported by Professor Sir Maurice Powicke to still be in existence in 1964.

The remains of the Priory of St Pancras, where Henry set up his headquarters before the battle and to which place he retreated after the battle, have recently been made fully accessible to the public with new pathways, seats and interpretation boards. A magnificent memorial to the battle in the shape of a knight's helmet stands in the grounds of the priory (TQ 414095) and is freely accessible to the public at all times. Around the top of the monument are scenes from the time of the battle, including a fine image of Simon de Montford. The memorial is also decorated by lines from the Song of Lewes. Next to the Priory is a large mound, some twenty-four-feet high. This is the motte of the original castle built at Lewes in the years immediately following the Battle of Hastings.

Amberley Castle (TQ 028132), a product of the Hundred Years War, has remained in private ownership and, since 1989, has been an hotel and restaurant of the highest order. The general public can view the castle and grounds but strictly by appointment only. It is still possible to mount part of the forty-feet-high walls and inside the castle are suits of armour, bills and pikes, and a crossbow. The restaurant serves excellent food in the most perfect setting Sussex has to offer the military historian!

Amberley Castle's main gate. The castle is situated off the B2139 (TQ 031132).

A reproduction of the "bombard" found in the moat of Bodiam Castle. It is currently on display in one of the towers of the castle. (By kind permission of the Director of Bodiam Castle and the National Trust.)

Bodiam Castle (TQ 785256) is one of the finest late-medieval castles in England. With its mighty towers reflected in the still waters of its vast moat, Bodiam Castle is magnificent. The exterior of the castle is in excellent condition and it is possible to climb the original steep, spiral staircases to reach the top of the gatehouse and one of the drum towers. Little remains of its internal buildings but in the base of one of the towers is a replica of the bombard cannon which was dredged out of the moat. In the gatehouse can be seen an original portcullis and the "murder holes" through which the defenders could drop objects – such as stones or boiling oil – upon the attackers. Within the castle grounds is a small museum with displays which include stone and iron shot, a Bill hook and a scale model of the castle in its heyday.

Herstmonceux Castle (TQ 646104), though built by a soldier in wartime, was of only limited military value. It has rising ground to the north, east and west, its gun ports are virtually useless and the water-filled moat encompasses only three sides of the castle walls. However, the enemies of the day were the French and all that they had been able to achieve during the Hundred Years War were hit-and-run raids.

Herstmonceux would have been quite capable of resisting such assaults. The grounds and gardens are open to the public, from which all sides of the castle can be inspected. Guided tours of the castle interior, which houses a working Study Centre, can be undertaken by prior arrangement.

Michelham Priory, near Arlington (TQ 558093), also dates from the Hundred Years War. This fortified monastery has a late-fourteenth century gatehouse with walls sixty feet high and four feet thick. It has a wet ditch and access to the Priory was originally over a wooden drawbridge. The Priory is open from March to October.

Rye's former role in the wars against the French is still recalled at its castle, the Ypres Tower, which is now a local museum. In front of the tower is the Gun Garden, complete with cannon. All that remains of Rye's perimeter defences, however, are the imposing Land Gate and a short section of the stone wall built to protect the exposed northern side of the town.

Winchelsea's defences date from just before the outbreak of the Hundred Years War. The remains of its three gateways – the New Gate, the Pipewell Gate and the impressive Strand Gate – still stand. In front of the New Gate can be seen the start of the huge ditch which protected the whole of the eastern side of the town.

Between Rye and Winchelsea is Henry VIII's Camber Castle, which is open to visitors for just a few weekends in the summer. Though its outer walls remain largely intact, the internal stonework has been badly damaged (TQ 922185).

At the same time that Henry was building his artillery castle at Camber, the first cannon in England to be cast as a single piece was made by the iron-master Ralph Hogg. His home, appropriately called Hogg House, can be seen by the entrance to Buxted Park on the A272.

Many of the former fire-beacon sites used to warn of the approach of the Spanish Armada are on public land and can be reached by footpath. A number of the beacons were located in old Celtic hill forts, such as The Trundle and Highdown Hill. Some of the others can be identified by their names, for example Firle Beacon (TQ 485059), Ditchling Beacon (TQ 333132) and Beacon Hill at Bishopstone (TQ 476017). Rottingdean also has a Beacon Hill which is crowned with a monument on the beacon site (TQ 366024). It was on Beacon Hill that Admiral de Vienne waited with his men to ambush the local militia in 1377 at the Battle of Rottingtdean.

The walk across the fields from Rye to Camber Castle goes besides, and then across, part of the Royal Military Canal, which reaches its conclusion at Cliff End (TQ 894138). It is possible to walk along the towpath for most of the canal's twenty-eight mile length with the Royal Military Canal Path marked with blue and yellow signs. It is hard to believe that during the Napoleonic Wars this lovely little waterway was considered a formidable defensive barrier.

From this era a surprisingly large number of Martello Towers still stand. The most westerly of this chain of forts, No.74 at Seaford (TV 485985), is now a local museum and is open to the public most weekends. With a cannon mounted on its roof, this fort provides a very good image of how a Martello Tower would have looked in the first decade of the nineteenth century.

Further east, No.73, known as the Wish Tower, is situated to the west of the pier along the seafront at Eastbourne (TV 613983). For a short period of time this was a Napoleonic museum run by the local council. No.66 at Langney Point close to Sovereign Harbour is in reasonable condition, having been taken over by the Coastguard Service as a lookout tower, though it is no longer occupied.

To the east of Sovereign Harbour, at the Crumbles, is No.64. This tower is sealed and has not been maintained. No.62 – the Grey Tower – is a private residence located in the Martello Beach Park caravan site. Nos. 61 and 60 are also private residences. The former (TQ 653035) is in remarkably good condition. In the Second World War it was used as an observation post for No.237 Coast Battery.

The brickwork of No.55 at the western edge of Norman's Bay (TQ 684053) is deteriorating and the building is unsafe, though planning permission has been granted for its renovation and conversion into a two-bedroom house. No.28 overlooks the estuary of the River Rother at Rye harbour (TQ 942188). It is now in very poor condition. No.30 is situated on the northern side of the A259 Winchelsea to Rye road, almost directly opposite Rye Harbour Road (TQ 918198). It was sited

A 32-pounder muzzle-loading gun on a traversing carriage on the gun platform of the Eastbourne Redoubt.

to defend the nearby sluices of the Royal Military Canal. It now sits on wasteland close to new housing.

The Eastbourne Circular Redoubt was the largest fortification built in Sussex during the Napoleonic Wars and it is still almost entirely intact (TV 623997). It is possible to walk around the parade ground and climb the walls to inspect a 32-pounder gun, on its traversing platform, which once formed part of the fortress's armament.

Within the casemates is the Redoubt Fortress & Military Museum. This first-class exhibition includes a large model of the Redoubt, as it was originally constructed in 1810, and a cut-away model of the other Napoleonic fort in Eastbourne, the Wish Tower. The main display is that of the uniforms, weapons, medals and other memorabilia of the Royal Sussex Regiment. There are also rooms dedicated to the presence in Sussex of the RAF, the Royal Artillery and the Royal Navy, including the Royal Marines. The museum also houses the Museum of the Queen's Royal Irish Hussars, its link with Sussex being that the 4th and 8th Hussars which combined to form this regiment were previously stationed at Lewes and Brighton. Admission to the Redoubt is free but a small charge is made to view the museum.

Bexhill-on-Sea's former importance as a barracks during Napoleonic times is recalled with a display of artefacts in the town's museum. Bexhill was one of the principal barracks of the King's German Legion which was composed mainly of soldiers from King George III's Hanoverian possessions. The items on display include a diorama of part of the battlefield of Waterloo, flags, portraits, and a brief history of this once-famous corps.

The Littlehampton East Bank Battery of 1760 now sits on the edge of the amusement park close to the mouth of the River Adur. Part of its earthen ramparts are visible but they are covered in shrubs and are scarcely recognisable as defensive works. Across the river, the West Bank Fort is no longer accessible to the general public but remains of the ramparts, part of the Carnot wall and one of the open bastions can be viewed from a public boardwalk which cuts through the sand dunes on the edge of West Beach (TQ 028012).

Shoreham Redoubt of 1857, though built in the same decade as the Littlehampton Fort, is in a much better condition. Apart from the removal of the barracks and rear walls, and considerable silting in the ditches, the fort is largely intact. It sits on the western arm of the harbour entrance with an uninterrupted view of the sea (TQ 233045). The fort is freely open to the general public and it is possible to walk around the parade ground and the gun emplacements but not the internal passages or inside the caponiers, the latter being blocked with debris.

Newhaven Fort (TQ 449001) has been completely refurbished after being allowed

One of a pair of cannon which originally stood at the entrance to a depot built on Horsham Common to house the arms of the troops in Horsham Barracks during the Napoleonic Wars. Currently these are on display at Horsham Museum (TQ 173304). (By kind permission of the Curator, Horsham Museum.)

to fall into ruin following the departure of the Army in 1962. It is now an award-winning tourist attraction open most of the year, with its barrack rooms displaying a wide range of military exhibits. The ramparts of the fort can be walked in their entirety and the 12-pounder and 6-inch gun emplacements – with each type of gun in situ – can be inspected. The views from the ramparts over the harbour and along the coast are wonderful as is the climb down the tunnel cut through the chalk to the caponier at the foot of the cliffs.

Though now overgrown, gun emplacements and magazines of the Lower Battery of 1855 can also be found at the bottom of the cliffs, between the caponier and the harbour entrance. On the clifftop beyond the confines of the fort are the well-preserved remains of a 1940s Emergency Coastal Battery.

Almost nothing remains of the Langney Redoubt. Just three iron gun pivots and part of a gun emplacement stand isolated close to the water's edge (TQ 643011) at Langney Point near to Martello Tower No.66.

There are so many reminders of the Second World War throughout Sussex that entire books have been written on the subject (see bibliography). Pillboxes, and the remains of gun and searchlight emplacements, still look out from points of tactical importance and a stroll along a quiet downland path is often a walk over one of the many tank roads that were laid in 1940. The most impressive concentration of pillboxes is at Barcombe Mills where ten works defended the tidal limit of the Ouse and the Newhaven to Lewes railway line. These formed part of the General Headquarters Line.

Most of the coastal defences of the 1940s, which formed what was known as the "coastal crust", have disappeared. However at Cuckmere Haven, one of the few relatively undeveloped areas of the Sussex coast, many of the defences of 1940–2 still remain. To the west of the River Cuckmere estuary is an anti-tank wall and, to the east, an anti-tank ditch and heavy machine-gun posts blend into the foot of the Downs. Guarding the beaches at Pett Level was an Emergency Coastal Battery (TQ 891135). The Battery Observation post and the Gun House are still largely intact.

Located close to the remains of the old runway at Tangmere is the Military Aviation Museum. As well as a fine display of medals, models, dioramas, uniforms and photographs the museum boasts a hall which houses a Hurricane and two Spitfires, one of which is an unusual early prototype. The Merston Hall also exhibits aircraft from Tangmere's post-war period. These include two aircraft that broke the world air speed record. The Gloster Meteor which established the record in 1946 and a Hawker Hunter, also flown from Tangmere, which achieved a new record in 1953, can both be seen.

Outside the museum building, other aircraft from the post-war period, not all of which have a direct relationship with Tangmere, are on display along with a number of military vehicles. Adjacent to the museum is a section of the runway at the end of which is the old Control Tower. Sadly, this historic building is not maintained and it is now in a poor condition. A few hundred yards down the road from the old airfield is the Bader Arms public house.

The deck gun from the German U-boat UB-130 *on display outside the Newhaven Maritime Museum in East Sussex. This 1-ton gun was recovered from the wreck, located off Beachy Head, in 1991. Recent reports from divers state that the wreck of* UB-130, *identified by numbers stamped on her propellers, is in three parts. (With the kind permission of Nick Hall.)*

Ford airfield, the former Fleet Air Arm base, is now the site of a weekly Sunday market which is held on part of the old runway. However, a Hawker Hunter in naval markings sits proudly above the market entrance to remind us all of its military past which began in the First World War and continued until 1958.

RAF Deanland (TQ 516114) was re-born in the 1990s as a small private airfield from which light aircraft, including microlights, still fly. Westhampnett, now known as Goodwood Aerodrome, also flourishes as a private airfield with many of the original buildings still standing around the site.

A new museum devoted to the aviation history of the Second World War opened at Balcombe in March 2010. The Wings Museum, which was originally located at Redhill, has an extensive collection of historically important "recovered" airframes, including the full-length fuselage of a Douglas C-47 Dakota used on D-Day. The exhibits include original items from the Battle of Britain, the Blitz, the Home Front, the Home Guard and RAF Bomber Command. There is also a V2 rocket engine and the relics of a V1 Flying Bomb. The museum is open every Saturday between March and October.

A reminder of the sights and sounds of the 1940s in Sussex is provided by the annual Royal Air Force Association Battle of Britain Airshow which takes place at the beginning of September at Shoreham Airport. This excellent event, which usually includes the Spitfire, Hurricane and Lancaster of the Battle of Britain Memorial Flight and the incomparable Harrier amongst its many displays, also has static exhibits from every period of aviation history.

In the years since the First World War, divers have discovered the remains of the Type UB-III boat lying on the seabed off Beachy Head, its only identification being the number *UB-130* stamped on one of its propellers.

This submarine was a 55.3m long UB-III type boat, also built by A.G. Weser, that was commissioned in June 1918. She joined I Flotilla in October of that year but only had time to make one wartime patrol before the Armistice. Her commander is reputed to have been the grandly named Heinrich XXXVII Prinz zu Reuss.

The 10.5cm (4.1in) gun from this boat was recovered by divers in 1991 and, after cleaning and preservation, was placed on display outside Newhaven Maritime Museum.

Lying at a depth of twenty metres some eight miles off Selsey Bill is an unusual assortment of Second World War armoured vehicles. Though the presence of these tanks and other relics had been known about for some time, the question of how they came to be there had always remained unanswered with any degree of certainty. For many years it had been believed that, because of the lack of a shipwreck nearby, that they had slipped or fallen from a Mulberry Harbour "Whale" section (a section of floating roadway) during its journey across the Channel on D-Day. Then, a team from the Southsea Sub-Aqua Club finally gathered the evidence needed to piece together the full story.

The initial breakthrough came after a preliminary survey during which the dive team realised that the tanks were not the more commonly used Sherman M4s that they had expected to find. They were British tanks and had a shorter-barrelled, larger-calibre gun. Staff at The Tank Museum at Bovington, Dorset, subsequently identified the wrecks as being Centaur CS IV tanks. This was a vital clue.

Fitted with a 95mm Howitzer Gun (HE ammunition) and one BESA machine-gun, and with their engines upgraded, some eighty Centaur CS IVs were provided for a specially created unit of the Royal Marines – the "Armoured Support Group". With their 95mm Howitzer, these tanks were intended to be used in the early waves ashore on D-Day to destroy beach obstacles, bunkers and defensive points. During the approach to the beaches, it was intended that some of the Centaurs would be mounted on ramps on the landing craft to allow their guns to fire over the bow at enemy positions using naval gunnery techniques. But only twenty-eight of these tanks, each of which weighed twenty-eight tons, had a maximum speed of 27mph, and a crew of five, made it on to the beaches and inland. At least two, we now know,

One of the D-Day Centaur CS IV tanks (CS standing for Close Support) that has been discovered by divers lying at a depth of twenty metres some eight miles off the West Sussex coast near Selsey Bill. (With the kind permission of Martin Davies.)

lie in the waters off West Sussex and after more than sixty years, one group of dedicated divers had finally answered a long-standing puzzle relating to one piece of surviving evidence of Sussex's part in the Second World War.

Areas of the Ashdown Forest are still designated for military use and are not readily accessible to the public. However, the remains of an Army camp can be seen to the west of Chucks Hatch (TQ 465 333) and the public can walk the length of the Second World War Emergency Landing Ground near Wych Cross (TQ 426305). The former Cold War radio installation can be seen from Camp Hill though the site is in a restricted area controlled and used by Sussex Police.

Thorney Island is the last military establishment on the Sussex coast still in the hands of the Ministry of Defence. Now known as Baker Barracks, it is the home of the 47th (Hampshire and Sussex) Regiment of Royal Artillery. Access to the barracks is strictly controlled by the Army, but a public footpath runs around the entire island. All walkers have to give their names and addresses before being allowed to follow the footpath through MoD property. The airfield can clearly be seen from the footpath and one of the runways is still used.

A military presence is also maintained at the Roussillon Barracks just north of Chichester on the A286 towards Midhurst. From 1873 until 1960 the barracks had been the Regimental Depot of the Royal Sussex Regiment. In 1964 it became a Training School of the Royal Military Police. The barracks are named after the French Roussillion Regiment which was defeated by the Sussex Regiment at the Battle of Quebec in 1759.

In The Keep of the barracks is housed the Royal Military Police Museum. It is

The Keep of the Roussillion Barracks on the A286 to the north of Chichester (SU 895065).

open on weekdays throughout the year and weekends during the summer. Admission is free, although visitors must report to the Guardhouse and sign a visitors' log before entry is granted. This compact museum depicts in paintings, photographs and words the surprisingly varied roles that have been performed by the RMP and the provosts since 1511. There are fine examples of uniforms, including those of the Mounted Troop and the Airborne Company, some of which are for sale in the small museum shop.

This then is the physical evidence of Sussex's military past. The true legacy of centuries of armed struggle against oppressive monarchs and aggressive invaders, however, is the freedom and democracy we now enjoy. In pursuit of these ideals the shores, seas and skies of Sussex have been the scenes of terrible slaughter. It should never be forgotten that the peace and prosperity we take for granted was won by the sword and defended by the gun.

Notes

Chapter 1: Celts and Centurions

1. D. Harrison, *Along the South Downs*, p.3. R. Bradley, "Stock Raising and the Origin of the Hill Forts on the South Downs." *The Antiquaries' Journal*, vol. 51, (1971), pp.8-29.
2. J. Armstrong, *A History of Sussex*, p.24. R. Penn, *Portrait of Ashdown Forest*, p.109. Other Iron Age forts in Sussex are to be found at Harting Down, Harrow Hill, Thundersbarrow, Offham Hill, Seaford Head, Saxonbury and Philpots in the High Weald and Castle Hill at Newhaven, see K. Leslie and B. Short, *An Historical Atlas of Sussex*, pp.20-3.
3. At Maiden Castle as many as 22,260 stones were found in a pit at one of the gateways; J. Dyer, *Ancient Britain*, p.126.
4. Harrison, p.9.
5. B. Darby, *The South Downs*, pp.82-3.
6. P. Beresford Ellis, *Caesar's Invasion of Britain*, p.70.
7. T. Newark, *Celtic Warriors*, p.18.
8. A. Down, *Roman Chichester*, pp.3-5, 7 and 52-4. Armstrong, *A History of Sussex*, p.25. G. Blaxland, *South-East Britain, Eternal Battleground*, p.28.
9. The other Saxon Shore forts were at Reculver, Richborough, Dover, Lympne and Porchester; E. Tetlow, *The Enigma of Hastings*, p.133.
10. Down, p.18.
11. Blaxland, p.35.

Chapter 2: South Saxons

1. M. Holmes, *King Arthur - A Military History*, pp.70-1.
2. A. Savage, *The Anglo Saxon Chronicles*, p.29.
3. H. Cheal, *The Story of Shoreham*, p.7.
4. Savage, p.35.
5. R. Whitlock, *The Warrior Kings of Saxon England*, p.17.
6. Heorepeburan, or Eorpeburan, has also been placed on the eastern Rother a few miles from Northiam, see *An Historical Atlas of Sussex*, pp.50-1.
7. P. Brandon, *The South Saxons*, pp.182, 183 and 185-6.
8. Savage, p.106.
9. D. Seaward, *Sussex*, p.35.
10. Savage, pp.107, 147 and 150-1.
11. J. Grimson, *The Channel Coasts of England*, p.53.

12. R. Abels, "Bookland and Fyrd Service in Late Saxon England", *The Battle of Hastings, Sources & Interpretations*, pp.60 and 68.
13. D. Harries, *Maritime Sussex*, p.9.
14. Here is one of History's greatest ironies. The Vikings had been using Normandy as a base for their attacks upon the south coast and in 1002 Ethelred married Emma, the sister of Robert Duke of Normandy (William the Conqueror's father), hoping that Richard would then put a stop to such activities. The result of this union was not the end of the raids but the invasion of England by the Normans in 1066!

Chapter 3: Fight for the Throne
1. Tetlow, *The Enigma of Hastings*. pp.62-4.
2. R. Wace, Le Roman de Rou, quoted by A. Clarke in *A Day That Made History*, p.6. A hauberk was a chain-mail tunic.
3. J. Gillingham, "William the Bastard at War", *The Battle of Hastings, Sources & Interpretations*, p.102.
4. *Ibid*, p.112.
5. *Ibid*, p.107.
6. S. Morillo, *The Battle of Hastings, Sources & Interpretations*, xxiv. E. Tetlow, pp.152-6. Strangely, we have no archaeological evidence for the exact site of the battle as there is no record of any bones or metal ever having been found on Battle Hill.
7. D. Howarth, *1066*, p.170.
8. M. Chibnall, "Military Service in Normandy before 1066", in *The Battle of Hastings, Sources & Interpretations*, p.90.
9. G. Regan, *Famous British Battles*, p.6.
10. S. Morillo, p.152.
11. M. Phillips, *1066 - Origin of a Nation*, p.19.
12. A. Clarke, *A Day That Made History*, p.20.
13. *Ibid*.
14. C. Lemmon, *The Field of Hastings*, p.44. D. Butler, *1066 The Story of a Year*, p.246.
15. B. Bachrach, "The Feigned Retreat at Hastings", in *The Battle of Hastings, Sources & Interpretations*, p.190.
16. Clarke, *Ibid*, p.25.
17. *Ibid*, p.26.
18. M. Rud, *The Bayeux Tapestry*, p.89.
19. Clarke, p.52.

Chapter 4: Conquerors and Castles

1. M. Salter, *The Castles of Sussex*, pp.28-31.
2. G. Blaxland, *South-East Britain, Eternal Battleground*, pp.60-1.
3. W.H. Blaauw, *Royal Licences to Fortify Towns and Houses in Sussex*, Sussex Archaeological Collections, vol.13, (1861), pp.104-7.
4. A. Emery, *Greater Medieval Houses*, vol.3, p.440; M.W. Thompson, *Medieval Bishops' Houses in England and Wales*, pp.168, 173.
5. D. Elwas, *A History of the Castles, Mansions, and Manors of Western Sussex*, p.269.
6. E.W. Holden, "The Excavation of a Motte at Lodsbridge Mill, Lodsworth", *SAC*, vol.105, (1967), p.103-5.
7. Elwas, p.113.
8. Emery, p.439.
9. R. Jones, "Hastings to Hertsmonceux: the castles of Sussex" in D. Rudling, *The Archaeology of Sussex to AD 2000*, pp.171-8.
10. Arlington Castle is not to be confused with nearby Burlow Castle for which there is no evidence of it being a medieval fortification. R. Musson, "Burlough Castle or Middleton Castle", *Sussex Notes & Queries*, vol.14, pp.19-22; H. Braun, "Notes on the Rookery, near Alfriston", *SNQ*, vol.5, pp.80-2.
11. T.S. Herbert, "Mounts at Lewes and Ringmer", *SAC* vol.63, (1922) pp.223-226.
12. M. Gardiner, "Recent Work on the Earthworks at Isfield", *SAC*, vol. (130), 1992, pp.140-6.
13. Thompson, p.163.
14. R. Jones, *Ibid*.
15. D.J.C. King, *Castellarium Anglicanum*, p.474; *The Gateway* internet site by Philip Davis.
16. H. Braun, "An Early Norman Castle Site in North Sussex", *SAC*, vol.77, (1936), pp.251-3.
17. A.H. Allcroft, *Earthworks of England*, pp.659-62.
18. Elwas, p.86.
19. R. Jones, *Ibid*.
20. Elwas, p.110.
21. D. Martin, "Three moated sites in north-east Sussex, Part 1: Glottenham", *SAC*, vol.127, (1989), pp.89-122.
22. R. Jones, *Ibid*.
23. King, p.475.
24. L.F. Salzman (Ed.), *Victoria County History: Sussex*, vol.9 (1937), pp.172-3.
25. Elwes, pp.189-90.
26. Emery, p.439.

27. King, p.475.
28. Guy, pp.135-6.

Chapter 5: Democracy's Dawn
1. C. Lee, *This Sceptred Isle*, p.88.
2. M. Powicke, *The Battle of Lewes 1264*, pp.22-3.
3. B. Fleming, *1264 The Battle of Lewes*, p.16.
4. D. Carpenter, *The Battles of Lewes & Evesham*, p.21.
5. *Ibid.*
6. Powicke, p.109.
7. *Ibid*, p.110.
8. Carpenter, p.25.
9. J.P. Gilson, "An unpublished notice of the battle of Lewes", *English Historical Review*, xi (1896), pp.520-22.
10. Carpenter, p.26.
11. *Ibid*, p.32.
12. In 1257 Richard was elected to succeed William of Holland as Holy Roman Emperor. He was never officially crowned and he usually adopted the marginally less presumptuous title of "King of the Romans".
13. Powicke, p.118.
14. G. Blaxland, *South-East Britain, Eternal Battleground*, p.77.
15. There were at least three fords, one at Southerham, one by Old Malling Farm and another by the bridge, T. Beamish, *Battle Royal*, pp.155-6.
16. *Ibid*, p.78.
17. M. Wade Labarge, *Simon de Montfort*, p.230.

Chapter 6: Defence of the Realm
1. J. Foster, *The Rye Guide*, pp.46-7.
2. I. Green, *The Book of the Cinque Ports*, p.17.
3. J. Collard, *Maritime Rye*, pp.12-3.
4. M. Bentall, *The Cinque Ports*, pp.121 and 145-7.
5. *Ibid*, p.163.
6. D. Seaward, *Sussex*, pp.12 and 179.
7. J. Guy, *Castles in Sussex*, p.32.
8. *Ibid*, p.34.
9. A. Bryant, *Freedom's Own Island*, p.122.
10. J. Goring, *Sussex and the Spanish Armada*, p.5.
11. A. Ankers, *Sussex Cavalcade*, p.129.
12. J. Goring, *Ibid*, pp.5-6.

13. J. Goodwin, *The Military Defence of West Sussex*, pp.13-16. L. Boynton, *The Elizabethan Militia*, pp.159-63.
14. Goodwin, *Ibid*, pp.11-12.
15. Boynton, *Ibid*, p.132.
16. Green, *Ibid*, p.29. J. Collard, p.24.
17. P. Kemp, *The Campaign of the Spanish Armada*, p.135.
18. J. Parry, *The Coast of Sussex*, pp.212-4.

Chapter 7: King Against Country

1. P. Brandon and B. Short, *The South East from AD 1000*, p.147.
2. G. Blaxland, *South-East Britain, Eternal Battleground*, p.94.
3. J. Guy, *Castles in Sussex*, p.24.
4. C. Thomas-Standford, *Sussex in the Great Civil War*, p.9.
5. A. Ankers, *Sussex Cavalcade*, pp.45-6 and 129.
6. P. Haythornewaite, *The English Civil War*, pp.24-56.
7. A. Fletcher, *Sussex 1600-1660*, pp.267-8.
8. Thomas-Stanford, *Ibid*, p.16.
9. Fletcher, *Ibid*, p.272. Rowkeshill, or Rooks Hill, was the name for The Trundle at that time because a medieval chapel dedicated to St Roche still stood on its summit, J. Armstrong, *A History of Sussex*, p.98.
10. Armstrong, *Ibid*, p.95.
11. D. Seaward, *Sussex*, p.151.

Chapter 8: The Bastion Shore

1. M. Brentnall, *The Cinque Ports*, p.163.
2. C. Barnett, *Britain and Her Army*, pp.187-90.
3. J. Parry, *The Coast of Sussex*, p.27. J. Goodwin, *Fortification of the South Coast*, p.2.
4. R. Grant, *The Brighton Garrison*, pp.12-15.
5. K. Leslie, *An Historical Atlas of Sussex*, pp.51-2. R. Cusick, "Signalling systems in use during the wars with France", *The Waterloo Journal*, December 2000, pp.5-14.
6. J. Goodwin, *Fortification of the South Coast*, p.16.
7. C. Woodford, *By the Crown Divided*, p.15.
8. S. Sutcliff, *Martello Towers*, p.47.
9. G. Hutchinson, *The Royal Military Canal*, pp.9-11.
10. The precise dimensions of the towers varied slightly from builder to builder, see S. Sutcliffe, *Martello Towers*, pp.64-79. The figures here are those given by J. Goodwin, *Fortification of the South Coast*, pp.10-11.

11. J. Goodwin, *The Military Defence of West Sussex*, pp.28-42.
12. *Ibid*, pp.45-51.

Chapter 9: The World at War
1. J. Goodwin, *The Military Defence of West Sussex*, p.75.
2. P. Longstaff-Tyrrell, *Tyrrell's List*, pp.10 and 19. B. Willard, *The Forest*, p.65.
3. R. Brooks, *Sussex Flights and Fliers*, pp.117-20.
4. M . Taylor, *This Was Rustington, In Times of War*, pp.2-9.
5. D. Harries, *Maritime Sussex*, pp.105-6.
6. K. Leslie, *An Historical Atlas of Sussex*, pp.58-9.
7. C. Alexander, *Ironside's Line*, pp.11-14.
8. G. Ellis, *The Secret Tunnels of South Heighton*, pp.51-4.
9. P. Longstaff-Tyrrell, *Operation Cuckmere Haven*, p.18. *Tyrrell's List*, p.7.
10. G. Hutchinson, *The Royal Military Canal*, p.16.
11. M. Mace, *Sussex Wartime Relics and Memorials*, pp.21-2.
12. Alexander, pp.64-5 and 74.
13. "The War in East Sussex", *Sussex Express and County Herald*, p.17.
14. M. Mace, *Frontline Sussex*, p.15.
15. D. Rowland, *Coastal Blitz*, pp.75-79.
16. *Tyrrell's List*, pp.11 and 19; M. Mace, *Relics and Memorials*, pp.49-50.

Chapter 10: Savage Skies
1. D. Wood, *Target England*, pp.7-9. Actual numbers vary from one source to another, see N. Franks, *Fighter Command*, p.71; A. Ward, *A Nation Alone*, p.94; L. Deighton, *Battle of Britain*, p.101; R. Brooks, *Sussex Airfields in the Second World War*, p.12.
2. Ward, *Ibid*, pp.86-9.
3. A. Saunders, *Channel Defences*, p.101.
4. Deighton, pp.97-101.
5. *Ibid*, pp.100-1.
6. E. Bishop, *Their Finest Hour*, p.40.
7. D. Rowland, *Spitfires over Sussex*, pp.37 and 40.
8. Burgess & Saunders, *Battle over Sussex*, 1940, pp.55-9.
9. Brooks, *Sussex Airfields*, pp.48-50.
10. *Ibid*, pp.68-70.
11. Wood, *Ibid* p.124.
12. Ward, *Ibid*, pp.154-8.
13. *Battle over Sussex*, pp.93-5.

NOTES

Chapter 11: Dieppe to D-Day

1. D. Sarkar, *Bader's Tangmere Spitfires*, p.28.
2. Burgess and Saunders, *Blitz over Sussex*, p.75.
3. R. Brooks, *Sussex Airfields*, pp.160-2.
4. *Ibid*, pp.149-53.
5. *Ibid*, pp.163-4.
6. *Ibid*, pp.153-5.
7. P. Longstaff-Tyrrell, *Operation Cuckmere Haven*, pp.45-6.
8. D. and S. Whitaker, *Dieppe*, p.227.
9. J. Gardiner, *D-Day: Those Who Were There*, p.33.
10. I. Greig, *D-Day West Sussex*, pp.12-4.
11. *Ibid*, pp.10-11.
12. *Tyrrell's List*, p.23.
13. Grieg, *Ibid*, pp.46-52. One of the Mulberry units sank off Pagham harbour and is now a popular diving site, see M. Mace, *Relics & Memorials*, p.142.
14. Grieg, pp.89-90.
15. K. Delve, *D-Day: The Air Battle*, pp.136-8.
16. P. Burgess and A. Saunders, *Bombers over Sussex 1943-45*.

Chapter 12: Witness to War

1. "Don't Touch", *Britain at War Magazine*, Issue 34, February 2010.
2. Police Miscellaneous Report No.MI491, dated 8 October 1944, West Sussex Wartime Archive.
3. Worthing Museum Archives.
4. First Report of the Select Committee on Estimates, 1947: House of Commons Sessional Papers 1946-47 (96) VI.
5. The National Archives, WO 32/16666.
6. Army Council Instruction No.472, 1 April 1944.
7. Army Notice Board Information Sheet No.87, April 1944.
8. Police Miscellaneous Report No.MI467, dated 3 September 1944, West Sussex Wartime Archive.
9. Police Miscellaneous Report No.MI586, dated 19 May 1945, West Sussex Wartime Archive.
10. Police Miscellaneous Report No.MI586, dated 19 May 1945, West Sussex Wartime Archive.
11. Letter in the Andy Saunders Collection.
12. This is believed to have been 32-year-old Lieutenant Commander (The Hon) Michael John Rance de Courcy RN, who was buried in St Mary's Churchyard, East Preston.

13. Letter held in the archives of the Fleet Air Arm Museum, Yeovilton.
14. Brooks, *Sussex Airfields in the Second World War*, p.69.
15. In many accounts, Corporal Hearn's surname is given as Avis-Hearn or Hearn-Avis (her surname as quoted in *The London Gazette*).
16. Though Joan stated she was in the "hut", she was in fact the person sent into the new "R" Block.
17. The famous noise produced by the Stukas as they dived was achieved by an external siren. This was intended to strike terror into the hearts of those on the ground. By the time of the raid on Poling, most of the Stukas had had these sirens removed. They were no longer attacking civilians, so there was no advantage to using the siren which only increased drag and slowed the Stukas down still further, M Korda, *With Wings Like Eagles*), p.200.
18. Interview with Joan Parsons on *Memories of Women at War*, produced by Kim M. Smith (KMS Productions, 2009).
19. Avis Hearn passed away peacefully at the RAF Benevolent Fund's Princess Marina House, Rustington, on 27 March 2008. She died a short distance from Poling, the scene of her brave action during the Battle of Britain.
20. "The War in East Sussex", *Sussex Express and County Herald*, Lewes, August 1945, pp.34-5.
21. Burgess and Saunders, *Bombers over Sussex 1943-45*, p.52.
22. "The War in East Sussex", p.71.
23. Chris Goss, *Luftwaffe Fighter-Bombers Over Britain*, p.224.
24. Some accounts quote O'Neil's surname as O'Neill. We have chosen to refer to the spelling used in the contemporary press accounts.
25. *War Illustrated*, No.33, Volume 2 (19 April 1940), p.411.
26. Martin Mace, *They Also Served*, pp.12-20.
27. Kendall McDonald, *Dive Sussex*, p.158.
28. Peter Marsden, *The Historic Shipwrecks of South East England*, p.31.
29. Martin Mace, *Frontline Sussex* pp.23-24.

Chapter 13: The Sussex Soldier

1. L. Boynton, *The Elizabethan Militia*, p.9.
2. C. Barnett, *Britain and Her Army*, pp.112, 172 and 282.
3. R. Glover, *Britain at Bay*, pp.211-17.
4. R. Cusick, *Barracks, Bounties and Beer in Sharpes Horsham*, paper presented to Horsham Museum Society, (April 2000).
5. J. Odam, *The Seaford Story*, pp.28-31.
6. The regiments were: The East Norfolks, The Berkshires, The West Essex, The Oxfords, The North Devons, The Westminster/Middlesex, The West Suffolks,

NOTES

The South Devons, The North Hants, The Dorsets, and the East Middlesex. R. Grant, *The Brighton Garrison*, pp.12–13.

7. R. Grant, *Ibid*, p.76.
8. P. Crook, *The Sussex Home Guard*, p.11.
9. Crook, *Ibid*, pp.4, 26-7 and 73-8.
10. S. Angell, *The Secret Sussex Resistance*, p.59.
11. J. Ainsworth, *The Royal Sussex Regiment*, pp.3-13.
12. J. Haswell, *The Queen's Regiment*, pp.20-1.
13. B. Peedle, *The Modern Territorial Army*, p.9.

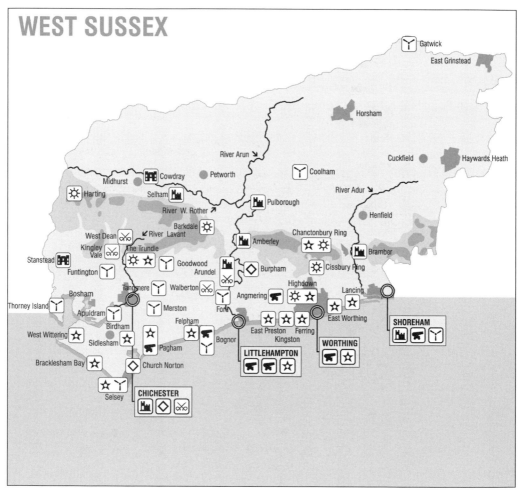

A map showing military features in West Sussex.

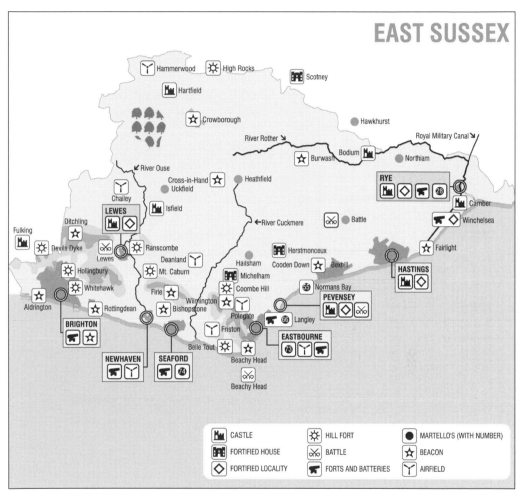

A map showing military features in East Sussex.

Bibliography

Ainsworth, J. *The Royal Sussex Regiment*, (Derby, 1972).

Alcock, L. *Arthur's Britain, History and Archaeology AD 367-634*, (Harmondsworth, 1971).

Alexander, C. *Ironside's Line, The Definitive Guide to the General Headquarters Line Planned for Great Britain in Response to the Threat of German Invasion 1940-42*, (Storrington, 1999).

Allcroft, A. H. *Earthworks of England*, (London, 1908).

Angell, S. *The Secret Sussex Resistance*, (Midhurst, 1996).

Ankers, A. *Sussex Cavalcade*, (Sevenoaks, 1992).

Armstrong, J.R. *A History of Sussex*, (Chichester, 1961).

Barnett, C. *Britain and Her Army 1509-1970*, (London, 1970).

Beamish, T. *Battle Royal; The Battle of Lewes*, (London, 1978).

Bishop, E. *Their Finest Hour, The Story of the Battle of Britain*, (London, 1972).

Blaxland, G. *South-East Britain: Eternal Battleground*, (Rainham, 1981).

Boynton, L. *The Elizabethan Militia 1558-1638*, (London, 1967).

Brandon, P. *The Sussex Landscape*, (London, 1974).

_____. *The South Saxons*, (Chichester, 1978).

Brandon, P. and Short, B. *The South East from AD 1000*, (Harlow, 1990).

Bradbury, J. *The Battle of Hastings*, (Stroud, 1998).

Bradley, R. "Stock Raising and the Origin of the Hill Forts on the South Downs", *The Antiquaries' Journal*, Vol.51 (1971).

Brooks, R. *Sussex Airfields in the Second World War*, (Newbury, 1993).

_____. *Sussex Flights and Fliers 1783-1919*, (Shoreham-by-Sea, 1992).

Bryant, A. *Freedom's Own Island*, (London, 1986).

Bugler, W. *The Story of a Sussex Gunner Regiment*, (Privately published, 1982).

Burk, J. *Sussex*, (London, 1974).

Butler, D. *1066: The Story of a Year*, (London, 1965).

Burgess, P. and Saunders, A. *Battle over Sussex 1940*, (Midhurst, 1990).

_____. *Blitz over Sussex 1941-42*, (Midhurst, 1994).

_____. *Bombers over Sussex 1943-45*, (Midhurst, 1995).

Carpenter, D. *The Battles of Lewes & Evesham 1264/5*, (Kccle, 1987).

Cheal, H. *The Story of Shoreham*, (Hove, 1921).

Clark, D. *Battlefield Walks: The South*, (Stroud, 1996).

Clarke, A. *The Battle of Hastings: a day that made history*, (London, 1988).

Collard, J. *Maritime Rye*, (Rye, 1978).

BIBLIOGRAPHY

Collier, R. *D-Day*, (London, 1992).

Corum, M. *D-Day: Brighton Remembers*, (Brighton, 1994).

Crook, P. *Sussex Home Guard*, (Midhurst, 1998).

Cusick, R. "Signalling systems in use during the wars with France", *The Waterloo Journal*, December 2000.

Darby, B. *A View of Sussex*, (London, 1975).

_____. *The South Downs*, (London, 1976).

Deighton, L. *Battle of Britain*, (London, 1980).

Delve, K. *D-Day, The Air Battle*, (London, 1994).

Denny, N. & Filmer-Sankey, J. *The Bayeux Tapestry*, (London, 1966).

Down, A. *Roman Chichester*, (Chichester, 1988).

Ellis, Beresford E. *Caesar's Invasion of Britain*, (London, 1978).

Ellis, G. *The Secret Tunnels of South Heighton*, (Seaford, 1996).

Elwes, D. *A History of the Castles, Mansions, and Manors of Western Sussex*, (London, 1837).

Emery, A. *Greater Medieval Houses*, (Cambridge, 2006).

Fleming, B. *1264 The Battle of Lewes*, (Hailsham, 1999).

Fletcher, A. *Sussex 1600-1660, A County Community in Peace and War*, (Chichester, 1980).

J. Foster & K. Clark, *The Rye Guide*, (Rye, 1997).

Franks, N. *RAF Fighter Command, 1936-1968*, (Sparkford, 1992).

Gardiner, J. *D-Day, Those Who Were There*, (London, 1994).

Glover, R. *Britain at Bay. Defence against Bonaparte, 1803-14*, (London, 1973).

Goodwin, J. *Fortifications of the South Coast. The Pevensey, Eastbourne and Newhaven Defences 1750-1945*, (Goring-by-Sea, 1994).

_____. *The Military Defence of West Sussex. 500 years of fortification of the coast between Brighton and Selsey*, (Midhurst, 1985).

Goring, J. *Sussex and the Spanish Armada*, (Lewes, 1988).

Goss, C. *Luftwaffe Fighter-Bombers Over Britain*, (Crécy, Manchester, 2003).

Grant, R.C. *The Brighton Garrison 1793-1900*, (Worthing, 1997).

Green, I. *The Book of the Cinque Ports*, (Buckingham, 1984).

Greig, I. *D-Day West Sussex: Springboard for the Normandy Landings 1944*, (Chichester, 1994).

Grimson, J. *The Channel Coasts of England*, (London, 1978).

Guy, J. *Castles in Sussex*, (Chichester, 1984).

Haes, E. *Natural History of Sussex*, (Hassocks, 1977).

Harries, D. *Maritime Sussex*, (Seaford, 1997).

Harrison, D. *Along the South Downs*, (London, 1975).

Haswell, J. *The Queen's Regiment*, (Canterbury, 1985).

Haythornwaite, P. *The English Civil War 1642-1651: An Illustrated Military History*, (London, 1983).

Hillier, D. *The Bulwark Shore*, (London, 1980).

Hogg, I. *Hill Forts of Britain*, (London, 1975).

Holmes, M. *King Arthur - A Military History*, (London, 1998).

Howarth, D. *1066 The Year of the Conquest*, (London, 1977).

Hutchinson, G. *The Royal Military Canal*, (Hastings, 1995).

Kemp, P. *The Campaign of the Spanish Armada*, (Oxford, 1988).

Kenyon, J.R. "A Hitherto Unknown Early Seventeenth Century Survey of the Coastal Forts of Southern England", Fort Magazine, vol. II, 1983.

King, D.J.C. *Castellarium Anglicanum*, (London, 1983).

Kinross, J. *The Battlefields of Britain*, (Newton Abbot, 1979).

Korda, M. *With Wings Like Eagles: A History of the Battle of Britain*, (London, 2009).

Labarge, M. Wade, *Simon de Montfort*, (Bath, 1972).

Lemmon, C. *The Field of Hastings*, (St. Leonards-on-Sea, 1956).

Leslie, K. and Short, B. *An Historical Atlas of Sussex*, (Chichester, 1999).

Longmate, N. *Defending the Island - Caesar to the Armada*, (London, 1989).

_____. *Island Fortress: The Defence of Great Britain 1603-1945*, (London, 1991).

Longstaff-Tyrrell, P. *Operation Cuckmere Haven*, (Polegate, 1997).

_____. *Tyrrell's List. The Artefacts of Two Great Wars in Sussex*, (Polegate, 1998).

Mace, M. *Frontline Sussex: The Defence Lines of West Sussex 1939-45*, (Storrington, 1996).

_____. *Sussex Wartime Relics and Memorials*, (Storrington, 1997).

_____. *They Also Served: The Story of the Sussex Lifeboats at War 1939-1945*, (Storrington, 2001).

Mackenzie, S.P. *The Home Guard*, (Oxford, 1996).

Marsden, P. *The Historic Shipwrecks of South East England*, (Norwich, 1987).

Mattingly, G. *The Defeat of the Spanish Armada*, (London, 1961).

Maynell, *Sussex*, (London, 1947).

McDonald, K. *Dive Sussex*, (Teddington, 1999).

Mee, A. *The King's England, Sussex*, (London, 1964).

Morillo, S. *The Battle of Hastings, Sources & Interpretations*, (Suffolk, 1996).

Morling, L. *Sussex Sappers: A History of the Sussex Volunteer and Territorial Army Royal Engineer Units from 1890 to 1967*, (Seaford, 1972).

Morris, J (Ed.) & Mothersill, J (trans.), *Doomsday Book: A Survey of the Counties: Sussex*, (Chichester, 1976).

Newark, T. *Celtic Warriors 400 BC – AD 1600* (Poole, 1956)

Newark, T. *War in Britain*, (London, 2000).

Odam, J. *The Seaford Story*, (Seaford, 1998).

Parry, J. *An Historical and Descriptive Account of the Coast of Sussex*, (London, 1833).

BIBLIOGRAPHY

Peedle, B. *Encyclopaedia of the Modern Territorial Army*, (Wellingborough, 1990).

Penn, R. *Portrait of Ashdown Forest*, (London, 1984).

Poole, H. *Lewes Priory: The Site and its History*, (Lewes, 2000).

Powell-Edwards, H. *The Sussex Yeomanry & 16th Battalion Royal Sussex Regiment, 1914-18*, (London, 1921).

Powicke, M. *The Battle of Lewes 1264*, (Lewes, 1964).

Rose, C. & Astell, J. *The Martello Tower at Seaford*, (Seaford, 1970).

Rowland, D. *Spitfires over Sussex*, (Peacehaven, 2000).

_____. *Coastal Blitz*, (Seaford, 2001).

Rudling, D. (Ed.), *The Archaeology of Sussex to AD 2000*, (Great Dunham, 2003).

Salter, M. *The Castles of Sussex*, (Malvern, 2000).

Sarkar, D. *Bader's Tangmere Spitfires*, (Sparford, 1996).

Saunders, A. *Channel Defences*, (London, 1997).

Savage, A. *The Anglo-Saxon Chronicles*, (London, 1982).

Seward, D. *Sussex*, (London, 1995).

Stephen, J. *The Roman Forts of the Saxon Shore*, (London, 1978).

Sussex Archaeological Society Collections.

Sussex Express and County Herald, "The War in East Sussex", (Lewes, 1945).

Sutcliffe, S. *Martello Towers*, (Newton Abbot, 1972).

Taylor, M. *This was Rustington, No.3: In Times of War*, (Rustington, 1989).

Terraine, J. *The Right of the Line, The Royal Air Force in the European War 1939-1945*, (Sevenoaks, 1988).

Tetlow, E. *The Enigma of Hastings*, (London, 1974).

Thompson, M.W. *Medieval Bishops' Houses in England and Wales*, (Aldershot, 1998).

Trimen, R. *An Historical Memoir of the 35th Royal Sussex Regiment of Foot*, (Southampton, 1873).

Ward, A. *A Nation Alone: The Battle of Britain – 1940*, (London, 1989).

Willard, B. *Sussex*, (London, 1965).

_____. *The Forest - Ashdown in East Sussex*, (Marsh Barton, 1989).

Whitaker, D. and S. *Dieppe*, (London, 1992).

Whitehead, W. *Dieppe 1942*, (Glasgow, 1982).

Wood, D. *Target England: The Illustrated history of the Battle of Britain*, (London, 1980).

Woodford, C. *By the Crown Divided. Hanoverian Sussex 1770-1800*, (Willingdon, 1983).

Yarrow, A. *The Fortifications of the East Coast. A guide to castles and other defences*, (Lewes, 1979).

Young, P. & Adair, J. *Hastings to Culloden*, (London, 1964).

General Index

INDEX